THE CULTURAL COLLAPSE

OF AMERICA

AND THE WORLD

DAVID E. SIRIANO

PRESS

The Cultural Collapse of America, and the World
by David E. Siriano

Printed in the United States of America

ISBN 1-60034-621-9
ISBN 978-1-60034-621-7

Unless otherwise indicated, Bible quotations are taken from:
    The King James Bible;
    New King James, Copyright © 1979, Thomas Nelson, Inc., Publishers;
    New International Version, Copyright © 1973, 1978, 1984, International Bible Society, Zondervan Bible Publishers;
    The New Living Translation, Copyright © 1996 Tyndale House Publishers, Inc.;
    The Amplified Bible, Copyright © 1954, 1958, 1962, 1964, The Lockman Foundation and Zondervan Publishing House;
    New American Standard, Copyright © 1960, 1962, 1963, 1968, 1971, 1972, 1973, 1975, 1977, The Lockman Foundation, Thomas Nelson, Publishers.

www.xulonpress.com

THE CULTURAL COLLAPSE OF AMERICA
AND THE WORLD

—⟋⟋⟋—

Chapter one - The Cradle of Civilization 19

Precious place to visit
World view
History is key
Creation versus evolution
Doubting Darwin
Beginning of beginnings

Noah's flood
Mass destruction
The grand struggle
Life cycles
Rock a bye baby

Chapter Two - The Shift of Global Super Powers 53

Messianic marvel
Look for clues
History is His story
Eye of God
Mighty kingdoms of old
Kingdom details

Palestine pre-occupation
European whirlwind
The latest super power
The new United Nations
The greatest warfare
Revelational warfare

Chapter Three - The Importance of War 99

God's view
Back to the future
War is necessary
God of war or peace
Peace
War
Religious wars
Early wars of America
20th century warfare
The War to end all Wars

The Second War
What did Korea do?
The short Cold War
Rushing Russians
Victor-less Vietnam War
The missing generation
What have we done/what are we doing?
10 wise men
Three views

Chapter Four - Why Terrorism will lead to Armageddon.. 145

What is terrorism?
20th century terrorism
I was terrified by terrorists
A just war on terrorism
WW III
Burning Bush
The majors

Who killed Christ?
Are the Jews, Jews?
Are Arabs who they say they are?
Jew and Arab occupancy
What the Bible says
Why the Jews are back

Chapter Five - When Catastrophe Strikes.................... 191

Potential catastrophes
Catastrophe in history
Earthquake inevitability

Catastrophe origination
Catastrophe in the Bible
The next big hit

Chapter Six - The Influence of Evil over Global Powers.. 217

A gentleman's agreement
Jeffersonian jargon
First Amendment
Burn, baby, burn
God is not in the Constitution?
Constitutional crises
Crazy courts
Life and death

Liberal media
Censorship is not a bad word
Hollywood hype
Music megalomania
Homosexuality is not gay
Abort abortion
Let's make a deal
Is there an answer

Chapter Seven - When History and the Bible Conflict 289

My family
Our predecessors
Christianity crush
Right wing, left wing, sound off
Stifle politicians and clergy?

Commandments – curse or cure?
Christianity corrects itself
Mainline versus evangelical church
The poor
Rich history of truth

Chapter Eight - 21st Century Internet Global Warfare

Chapter Eight - 21st Century Internet Global
   Warfare.. 327

The imperfection of American freedom
Internet isolation
An angry America
Porn-net
Rumors of war
The beginning of the end
Four terrifying horsemen
The earth moves
Internet warfare

The three terrors
Antithesis of Christ
Arrival at Armageddon
Mysteries
Mystery Babylon
Second Coming of Jesus Christ
Judgment of the nations
New heaven and earth

DEDICATION

—⚡—

To my wife, Elsa May who has given me all of her support and love. To my son David, his wife Glenda, and children, Karina Nicole, Andrea, Karina Lynn, Katie, and Alyssa. To my daughter Darla, her husband Steve, and children, Tyler, Kaci, and Colin Edlin. I would not be where I am today without each of them!

IN MEMORY

—ɯ—

Of Joseph Siriano, (1935-1987) my older brother, my friend, my mentor, with whom I have spent countless numbers of hours with, talking about life, people, history, current events, and the Bible. Thank you Joe!

ACKNOWLEDGEMENTS

—⟋⟍—

There have been a number of messages and subjects over the past 43 years of Pastoral ministry that I have enjoyed preaching and teaching from God's Word and that I have been very passionate about. One of those subjects has been Eschatology, or the study of the "End Times."

I have had the opportunity to lecture on the college level about this all-important subject as well as travel to numerous churches as a guest speaker. Many individuals have had to endure and hear my endless devotion to "my passion" over the years.

One such person has been my wife Elsa May who has been a faithful Pastor's wife and has stood by my side all these years. She has helped with our ministry in so many ways. Not only has she been devoted to helping others but she has traveled with me extensively, listening to my thoughts about the "End Times" over and over again. To her I owe a deep and abiding appreciation for all the many ways she has been there for me and encouraged me.

I wish to thank Sam and Jean Shearer of Essex Jct, Vermont, Wally and Joanne Lundstrom, of Cape Cod, Massachusetts, and Larry and Sherryl Ford, of Ft. Myers, Florida. These are friends whom my wife and I visited and where I continued writing and finishing much of the work of this book in their homes.

I owe a deep sense of gratitude to my wife Elsa May Siriano, Rev. Ed Shearer, David Livingston, Kara Simpson, and my secretary Cindi Wilkins, who helped in one way or another in the editing process of this book. Also, thank you Jonathan Burow for a beautiful cover design and graphics.

Thank you to all my other friends and colleagues whose names are too numerous to mention, who have encouraged me to not give up my passion for writing this book. I owe a deep sense of gratitude to all my church family who had a great hunger to hear about the end times as it pertains to the Second Coming of Jesus Christ and had to tolerate my continuous speaking about my writings.

I pray that this book is a source of inspiration, blessing, and understanding to all that read it and believe that Jesus Christ is returning to bring everlasting peace to this world!

David E. Siriano

INTRODUCTION

—ᘉ—

Could there be such a thing as the collapse of our culture in America and the cultures in the world today? How frightening can that be, and what will come out of the chaos of a cultural behavior that is gone awry, or a global war or catastrophe if there is an end to this world? For those who view the world as evolving from innumerable transitional changes through the process of evolution, it just seems impossible that an end will come to this world. Will life, as we know it end or just change?

First, is the lowering of moral standards in many of our cultures leading to the collapse of society as a whole? The dictionary describes culture as a pattern of human behavior that includes our thoughts, speech, and actions. We learn and transmit that knowledge to succeeding generations, including our beliefs, social group ideals, racial, and religious instruction. There is a cultural problem in our world that is affecting the type of information and moral instruction that we are passing on from generation to generation. What we recognize and appreciate as our philosophy of moral behavior and principle is often misguided and can lead to the destruction of any society. Our children are not born with any predisposed cultural behavior pattern but we develop and program much of our behavioral patterns into them and into our culture.

Second, is the thought of a global war ending the world, an unacceptable thought to any person who believes that the world will last forever? One can hardly imagine any nation or groups of nations to be so callous that they would lead us to the brink of annihilation either through conventional, biological, chemical, or nuclear warfare. Some may say that it is impossible for the world to be involved in a nuclear exchange between two or more nations. They wouldn't have to go back very far in history to see its possibility. We were brought to near nuclear disaster during the Cuban missile crisis of 1962. Everyone was fearful that a major war was going to break out across the globe.

Just as a global cultural war was possible then in bringing the world to near annihilation, it is possible that a global cultural warfare could end the world in the 21st Century. This could happen if man continues down his prideful path without bringing God into his thoughts and deliberations.

Third, is there a connection between the downward slide of excellent moral living in any part of the world and the upheavals of geological tremors felt around the world? Is God trying to get our attention? Is He trying to tell us something? To some, the thought of a worldwide catastrophe ending the world is out of the question. Many of us cannot collate the connection of our unacceptable moral behavior in the eyes of God and the catastrophes that come as a result of a society that is out of control and sick with incurable symptoms.

The earthquake and Tsunami that occurred the day after Christmas in 2004 brought devastation to a score of Southeast Asian nations with approximately 225,000 people killed and missing. With many still missing who may never be found, it proved to us that a mini-global catastrophe could happen. In satellite photographs the ripple effect of the Tsunami was seen throughout all the oceans of the world as the waters of those oceans were movably impacted by the Tsunami's power. That region of the world that is rife with child sexual trafficking and immoral behavior is somewhat reminiscent of the worldwide flood of Noah's day, when God was displeased with the world and sent a great catastrophe. Three months after that Tsunami another aftershock earthquake hit the same region in Southeast Asia and over 400 people were killed. Then a 6.3 earthquake hit that region again in May of 2006 with over 6,200 killed.

Some would argue that it would seem strange that all the good that we have in this world could come to an end. If only we would practice peace and not war, the world would be able to continue as it always has.

The idea that the world will end can only be thought as a good thing if you believe in a Creator God who has all things in His control. The disciples were concerned about the end of the world; therefore they came to Jesus about this very issue.

Matthew 24:3 says, *"Now as He sat on the Mount of Olives, the disciples came to Him privately, saying, tell us, when will these things be? And what will be the sign of your coming, and of the end of the age?"*

Jesus explains very thoroughly how the world will come to an end when one reads the entire chapter of Matthew 24 and similar chapters in Mark 13 and Luke 21. It is through His power and authority that He has a plan for time and eternity. If the world comes to an end, it is because of man's sin and his penchant for war that will move the hand of God, bringing the end of all things according to His will. If one does not trust in God, the words of Jesus in Luke 21:26 indicates that their fear will be indescribable.

The purpose of this book is to explain how the events of this world such as wars, cultural lifestyles of evil, and the potentially built in catastrophes as earthquakes and other natural disasters, are events allowed by God because of man's sin. These events lead to the interruption of man's plans in the end-time by a loving creator God.

CHAPTER ONE:

The Cradle of Civilization

—⧟—

Before we understand the collapse of culture in a country like the United States, we have to understand what God is planning for the world as a whole. If societies in our world begin to collapse and we are in a survival mode, we should try and discover what is inbred in man that would bring the world to that point, and what seed of destruction is sown in his heart that would help precipitate that event. Has man's thoughts always been bent toward war? Is a dangerous jingoism built into our genetic code and did it start somewhere when civilization began? What happened in the beginning of time to make man the way he is today? We must go back to the Middle East to answer these questions. We will discover that there will be no peace in the world until the peace of the Cradle of Civilization has been settled in that part of the world. The Cradle of Civilization is currently a cradle in crisis.

Without peace, cultural wars will bring an end to the world as we know it unless Jesus Christ the Messiah returns in great power and glory to intervene. As we will see in God's Word, He does return to this earth to bring a peaceful solution to the failure of government and the crises of culture, and He will bring an answer to all the bloodshed and war in our societies.

PRECIOUS PLACE TO VISIT

My wife, two children, and I had a wonderful opportunity to visit Europe and the Middle East a number of years ago. After a stopover in Amsterdam, Holland, we flew over Germany, the Austrian Alps, Greece, and Yugoslavia, on our way to Tel Aviv, Israel. The sun was bright during our flight and when we landed, we were thrilled to see people from all over the world, young and old, all on Israel's soil. We took a bus to our hotel, spent the night and woke up to a beautiful morning the next day. Our very soul was thrilled and tears came to our eyes for being able to share this wonderful experience together.

The next few days we visited the usual tourist stops such as the Mount of Olives, Garden of Gethsemane, and Bethlehem. We visited Jericho, the Jordan River, Masada, and the Dead Sea. There is so much history to this land. Driving south of Jerusalem, all of a sudden, in the midst of nowhere, we came to Arad, a modern town of beautiful buildings, trees, grass, and flowers. We will never forget that place. We remembered God's Word as it reminded us of how God will bless the whole world through Israel and will rejuvenate her desert land.

Isaiah 27:6 says, *"The time is coming when my people will take root. Israel will bud and blossom and fill the whole earth with her fruit!"*

Isaiah 35:1-2 says, *"Even the wilderness will rejoice in those days. The desert will blossom with flowers. Yes, there will be an abundance of flowers and singing and joy! The deserts will become as green as the mountains of Lebanon, as lovely as Mount Carmel's pastures and the Plain of Sharon. There the LORD will display his glory, the splendor of our God."*

Isaiah 41:18 says, *"I will open rivers in desolate heights, and fountains in the midst of the valleys; I will make the wilderness a pool of water, and the dry land springs of water."*

We toured much of the old section of the Jerusalem area and saw the display of the Dead Sea Scrolls. As we neared the Western Wall, we could hear the prayers of God's people and felt a spiritual rush that was overwhelming. Just seeing and hearing the Jews pray was one of the most beautiful experiences of the entire trip. We knew however, that times were tense for everyone when we saw the armed Israeli soldiers on the walls, while people were praying. Later on, after driving to a fruit stand, you could feel the tension between the Arab proprietor and one of the soldiers who was trying to buy some fruit. This part of the world needed a lot of prayer for both the Arab and the Jew.

A bus ride north to the plain of Megiddo brought us to the Mount of Beatitudes. Our boat ride across the Sea of Galilee allowed us to see the surrounding hills, and at nighttime, the lighted cities that were set on the hills, just as the Bible says.

Later in the week we took a plane ride to Istanbul, Turkey and then a forty-minute bus ride to Izmir where our hotel was located. Izmir is the ancient site of Sardis, one of the Seven Churches of Asia found in the Book of Revelation. Izmir was the third largest city in Turkey and it is 98 percent Muslim. We saw the Aegean Sea and the lights across the bay that looked like Christmas tree lights. Another bus tour took us to the ancient ruins of Ephesus, Smyrna, Pergamos, and Thyatira, where some of the other seven Churches were located.

In Turkey we found out that every Muslim family buys a lamb and sacrifices it according to the tradition handed down to them from Abraham and Isaac. It was back again to Istanbul, a city that is on both continents of Europe and Asia. We had breakfast, did some sightseeing, visited a mosque, and then went to a showroom for Turkish rugs. We thanked God for this golden opportunity to see the land of the Middle East, the land of the Bible, and of God's people.

The Middle East is a breath-taking place to visit given the history of that geographically important part of the world, the Cradle of Civilization.

WORLD VIEW

Not everyone will agree that Christ will stabilize the world and bring peace to the land of the Middle East where so many people visit. How we think peace will come will depend on our "world view" and how we interpret what happened at the beginning of time. Our world-view depends on how we ponder the beginning of our own existence. To determine our world-view, one usually has to ask themselves these intensely personal questions, "Why am I here? Who made me? How do I determine right from wrong? If there is a God, who is He and what is He like?"

How these questions are answered, how we view the nature of man, and our purpose in life, is typically referred to as our world-view. This will help us determine many facts about the beginning of civilization and where it goes from here, and whether or not we believe peace will come and how we believe it will come.

"A person's world-view is usually the sum of their basic under-standing about life and how they see reality. It becomes their core belief. How they look at their world-view becomes the center of their life. All of us find our place within that world-view and our responsibilities to it. Our values, the actions we perform, and decisions we make are based on our world-view. If we don't believe that there is a God, then our world-view will have no consideration of an afterlife and of our responsibility to prepare for it. Therefore, our morals, ethics of life, and belief system would not matter for all of eternity because responsibility to them ends at death. There would be no afterlife accountability, so we could easily give way to situational ethics that pleases our senses here and now." (1)

Without God, moral absolutes would not be a part of our belief system so therefore we can do as we please. The Bible predicted that there would be people living like that as time for this world draws to a close.

If you are an atheist then you really have a problem. Not only will you have to stand at the end of time before a God you don't believe in, but you also have to constantly deal with the idea of God while you're living on earth. The atheist's biggest problem this side of eternity is that he can never stop thinking about God because he has to continually state his atheistic position in a world that is affected in its entirety, by God. He constantly has to defend the fact that he doesn't believe in a God or an afterlife. He is consumed with arguments and dialogue about a God that he says does not exist. Atheists spend just as much time and energy thinking about God as believers do. Their stand against God is the biggest endorsement that there is for a belief in God. Having to make a God that they do not believe in such an overwhelming part of the structure of atheism, is what makes atheism a religion. God's word makes it clear concerning the person who is an atheist.

> Psalm 14:1 and Psalm 53:1 *says, "The fool has said in his heart, there is no God."*

I heard Pastor Paul Beck of Christ Chapel in Centerville, Massachusetts speak about a person's world-view, the atheist's difficulty with a belief in God, and about the following questions that we need to ask ourselves about those issues.

[1] Why is there something rather than nothing? Is matter eternal or did matter come from nothing?

[2] How do we explain human nature? Why does man go wrong and why were we born with the absence of absolute goodness?

[3] How do we determine right from wrong? Are ethics merely situational? Do others bring their morality upon us or is it rooted in us at birth?

[4] How do we know what we know? Is in Intrinsic within us or does our education tell us what we know?

[5] What happens at death? Is there a dark void in the afterlife or is there something beyond the grave?

[6] What is the meaning of the history of life? Is life a series of random circumstances or is there a meaning and purpose to bring about a qualified end to all things? Is there a Christian world-view?

Believing in a Christian world-view is something that has impacted the Western world since the birth of Christianity and has made it easy for the Christian to believe in a Creator God. For the Christian, having a world-view that includes God creates responsibility and accountability to life, both now and in eternity. Our belief in Creation is based on scripture.

Genesis 1:1 makes it clear, *"In the beginning God created the heavens and the earth."*

Nehemiah 9:6 says, *"You alone are the LORD; You have made heaven, The heaven of heavens, with all their host, The earth and everything on it, The seas and all that is in them, And You preserve them all. The host of heaven worships you"*.

In Job 26:7 we read, *"He spreads out the northern skies over empty space; he suspends the earth over nothing"*.

Hebrews 11:3 says, *"By faith we understand that the universe was formed at God's command, so that what is seen was not made out of what was visible"*.

Pastor Beck went on to say that beside the Christian world-view, "we are confronted with world-views everyday in the newspaper, the university classroom, at work, on television, and on the Internet. It is seen in popular culture, in music, and the arts. All of these processes of information and education display a particular world-view." Your response to what you are confronted with determines your world-view and will cause you to ask where we all came from and where we are going. Our world-view determines how we view the beginning of civilization and the world and whether or not God figures into the process of peace for the Cradle of Civilization.

The beginning of civilizations across our globe plays a vital role in discovering who we are and from where our roots have come. As we check our history, we find that we came from a single family and can trace the beginning of our ancestry back to a single place and a single civilization. We are all related and someone began this whole process and it's not as long ago as most evolutionary thinkers believe that it is.

HISTORY IS KEY

Going back far enough, we discover that from the early beginnings of society there has been a prevailing evil that has caused man to be at war with each other that continues to this day. It now threatens the very societies that we live in because of the multiplied millions of people who are now living who can raise the threat of violence at any given moment anywhere on the globe.

To begin with there was the first murder when Cain killed his brother Abel which was followed by the first war among the nations. Some of the most ferocious wars in history were fought among brothers. When Abraham, the father of the nations bore his children Isaac and Ishmael, their descendents were bitterly opposed to each other and that's what in part has led us to the cultural conflicts of the Middle East to this day. Ishmael was born first but Isaac was given key promises and an inheritance that made Ishmael jealous and angry even though he was given promises as well.

Genesis 16:12 says that Ishmael *"will be a wild man, his hand will be against every man, and every man's hand against him"*.

That scripture is an indication of the problem that the sons of Ishmael would have with other nations in the world, including the Jews who were the sons of Isaac. We can understand the defense mechanism built into the Arab of today and why some of them and their world-view belief system are at the center of terrorism around the world. It was evident then, and persists even unto this day, that the Jew and Arab in conflict are at the core of destruction and terrorism. We can also see that our present and future are most definitely influenced by our past and where we began as a civilization.

The birth of these and other nations is an interesting pattern as you discover that one nation would rise to power and another nation would come to be influenced by it. Later, in succeeding generations, one of the nations would perhaps eventually overcome the other either through war or cultural influence.

Where and when did the nations begin and how did these nations rise to such greatness above all the other nations and for what purpose? Was there a master plan that was to bring the world to where we are today? How did they formulate their power? What were the first nations and when did civilization begin? These questions are critical if you want to understand the influence that nations have over each other and over the future of the world.

After creation, the peoples of the world moved south, east, and northwest away from the central part of the globe. South to Egypt, east to India and China, and northwest to Europe, civilizations flourished and developed. Cultures, languages, and territory had a way of developing out of the one common source.

CREATION VERSUS EVOLUTION

The story of the beginning traces back to Adam and Eve. God created mankind or Adam, the first human being. He then created Eve, out of or in contrast to Adam. She became the man with the womb, or "womb man," hence Woman. Their story is sometimes used satirically but it is the clearest picture that we have of how things began. They were made in God's image, not necessarily in the physical sense, but in life, character, spirit, and attributes.

Creation of the heaven and earth can be seen in Albert Einstein's general scientific theory of relativity, $E = mc^2$. Through this equation we can understand Creation and the idea that there was a higher power of unimaginable genius that became the cause of our world and the universe. Einstein's equation in his own words says "energy is put equal to mass, multiplied by the square of the velocity of light, showed that very small amounts of mass may be converted into a very large amount of energy, and vice versa."(2). That theory became the basis for the Atomic Bomb.

In support of Einstein's theory, other physicists had also stated that not only can mass be converted into energy but energy can be converted into mass. In Paris in 1933, physical chemists Irène and Frédéric Joliot-Curie took a photograph that shows energy along with light converting into mass. Another physicist said about Einstein's theory that, "90 percent or 95 percent of the mass of matter as we know it, comes from energy. That's the deeper vision."(3). That interpretation leads us to Creation. The Bible says that God created the heavens and the earth. How did He do it?

Genesis 1:2-4 says, *"The Spirit of God was hovering over the face of the waters. Then God said, "Let there be light"; and there was light. And God saw the light, that it was good; and God divided the light from the darkness."*

If Einstein's equation can be applied to Creation, those scriptures show us that God's Spirit, or His powerful energy, moved over the waters that He had created. That's the *E* or the energy in Einstein's equation. The Bible informs us that "God is Light" so during Creation, God easily spoken light into existence. He created light which no doubt would have been at the speed of light as we know it today, 186,000 miles per second. That became the speed of light constant in Einstein's equation or c^2, a very large number.

The energy of God moved through the timelessness of space by the power of His Holy Spirit and when He spoke the energetic words of Creation, they became worlds as they erupted through space by the speed of light that He had just created. His energy produced mass as it united with the power of His light multiplied to the highest degree and is the force that is behind the continued expansion of the universe. The land, the seas, the sun, the moon, the sky, the planets, and the stars appeared, as our solar system became part of our universe as it erupted by the power of His Spirit and light. His energy and light moved at a fantastic rate of speed in order to create the worlds. In other words, $E = mc^2$. In order to bring all things into existence, His energy had to be propelled at or faster than the speed of light by the power of His word which formed the mass of universe as we see it today. So you see, Einstein didn't create relativity, God did!

Einstein's theory of traveling at the speed of light also involves the slowing down of objects in relationship to other objects and in relationship to time. Imagine moving faster than fast, or beyond the point of fast, and at a speed much greater than the speed of light, where time stops. This helps us to envision and theorize about our

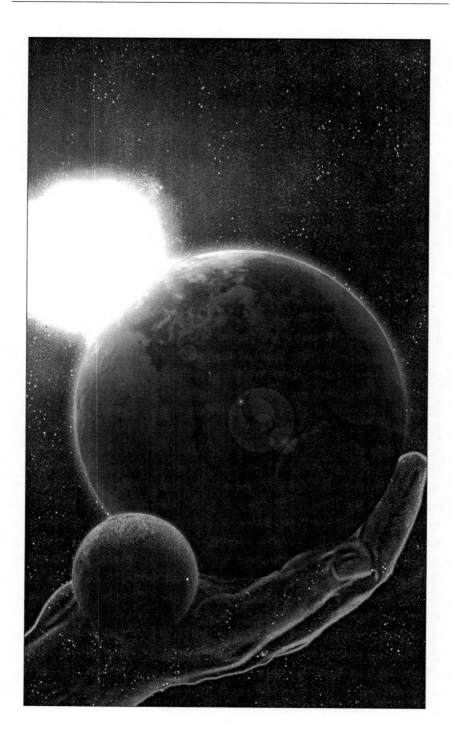

eternity with God. At the future resurrection of the saints of God, we will eventually break free from the spherical enclosure that encases us in dimensional limitations, to form a continuum of time that will empower us to become eternal beings. Of course, no one has traveled at the speed of light to prove whether or not Einstein's theory is true, but we can see how this could easily fit into an eternity that God would share with His created beings.

Creationism has been a central part of our worldview and of our Judeo-Christian heritage for the past 4,000-6,000 years, whereas evolution has been a prominent theory for only about the past 150 years. Some have forgotten that, such as former President Jimmy Carter, a Baptist who has indicated that creation should not be taught in the science classroom even though he personally believed in it. In one sweeping statement, he has ignored all the thousands of years of science that has been an outgrowth of creationism and religion. That's what the John Scopes "Monkey Trial" in 1925 was all about, the fact that Creation was taught in the American classroom and there were people fighting it! Creationism was there and had been there for years. It appears that Jimmy Carter doesn't want to mix religion and science. Small wonder, because he doesn't want to change Roe v. Wade either. He doesn't believe in abortion but rides the fence and straddles both sides, like many other politicians who are afraid to take a stand on the side of life. What are they afraid of?

There is a real conflict between the story of creation and the idea of evolution. I don't believe in the theory that the earth evolved gradually over a lengthy period of time nor do I believe the "Big Bang" theory, which was only recently postulated in 1927. In my mind, the only big bang was the booming power of God's voice speaking and bang, it happened. Without God is unrealistic. An opposing view to the theory says, "The Big Bang Theory is the dominant scientific theory about the origin of the universe. According to the Big Bang, the universe was created sometime between 10 billion and 20 billion years ago from a cosmic explosion that hurled matter in all directions. Although the Big Bang Theory is widely accepted, it probably will never be proved; consequentially, leaving a number of tough, unanswered questions."(4). In other words, not everyone accepts the Big Bang Theory as fact. "The demise of the Big Bang theory will not discourage evolutionary theorists from proposing other theories. Eventually, all such theories will fail."(**5**).

The problem and the confusion of evolution engulf us today. We have to continually hear various theories invented by man that are thrown at us, offering nothing but misinformation that they call science. It isn't just evolution and Darwinism that confuses people. Some Christians want to appease the evolutionists. They try to fit the Dinosaurs in somewhere by placing them in a world prior to Adam and Eve. They believe God created a world before Genesis chapter one and then say that first world was destroyed by the Devil when he was cast out of heaven.

I heard a scientist who happens to be a Christian say that some Christians, who sincerely believe the Bible, treat the Genesis text of creation in a separate manner from the rest of the Bible. He said that they believe in a loving, redeeming God, but doubt that God could create the world in seven days. Some of these same Christians say that the creation days of Genesis chapter one is perhaps 1,000 years or eons of time in length. They try to mesh creation and evolution in other ways to find a middle ground. They want to make creation and evolution more palatable to each other. The possibility of a 1,000-year creative day is based on a scripture found in II Peter.

II Peter 3:8 says, *"...do not forget this one thing, that one day is with the Lord as a thousand years, and a thousand years as one day"*.

That scriptural context is meant to show that God's eternity waits patiently for His plan to unfold, and is not meant as a theological argument concerning creation. If the creation days were 1,000 years long then the Lord would have rested for a thousand years on the seventh day, and that would be unacceptable. Also, to say that those days could have been different lengths of time or eons of times does a grave injustice to the Genesis text. The truth of the 24-hour creative day can be seen as it is compared with the 24-hour Sabbath day period. You can see that Moses had a 24-hour day in mind when he was speaking about creation.

Moses wrote in Exodus 20:11, *"For in six days the Lord made heaven and earth, the sea, and all that in them is, and rested the seventh day: wherefore the Lord blessed the Sabbath day, and hallowed it"*.

He also wrote in Exodus 31:17, *"It is a sign between me and the children of Israel forever: for in six days the Lord made heaven and earth, and on the seventh day he rested, and was refreshed"*.

Many Anthropological experts have tried to convince us that our ancestors emerged millions of years ago, evolving from apelike primates. Their story centers around a small number of genetic and anatomical studies of fossils and their interpretation of the geological record that they say dates back to millions of years ago. They try to convince us that there may have been some "missing link" in the human race that traces back to those early primates. Evolutionists would have us believe that the various pieces of bone and fossils come from various periods of time, anywhere from three to five million years ago. They have affectionately named some of the species of that time, "skillful man, believed to have used stone tools," "upright man" a humanlike primate coming from Africa, and "Lucy, found in Ethiopia,"(6) the earliest and perhaps mother of us all.

Their theory is that an extinct species of humans that evolved from that time are believed to be the ancestors of modern humans and may have had some type of primitive skills in tools, fire making, primitive language skills or cave writing. However, nothing denotes any intelligence in written or oral history prior to approximately 4,000 or 6,000 BC, and nothing is seen as coming from an organized civilization that made any influence prior to that period of time. The ancient evolutionary man may seem plausible to the scientist who espouses theory after theory to try and prove his evolutionary position, but it is not practical for the serious historian.

Taking Carbon Dating into consideration doesn't come close to their guesses as to how long man has been on the earth. According to the dictionary, Carbon Dating is "a chemical analysis used to determine the age of organic materials based on their content of the radioisotope (atoms of a chemical element) carbon-14; believed to be reliable up to 40,000 years." Did you get that? Reliable up to 40,000 years! The amount of these atoms decreases over time until they cannot be registered anymore. That's why the time clock is 40,000 years. How can one determine anything to be three to five millions years old, other than guessing? Here is another problem for the evolutionist; Carbon Dating does not work for rocks or other inanimate objects but only for things that at one time were living beings. Guess, guess, and guess! That's all the evolutionist has. Carbon Dating is not the foolproof answer. Evolutionists are having trouble with Carbon Dating because many of their findings fall into a timeline that is much later than the ancient history that they project the world to be. Carbon Dating is just not as well accepted anymore, period.

Now the latest is radioactive isotope dating of minerals and rocks, as scientists try to fit facts into their theories. They feel this is more accurate in proving the age of the earth but they continually move from one theory and concept to another. They try to follow scientific law, which should remain a constant, but they try to fit it into evolution, which is not a constant, because evolution says that one species changes into another. Assumptions are made on their part as they try to work with scientific law.

Attempts by evolutionists have been made to piece together a dramatic tale of missing pieces of bone and fossil data. But there has been no hard-fast evidence of history to underscore their "evidence". It has been a best-guess scenario. Their ideas when finding ancient tools, bones, or items in caves such as cave paintings is to place them in the "millions of years ago" category, rather than date them to a more reasonable time period that fits in with recorded time and history. There are simply no records or data from the period of time of "millions of years ago". The influence of Charles Darwin is noticeably seen in their conclusions as much of their ideas have missed the "mark" time and time again.

The Encyclopedia Britannica as well dates some civilizations back millions of years prior to the book of Genesis but without any detailed and logical record, they are just guessing at the dates. Instead, understanding that a Creator God had everything to do with the cradle of civilization helps all of us sense the significance of the origin and importance that it plays on the future of the world. The plan that God has can clearly be seen as one studies the Bible with the future of a world that will be changed by Him.

DOUBTING DARWIN

The evolutionists tell us that the earth began billions of years ago with a tremendous energy. A few billion years later, the stars appeared and then after the passing of a few more billion years, our solar system came into being. A few more billion years later, life began in the sea. Down to a few hundred million years ago there appeared plants, and then insects emerged. Trees begin to grow and dinosaurs came on the scene. On and on the scene is painted in the minds of gullible Americans including our children, as the evolutionist equations continue.

In 1859, Charles Darwin set the pace, but much of the material that we have about evolution has been written after his time. His idea about natural selection where the strongest of the species survive is one thing, but to leap from that to the idea that the species have cross-mutated and evolved over millions of years is quite another.

Adam and Eve would have had all of the necessary components for blond or black hair, or blue or brown eyes built into their genetic code. It would have been passed down through Noah, when he became the father of the New World after the flood. My wife, my son, and I all have dark hair but our daughter has blond hair due to the genetics on my wife's family who happen to be Swedish. *Species naturally change within the sphere of their own genetic code such as different colored hair or eyes and different features and complexions but there is no proof of the popular evolutionary thought of today that one species has changed into another species.*

Dr. D. James Kennedy said that even Darwin could not prove the transmutation of the species, whereby "one species turn into another, into another, and into another." He further stated that Darwin said, "When we descend to details, we can prove that no one species has changed. That is, we cannot prove that a single species has changed"(7).

Various comparisons have been made between the orangutan and other members of the ape family with the human skeleton. Continued reference is made to their similarities suggesting a relationship between man and the ape. Well of course there are similarities! They were both created on the sixth day in Genesis chapter one! That is why you see similarities of species in all of God's creatures that were created on the same day and after their own kind.

In Genesis chapter one, it says that vegetation, sea creatures, fowl of the air, and land animals were created after their own kind. That means there were no cross mutations as far as breeding was concerned, and none of the creatures evolved into another creature or changed over time to form another species. Any two different species of animals are separated in terms of reproduction because their DNA is distinctly different. Their chromosomes are so different that it makes them genetically incompatible for the reproduction process. In other words, they reproduce after their own kind.

An example would be the horse and donkey whose species are similar in origin but have different sets of chromosomes. When they mate, they reproduce the mule that is sterile, that cannot reproduce. Thus its line of reproduction can go no further. Thousands of years of recorded history has proved that not one species has evolved into another. For the survival of any species, they must have similar genes or chromosomes. Today, scientists are trying to force splice genes in order to reproduce a desired offspring in genetically incompatible animals. Of course, that opens the door for questions regarding its moral and ethical decency.

As far as the orangutan is concerned, it's laughable to what extent evolutionists will go to try and prove their theories. For over 40 years the Piltdown Man, found near Piltdown Common in Sussex, England in the early 20th Century, was considered a great archeological find as evolution's "missing link" between humans and primates. The Piltdown Man was eventually uncovered as one of the most incredible hoaxes in science. An orangutan had been stained to look fossilized and its teeth were filed to appear humanlike. The lie was uncovered as X-ray fluorescence was used to debunk the discovery. What more can be said about such other discoveries that supposedly link us to some distant past? Is the Neanderthal Man found in

Germany, as well as the Cro-Magnon Man found in France during the 19th Century, and the Kennewick man found in South America in the 20th Century an evolutionary Darwinian bias and archaeological figment of some scientist's imagination?

As of this date, some of the evolutionary conclusions attributed to Darwinism have now been viewed with suspicion and some evolutionists now believe that intelligent design brought us here, not evolution. For example, noted professor of philosophy at Oxford, Dr. Antony Flew, for years had supported the atheistic position against intelligent design in the creation of all things. He was regarded as the all-knowing guru on promoting atheism and has had a profound affect on colleges and universities where he spent decades making his impact on colleagues and students alike. At the age of 81, he has concluded that after more than fifty years of research, DNA has "provided materials for a new and enormously powerful argument to design. It has become inordinately difficult to think about constructing a naturalistic theory of the evolution of that first reproducing organism."(8). It seems that Dr. Flew has changed his thoughts about a God with power and intelligence. His thinking is more like becoming a Deist instead of a "born again" Christian, but nevertheless, he has renounced naturalistic theories of evolution. Basically, I take his thoughts to mean that the human race didn't start from amoebae, neither did we come from a type of amphibians that came out of the water to evolve into the human race such as the fish fossil that was recently found in 2006. He and many other evolutionists have changed their minds because of DNA, and have now determined that something more intelligent than evolution has brought us all here. Wow!

It's very sad because evolutionists have done irreparable harm to thousands of young lives and have helped spawn decades of atheistic thought in academia where there is a predominance of liberal educators and bias. They have ignored the evidence and work of many great men who have connected the idea of creation and the catastrophe of Noah's flood as evidence of the validity of the Bible. Maybe not all of the early scientists had a Christian perspective but men like Copernicus, Galileo, and Sir Isaac Newton, all studied astronomy, mathematics, and philosophy at prestigious Christian universities and monasteries. They may have debated science such as the earth's centrality in the universe as it relates to the Bible, but they stood to defend their Christian view of the world and its creationist thought, making a compelling story of good versus evil. Some modern day scientists don't realize that it was Christianity that gave science the initial impetus for its theories and conclusions that are its foundation today. Science and religion should be viewed as complementary rather than conflicting ideas.

We now have to unravel the faulty belief systems of the generation of the 1960's and 1970's who helped build on top of the atheism that had already found it's way into the early part of the 20th Century in America. The teachings of our universities and colleges are immersed in the teachings of evolution. They have accepted that theory but will not consider Creation as a part of their discussions. It may take decades to reverse those teachings if it is even possible. May God help us all!

Evolution has its greatest friend in western Christian nations such as the United States. Even Islam, Hinduism, and Buddhism, the largest religions following Christianity believe either in a Divine God or gods, an Eternal Being, or a Creator God that man can commune with. Western civilization that was at one time profoundly Christian is beginning to take a unique place as an anti-god culture.

The bottom line is that it takes faith to accept either evolution or creation. I choose creation and a Creator God because there isn't a thing that man has made or invented that has evolved into what it is today. Nothing that man has brought into his possession arrived by hocus-pocus, wishful thinking, or evolution. It always takes mans "hands on" experience to create what he has today, whether it is in agriculture, manufacturing, construction, or science. The pattern of things made by man fits the pattern of things made by a Creator. With man being made "in the image of God" it is therefore inconceivable to think of evolution as the source of this universe and of man's arrival on this planet. It takes faith to believe in creation.

Hebrews 11: 3 says, *"By faith we understand that the worlds were framed by the word of God, so that the things which are seen were not made of things which are visible."*

BEGINNING OF BEGINNINGS

Contrary to the teachings of the Church of Jesus Christ of Latter Day Saints, early civilization did not immigrate to America after the Garden of Eden and become the ancient civilizations of the Mormons. Their belief that ancient peoples came to the central part of America is a historical misconception of overwhelming proportions and their belief could be nothing further from the truth. It's one thing to have a belief that is contrary to what the world-view might be when it comes to theology or a relationship with Jesus Christ. It's quite another thing to ignore overwhelming evidence found in credible historical writings and in the very book that they are called to defend, the Bible. Their reliance is on the book of Mormon that was written thousands of years after the Genesis record and runs contrary to its account. It's no wonder they consider that "revelations" given to their leaders throughout the history of their church takes precedence over the interpretation of the Old and New Testaments. In other words, their revelations can take the place of the inspired text of the Bible. That's unfortunate because their penchant for digging for historical data runs contrary to how they interpret the Biblical historical record. They categorically and conveniently dispense of the Biblical record to fit their dogmatic interpretations, when instead, if they practiced more Orthodox accuracy, they could be so beneficial to the church at large. They believe that God is a physical God and that the cross of Jesus Christ does not provide complete atonement for the sin of man. If only their church would become like the Worldwide Church of God that stripped their unorthodox theology from its core teachings and joined the mainstream of doctrinal analysis and truth.

As to our question of what were the first nations and when civilization began, there are four recognized major centers of early civilization throughout the world. These early settlements were in Central America, China, Africa, and Mesopotamia. Despite the fact that some have tried to say that Africa is where early man first appeared, the earliest development of skills and settlements is deemed to belong to Mesopotamia where the modern nation of Iraq is currently located. This is where the earliest settled communities emerged, and eventually where urban centers with social and religious organization developed. Secular historical records place the earliest civilization at the Tigris and Euphrates Rivers in Mesopotamia. This is in agreement with the biblical historical record of Genesis 2:8-14 that says life began in the Garden of Eden where these same rivers flow through modern day Iraq.

The humble beginning of life in Mesopotamia is the time when organized civilization began in what is referred to as the Cradle of Civilization. History began for all of us at that time when skills developed such as the wheel, tools, pottery, and musical instruments. Some time later, an early alphabet, and writings on clay tablets, using pictographs or hieroglyphic symbols also appeared. We also see the beginnings of the discovery of mathematics, medicine, commerce, agriculture, astronomy, and of course religion.

The other civilizations in Central America, Africa, and China more than likely appeared sometime after the language of the world was confused and disbursed at the oft quoted Tower of Babel experience, in Genesis chapter eleven when the whole earth had only one language. Those at the Tower of Babel had foolishly tried to build a tower that would reach the heavens. It was sort of a primitive attempt at "space exploration."

Genesis 11:1-8 tells the Tower Tale. The people of the world said, *"Let us build ourselves a city, and a tower whose top is in the heavens; let us make a name for ourselves"*.

God recognized the futility of those efforts and said, *"Let Us go down and there confuse their language, that they may not understand one another's speech. So the LORD scattered them abroad from there, over the face of all the earth, and they ceased building the city"*.

God thwarted the plans that they had devised by causing them to speak different languages to confuse them and scatter them. After that, the other far reaching civilizations of the world began. This happened not long after the worldwide flood that is mentioned in Genesis chapters six through eight.

NOAH'S FLOOD

The story of Noah's flood is an important event that shows that God's hand was in control of the world during the early years of the cradle of civilization. In just a few thousand years after creation and the first sin, the people of the world had multiplied greatly. They lived much longer than what we live today due perhaps to different atmospheric conditions at the time. They filled the earth with many sons and daughters, who did anything that the imagination could think of and much of it was evil. In the Bible record, it didn't take long after creation for God to do something about their sin, so He decided to destroy the earth.

> Genesis 6:5 says, *"And God saw that the wickedness of man was great in the earth, and that every imagination of the thoughts of his heart was only evil continually"*.

This led to the flood that God brought during the days of Noah. Afterward, God restarted the peoples of the earth, and nations were formed to fill the earth. God had to deal with many firsts before and after the flood: the first sin, first murder, first destruction of the earth, and many other firsts that showed his anger. Eventually, God had to get past all of His anger and reveal His mercy, love, and forgiveness.

The evolutionist has no use for the record of the Biblical Flood. That's because the evolutionist's belief is based on Uniformitarianism, defined in the dictionary as "The theory that all geologic phenomena may be explained as the result of existing forces having operated uniformly from the origin of the earth to the present time." That means that the world slowly evolved over millions of years and the idea of a catastrophic flood is out of the question. It is taught as fact rather than theory.

The creationist's belief is based on Catastrophism, defined in the dictionary as "The doctrine that major changes in the earth's crust result from catastrophes rather than evolutionary processes." That means that a great global havoc or catastrophe came upon the earth and brought sudden changes to the crust of the earth, the oceans, and the atmosphere.

That's where Noah's flood fits into the picture. It wasn't gradual geological evolution but sudden geological change. It is believed that the world was made up of one or two super continents throughout most of geologic time known as pangaea. My thought is that before the flood the world was not comprised of the vast ocean depressions that there are today, instead, there were many large seas. Neither were there the high mountains of the Alps, Himalayan, or the Pacific Ring of Fire volcanoes as we see them today. The sudden geologic changes which the Bible describes as "fountains of the great deep," broke open from the depth of the earth and magma (lava) as well as water, would have come gushing over the earth making all the changes as we see them today. Rain poured forth from the heavens, and filled the depressions of the Atlantic and Pacific basins as the earth's crust heaved and caved in. It tore apart to form the tectonic plates and high mountains of the Alps, the Himalayas, and the Pacific Ring of Fire as well as other regions of the earth.

Contrary to evolutionary thought, places like the Grand Canyon in Arizona and the Niagara Falls escarpment in New York were given over to a catastrophic, metamorphic pressure that created a soft strata stone, developed by the intense and powerful global impact of Noah's flood. Instead of billions of years, the multiple layers of sedimentary rock of the Grand Canyon captured the vastness and astronomical power of a tremendous movement of water that was part of an immediate restructuring of the geography of our planet. The erosion of Niagara Falls that scientists say occurred over a period of 8,000 years, actually displays the power of the water of Noah's flood that helped form that escarpment about 4500 years ago. Even the Ice Age that would have occurred at that time was far shorter in length than what evolutionists depict.

Before the flood erupted, all species of animals were able to trek across every part of the globe to arrive just in time at Noah's Ark. Those that were not a part of God's plan, in which two would survive from each species, were caught in the floodwaters, or mountains of lava pouring forth from the earth. They were either drowned, burned alive or fossilized for all eternity. It was the catastrophic pressure that fossilized these mammals instantly.

There are hundreds of global or partial-global flood legends mentioned in one form or another in almost every culture in the world. This shows that it is something that should be taken seriously. In these legends, there are different names or survivors that came through a sizable proportionate flood, and in different areas where the flood took place. The fact that a flood has been so dramatically reported, even though the details are reported differently in each culture, proves that it was not a figment of someone's imagination or written with a particular religious bias. It is a cultural historical fact and phenomena that was passed throughout the world from generation to generation. The differences aren't proof that the flood didn't happen, but proof that it more than likely did. The fact that there are different names or survivors in practically every culture shows that there was no coercion or corroboration of a flood story.

Their ancestral heritage truly believed that it happened and they transmitted their knowledge of the flood to each succeeding generation. They simply reported what they believed to be an historical event much like any other family event that was passed on from one generation to the next. Anyone would know the family story to be true with a slight variation of facts, depending on which person would be telling it. The story would be altered, or some of the information would be lost is its transmission but the fact remains that the multi-cultural reporting of the flood as best they remember gives credence to the evidence found in the Bible.

Of course there are those who would challenge anyone's belief that there was an actual flood. Reading the likes of Charles Darwin, Carl Marx, and Sigmund Freud, one would find that these men who were tied in with Humanism did not accept the Biblical flood record. Their teachings and those who follow behind them in their views actually look at the flood during the time of Noah as something of a myth, a classic story of fiction and legends.

Why these "flood legends" then? Because they were based on the facts recorded in the early writings of Moses 1500 years before the time of Christ, and eventually recorded as part of one of the oldest and most comprehensive historical records available, the Bible. The flood story in the Bible has its roots tied to the earliest record of civilization. That makes the Bible a book that we can accurately compare other historical events to and feel comfortable in its reliability. That book with its accurate recording is religiously based and we know that religion has not only been the bedrock of every society, but it has permeated our thinking, our languages, and how we act and conduct ourselves, whether atheists like it or not. Once the flood took place, the stories of the flood went with everyone in their different languages as they were scattered over the face of the earth after the Tower of Babel. The flood story could not help but be in every culture and society.

The flood was of such cataclysmic and mammoth proportions that ancient cities along the coasts of various nations were buried in deep waters, as the floodwaters did not recede to their earlier levels. The recording of the flood and the unearthing of other archeological findings dating back to Old Testament time coincides perfectly with Bible history and records, which dates the beginning of civilized history at approximately 4,000 to 6,000 years before Christ. There are some Creation Scientists who are Christians that date the beginning of civilization a few thousand years earlier than that.

Dinosaurs would naturally fit in with the events of Genesis and the epoch of Noah's flood. Dinosaurs either became extinct before the flood or it is quite possible that Noah took small species of dinosaurs as well as other small or infant animals into the Ark. The Ice Age would have occurred at this time and if there were dinosaurs still outside the ark, they along with other great "mammoths were quick-frozen by the millions under sudden and extremely cold conditions. There must have been a sudden and permanent change in the climate, from sub-tropical to Arctic. Every indication is that the mammoths died suddenly, in intense cold, and in great numbers. Death came so quickly that the swallowed vegetation is yet undigested in their stomachs and their mouths."(9). This perhaps would be when the dinosaurs that were not aboard the ark were buried and fossilized. The surviving dinosaurs that would have come off the ark could have eventually become extinct after the flood just as we have lost other animals over the thousands of years since the flood. It is entirely plausible that conditions on the earth changed dramatically after the flood so that the dinosaurs and other species of animals could not survive, and they died off.

Then you have the amazing stories of the numerous sightings of Noah's Ark high in the hills of Mount Ararat. Throughout the 20th Century, expeditions were conducted in that area and researchers have come back with amazing stories of what they say is a great structure shaped like a huge ship on the side of the mountain embedded in ice. We are not positive these sightings to be true, but we have been told that satellite photos were taken in various years of an apparent structure that some believe is the bow of a ship. Other than the few who have supposedly seen the Ark, the local government has not allowed extensive research to verify whether or not it could be Noah's Ark. If it is Noah's Ark, and if it can be verifiable, it would be the greatest archeological discovery since the miracle of the resurrection of Jesus Christ.

If you believe the genealogy of the Bible found in Genesis chapter ten, you would understand the impact and disbursement of the nations after the time of Noah's flood. Some question the historical credibility of these records, but recorded there are the names of these great peoples and where they were scattered.

After the flood, the world was divided between the three sons of Noah. Many good Bible Concordances will list where the families were disbursed after the Flood. The family of Shem occupied the region from Iraq westward to the Mediterranean Sea. Some of those nations were Assyria, Arabia, Israel, Edom, Moab, and Syria. The family of Ham settled in the central nations and southwestern nations that were in Africa. Some of those nations were Libya, Ethiopia, and Philistia. Japheth and his family were part of the great northern nations of Asia and Europe. Some of those nations are today's Britain, Germany, Italy, France, Russia, Greece, Ireland, Spain, and Portugal.

MASS DESTRUCTION

According to scripture, God promised Noah that a flood to destroy the earth would never again occur. I'm sure Noah must have felt a great sense of relief as God gave him the following wonderful promise.

Genesis 9:11-13 says, *"And I will establish my covenant with you; neither shall all flesh be cut off any more by the waters of a flood; neither shall there any more be a flood to destroy the earth. And God said: 'This is the sign of the covenant which I make between Me and you, and every living creature that is with you, for perpetual generations: I set My rainbow in the cloud, and it shall be for the sign of the covenant between Me and the earth.'"*

Every time we see a rainbow in the sky after it rains we can be reminded of that Old Testament promise. That promise of the protection of life is good not only for mass flooding, but for mass destruction of any kind by God. There is no indication in the Bible that God will destroy masses of people again on the earth in one fell swoop by His hand as He did during the days of Noah. True, the Bible says that the next time the earth will be destroyed will be by fire but that's after the horrible judgments of what the Bible calls great "Tribulation," and "Armageddon," recorded in the book of Revelation. It is also after the rewards given to the people of the earth as determined by God, and after we are with Him. Then the end of time will occur, and one of the last things God will do is remake the earth through fire.

God is waiting for that day, the right moment in history when He will close the events of time. Could there be a connection between the sin of our day and a possible collapse in society as in the days of Noah? There seems to be a definite link between the flood in Noah's day and the fiery destruction of the world in the future as God can use much of the storms and disasters in our oceans and climate to change the world. The following scripture is one of several verses that some misapply to try and prove that there was a world prior to the present one and that it was destroyed by the Devil. Instead, the following verses definitely belong to the days of Noah and the flood, and they connect with what God plans to do with our world in the future.

II Peter 3 verses 6-7 and 10 say, *"The world that then existed perished, being flooded with water. But the heavens and the earth which are now preserved by the same word, are reserved for fire until the day of judgment and perdition of ungodly men. But the day of the Lord will come as a thief in the night; in the which the heavens shall pass away with a great noise, and the elements shall melt with fervent heat, the earth also and the works that are therein shall be burned up".*

Just as in the days of Noah, the earth is reserved for a future time of judgment. Not only will God remake the earth in the future; He has a change of plans and a design for the entire universe. The book of Revelation reminds us that at the end of time God will bring in a new heaven and a new earth.

Revelation 21:1 says, *"And I saw a new heaven and a new earth: for the first heaven and the first earth were passed away; and there was no more sea".*

The world and indeed all of creation itself is waiting for the right timing of its deliverance. If there is to be a collapse of the world and its cultures, we His created joy are waiting for this change with great anticipation!

Romans 8:19-23 says, *"For the earnest expectation of the creation eagerly waits for the revealing of the sons of God. For the creation was subjected to futility, not willingly, but because of Him who subjected it in hope; because the creation itself also will be delivered from the bondage of corruption into the glorious liberty of the children of God. For we know that the whole creation groans and labors with birth pangs together until now. Not only that, but we also who have the first-fruits of the Spirit, even we ourselves groan within ourselves, eagerly waiting for the adoption, the redemption of our body."*

THE GRAND STRUGGLE

The struggle revealed in the previous scripture is a depiction of what we are still faced with today as the whole world is reeling in utter chaos and turmoil. We see a microcosm of this grandiose struggle everyday that we see acts of war and terrorism, as these acts have become global in their proportions.

The Middle East cradle of civilization, the very place where it all began is where the biggest problems seem to be rooted. There is something about the fact that this unsettled part of the world needs to be settled or the world will continue to hang in the balance because of the worldwide fear and terror that the cradle of civilization has spawned throughout the centuries by warfare and vengeance. The world's birthplace and oldest settlement of bad sentiments has been full of bloodshed. It affects and impacts everything else in a ripple effect that has stretched around the world, similar to a Tsunami. Much of the world's philosophical, psychological and emotional well being is tied to that part of the world.

Why is that? Because it is the place where our early civilization was formed and it needs to be brought to a state of peace. Nothing else will matter until it is. It started there and it will end there. Unbeknownst to most of us, the heart, mind, and soul of the world is crying out and wants to return to that cradle of civilization, back to where all these early events of the Bible took place because it wants things to turn out right. Call it whimsical, practical or psychological. In order to try and make things right at the core of our past, there is something bred deep within the nature of the world that creates a response in us to make us want to return to where it all began, "in the beginning".

The world is in a state of constant turmoil, as God has not let us live down the lack of peace in that region. Therein lies the dilemma. The moment we may think that we have won the peace, according to the Bible an unraveling of events will be unleashed that find their dramatic cataclysmic conclusion at the Battle of Armageddon. The Jews, Christians, and Muslims have been disobedient over the centuries, and have clashed over that part of the world. God wants to finalize His plans and fight against those who have not followed His way. Jesus Christ does return to the earth for a day of final battle, which will bring peace.

Part of Zechariah 14:1-5 says, *"Behold, the day of the LORD is coming...For I will gather all the nations to battle against Jerusalem; Then the LORD will go forth and fight against those nations, As He fights in the day of battle. And in that day His feet will stand on the Mount of Olives, which faces Jerusalem on the east". Thus the LORD my God will come, and all the saints with You.*

The leaders of the world will try and win the peace without Christ. The peace will unravel and things will become disastrous until Christ appears to bring peace to the cradle of civilization and the rest of the world. The utter chaos and collapse of the world will find a reversal of its fortunes as a just and loving God recreates the world.

Every recent American President has tried to find a solution to the Arab/Palestinian and Israeli problem. With the most recent political victories in Afghanistan, Ukraine, Iraq, and the Baltic's, the push is for democracy around the world. The quest is for Palestine and Israel to live side by side in a land that is ripe and being readied for the Second Coming of Jesus Christ! Other countries of the Middle East and Asia are at the doorstep of democracy. While visiting Europe in 2005, President George W. Bush declared that the world could not rest until there is peace between the Israelis and Palestinians. Each President has wanted to heal the hurt in that part of the world.

LIFE CYCLES

The reason there is the need to heal the hurt at the core of civilization is because it is similar to the life cycle of any person who lives from infancy to old age and wants a psychological healing before they die. They begin as a baby and depend on everyone else for sustenance in their early years. Then in later years, at the end of their life, their health may fail and they have to depend on others again because of old age and infirmity. Many times they suffer with Alzheimer's or some other disease and cannot take care of themselves. They may live with a relative, in a retirement village, assisted living, or a nursing home. They live a full and complete life, reminisce and think about their childhood, and then return to that same reliance on others before their body decays and dies. It's the cycle of life that causes them to sometimes think about their childhood and in their mind return to it again.

Many times before a person dies, they become tender hearted and they make peace with family members and old enemies. There is something about returning to the core of their existence when they were tender and pliable, in order to make sure that everything is right before they leave this life. It's important to go back to those unsettled differences and to be at peace with yourself, your spirit, and with God.

I have had the opportunity to be at the bedside of many individuals who have passed from this life to the next. My own grandmother Teresa Cecchini, who came from Italy, died at the age of 94 with her body spent but her mind still intact. Before she died, she life-cycled and just like a baby, she cried out for her own mother whom she hadn't been around or seen in years, and who had passed away many years before in Italy. Something in her cried out like in infancy, in order to enter into her rest and to subside into peace at her moment of death. My wife's mother did a similar thing when at the end of her life she cried out for her father.

Civilization is like an aged person who needs to settle all things in its heart, mind, and soul. Not knowing what the dilemma is, we fight cultural wars here and there, and we have ambassadors representing us to broker peace around the globe. We are unwittingly trying to settle the peace and come to grips with the problems in the Middle East. Peace is the missing element at the core of our existence, the cradle of civilization. Peace has to come and must come to the Middle East. It has to be done, and it will be done, at least temporarily.

Great horror and troubled times will then occur before Jesus Christ returns. When the Four Horsemen of the Apocalypse begin their rampage at the end of time, the world will be shocked into a beginning of sorrow and calamity as the Antichrist, war, famine, and death are introduced. Revelation chapter six describes their march. The fourth and final horseman makes his awful appearance as death.

Revelation 6:8 says, *"So I looked, and behold, a pale horse. And the name of him who sat on it was Death, and Hades followed with him. And power was given to them over a fourth of the earth, to kill with sword, with hunger, with death, and by the beasts of the earth."*

The ninth chapter of Revelation describes more death from the hands of an army of 200 million that comes from the east region of Asia, the most populated area of the world. Great havoc will be unleashed upon the world at this time.

Revelation 9:16-18 says, *"By listening, I could tell there were more than two hundred million of these war horses. In my vision their riders wore fiery-red, dark-blue, and yellow armor on their chests. The heads of the horses looked like lions, with fire and smoke and sulfur coming out of their mouths. One-third of all people were killed by the three terrible troubles caused by the fire, the smoke, and the sulfur."*

ROCK A BYE BABY

Of course those scriptures and the conflagration that results from those battles opens up a scenario that has challenged the minds of brilliant scholars and historians who want to know what our future holds. It has long been reported throughout history of the battles that have ignited in and around the Middle East for ages. The Arabs who invaded Israel in 637 AD took control of the land of Palestine and they were a dominant force there for over 1200 years. The response from the Christian world was to conduct Crusades of war to try and win Palestine back. The Crusades that took place after the turn of the first millennium AD were considered unsuccessful, and it took wars at the end of the second millennium to wrest control of Palestine from the Arabs. God's master plan was being unfolded in the Middle East.

The mammoth struggle and conflict for peace in civilization throughout the millennia that never seems to find an answer and never seems to be settled, has not centered in Mexico or Central

America. It isn't in the Niger River in Africa or the Yellow River valley in China. These regions have had their difficulties throughout the centuries, but the conflict of all conflicts is in the cradle of the world's civilization. The shifts of the greatest struggles for global cultural power throughout the millennia seem to have centered on the Middle East and much of it has been between the descendants of the two sons of Abraham. It is where it all began, in and near the heart of God and the cradle of civilization, the Tigris and Euphrates Rivers in Mesopotamia and in the rest of the Middle East.

The world's heart and soul is restless. The cradle has been rocked in an unsettled manner. The baby is crying. In essence, the aged civilization is crying for its mother. The civilizations of Mexico and Central America, Africa and China have not pained or cried as much as the earliest civilization of Mesopotamia. Nothing will get done until that score is settled.

When will everything end? Will we look for a world leader of profound social utterance and religious graces to help us look into the soul of our earliest civilization? Are we to expect someone that is perfectly suited to give answer to the struggles of our physical and geographic dilemmas?

Will powerful dictators rise to conquer and destroy, or will they lay down their weapons of terror? Will super powers finally settle the score and win the peace? Will the rest of the world be lulled into peace and contentment? Will negotiations and peace accords finally take hold and last for a lifetime?

We shall see, for there will be no peace in the world until there is peace in the Cradle of Civilization, the Middle East. The Middle Eastern area of Mesopotamia is a strategic spot. The lines in the sand have been drawn. No one is sure where the lines will fall politically, between Europe, the United States, the Middle East, and the Far East. There is only one who can bring the peace and that person is Jesus Christ, when He returns again to this earth.

The traditions of Islam say that Jesus will return to earth for a special role in the future day of judgment to turn the hearts of the world to the Islamic faith. The Christian believers do agree with Islam that Jesus Christ will return to the earth, but they also know that the hearts of the Christians will embrace the Coming Savior instead of a world religion.

How we survive the end of the world and the coming of Jesus Christ depends on our world-view, which of course is shaped by how and when we believe the cradle of civilization to have started and whether or not it was God who started it all. This has been the grand struggle, with creation being the force that leads us to the conclusion, that God is interested in the people that He has created and His master plan for the world.

CHAPTER TWO:

The Shift of Global Super Powers

—⚊—

Global and cultural power shifts take place when one nation that has been a super power over the nations of the world, loses the status of that position through military combat, cultural change, or weakness. That privilege is then passed to another nation that rises in power greater than the nation it is succeeding.

God has used these great power shifts while the human race has continually been disobedient. God waited patiently as one power rose above another as He continued to protect His chosen people, or a selected remnant of believers, or a massive nation that He used to bring his future final plans to fruition. Remember, the Bible says that a thousand years is only like a day to God. Therefore, if the earth has been here for 6,000 years, that's nothing in all of God's eternity. He is working on His future plans to bring all of His creation to a climax of belief in Him.

Birthed right in the middle of the great global super power shifts since the beginning of civilization, was a plan that God had to once again walk the earth as a man in order to bring His master plan for the earth to a close. God lost His place walking with man when Adam and Eve were cast out of the Garden and out from the direct presence of God. He made a number of appearances in the Old Testament but He had not walked with man until Jesus Christ came. After they disobeyed God, Adam and Eve's eyes were opened because of their sin.

Genesis 3:7-8 says that Adam and Eve *"...knew that they were naked; and they sewed fig leaves together and made themselves coverings. And they heard the sound of the LORD God walking in the garden in the cool of the day, and Adam and his wife hid themselves from the presence of the LORD God among the trees of the garden."*

MESSIANIC MARVEL

Immediately after the sin of Adam and Eve, God developed His plan to walk with man and save him in the midst of all the coming global destruction. In Genesis we read of the future demise of God's enemy the Devil and an indication of a future hope of salvation for mankind. Here is the word that God spoke to that tempter of the problem he would have with the one who would eventually be birthed from the woman. I believe that the woman's seed mentioned here is an indication of the birth of Jesus.

Genesis 3:15 says *"And I will put enmity between thee and the woman, and between thy seed and her seed; it shall bruise thy head, and you shall bruise his heel"*.

It was a prophetic picture of God's plan for a future Messiah. The Devil would be fatally harmed with a blow to the head by the plan of God's redemption of man. Christ would pay a price to redeem mankind with death, but His resurrection would make it seem as a bruise to His heel.

The introduction of sin through Adam and Eve had a tremendous impact on humanity. It set the stage that helped create powerful nations. Global super powers would eventually be formed from their offspring and the shifts of those powers across the world would impact people globally after Noah's flood. With those great nations challenging the peoples of the world, the appearance of a Messiah for the Jewish people had been believed in and revealed over and over again throughout their history. The miracle of a messianic messenger was God's answer to man's dilemma of sin. A nation had been chosen and a family ancestral line was put in place for God to walk again with His creation.

To say that God as man would walk with man, is something that Islam and other religions do not understand or believe. Even though the Jews and the Muslims believe that Jesus came to this earth, the fact that it was God who came and walked with man, is what has placed a wide chasm between these religions and Christianity. The following verse was given to Moses and is what the Bible indicates about a coming Savior who would speak to mankind.

Deuteronomy 18:18 reveals, *"I will raise up for them a Prophet like you from among their brethren, and will put My words in His mouth, and He shall speak to them all that I command Him."*

This scripture in Deuteronomy says a prophet would come and was a prophetic promise of this future Messiah. It was confirmed in the New Testament by Peter in Acts 3:22 and by Stephen in Acts 7:37 as they repeat that verse in Deuteronomy practically word for word – Jesus Christ was indeed that prophet. However, there are other scriptures that speak of the coming Messiah as well. The following passage reveals His birth to fulfill prophecy that a Messiah was to be born to govern Israel, be responsible as a son who would become a man, and be the ruling heir in that government.

Isaiah 9:6 says, *"For unto us a Child is born, Unto us a Son is given; and the government will be upon His shoulder. And His name will be called Wonderful, Counselor, Mighty God, Everlasting Father, Prince of Peace."*

Isaiah 53 also reveals even more about the Messiah that would come. I heard that scripture read during a seminar at a Jewish Synagogue in Hartford, Connecticut a number of years ago. The Rabbi who was conducting the seminar said that Isaiah 53 was talking about Israel and not Jesus Christ. I thought the interpretation the Rabbi gave was a bit of a stretch for a chosen people who were looking for the Messiah to come as a person, to then say that the scripture meant the nation of Israel. Far from it! Isaiah was talking about someone in the singular and not the plural, not a nation or a group of people. Isaiah 53 is powerfully prophetic for all the peoples of the world.

> Isaiah 53:3-6 says *"He is despised and rejected by men, a Man of sorrows and acquainted with grief. And we hid, as it were, our faces from Him; He was despised, and we did not esteem Him. Surely He has borne our grief and carried our sorrows; yet we esteemed Him stricken, Smitten by God, and afflicted. But He was wounded for our transgressions, He was bruised for our iniquities; the chastisement for our peace was upon Him, and by His stripes we are healed. All we like sheep have gone astray; we have turned, every one, to his own way; and the LORD has laid on Him the iniquity of us all."*

This scripture shows us God had a plan for the future of the world that brought the Messiah to man. It happened right in the midst of the power of the Roman Government Super Power. Christ's entrance into the world was so powerful that it caused a change in how the Roman government treated the early Christians as Christianity eventually became the "in vogue" religion of the Western World. Christ's birth also caused the western world to change the calendar to reflect His birth. That's why the west is living in the 21st Century, and not the Islamic, Jewish, Hindu, or Chinese Centuries.

> According to Galatians 4:4, Jesus the Christ was born in *"the fullness of time."*

In other words, He was born at the right moment. Jesus had come to the nation of Israel but the Jews rejected the offer made by God that Christ would bring them salvation. The Jews who knew plenty of suffering throughout their history couldn't understand that principle of suffering later recorded about Jesus in the book of Hebrews.

Hebrews 2:9-10 that says, *"But we see Jesus, who was made a little lower than the angels, now crowned with glory and honor because he suffered death, so that by the grace of God he might taste death for everyone. In bringing many sons to glory, it was fitting that God, for whom and through whom everything exists, should make the author of their salvation perfect through suffering"*.

The Jews could not fathom that a Divine Messiah had to suffer and die for the sins of the people. That Divine Messiah was none other than God Himself in the form of Jesus Christ. Caiaphas the Jewish High Priest who was motivated by political ideology, mentions in the Gospel of John in purely Jewish Messianic terms that it was important that someone should die not only for the nation of Israel but for all the people of the world.

John 11:49-52 says, *"And one of them, Caiaphas, being high priest that year, said to them, 'You know nothing at all, nor do you consider that it is expedient for us that one man should die for the people, and not that the whole nation should perish.' Now this he did not say on his own authority; but being high priest that year he prophesied that Jesus would die for the nation, and not for that nation only, but also that He would gather together in one the children of God who were scattered abroad.*

Christianity is the only major religion that says that the God of Creation became a man in order to understand the sufferings and pain of mankind. Christianity is the only religion that says that the Son of God died for the sins of the world, resurrected, and is sitting on a throne at the Father's right hand. That God who became a man is none other than Jesus Christ.

The birth of Christ was right in the midst of the shifting of global powers. He was the answer to the cultural power struggles that was bringing destruction to the world through sin. Sin brought murder, murder brought nationalism, nationalism brought war, and war brought destruction. Christ brought peace in the hearts of humanity even though humanity continued to instigate war throughout the world in every millennium since that time.

LOOK FOR CLUES

If the world is to come to an end, it is important to discover what would bring us to that point. How have the nations of the world interacted and what could bring us to such a world disaster? How did they get along over the years and will things get so bad that everything will finally reach a climax that will bring total chaos and annihilation? The history of international wars and the challenges that nations have made toward each other can give us a clue.

With nations and terrorist groups having super nuclear, chemical, and biological weapons, whether or not we can survive as a people becomes a critical question. The shift of global super powers gives us a clue as to how nations respond to each other and which nations will rise in power next in order to bring us closer to the end time.

Global power shifts among major super power nations happen infrequently, but when they do, they are consequential and last for numbers of years and even generations. Generally speaking, power shifts occur among two or three nations that are vying for power over restrictive areas that affect their nations and also when they vie for power over sub-nations of lesser rank and power. They seek to overcome other nations until their war machine or their influence is the greatest in the world. In many instances they run roughshod over other nations and imprison the vanquished people and culture with their own culture. In essence, they become a super power, similar to the Soviet Union of the recent past and of the lone super power of the United States today. The other nations of lesser rank or power also struggle to make their impact felt throughout their local region or throughout the world.

With these power shifts come the seemingly inherent feeling of destiny in those nations that they have their power and rank because of psychological, political, or perhaps religious reasons. The leaders usually think that they and their nation have a place in history and give little or no regard to other nations that they feel rank second place to their destiny. The world seems to center around their nation and place in history. They move within that dynamic and geo-political power and usually wreak havoc of global proportions. Their war machine rumbles over everyone.

The United States seems to be an exception to the cruel super powers of the past. There are people that would disagree with me and say there have been times when the United States has behaved ignobly in the past. That may be true, but as the United States has fought wars, it has always seemed to be able to reach out to the people they have disagreed with and eventually soundly defeated in war. Many times they have helped their enemies physically, financially, psychologically, and morally. They have even allowed them to keep most of their own culture. These shifting of global and cultural powers over the centuries is what will cause God to eventually put an end to all the destruction and mayhem. God will bring in His plan for peace that will replace all the war.

HISTORY IS HIS STORY

Unless history lives in the present, it has no future. Until we learn from history and how to apply it to today, our future lies in question because what we live today becomes the history of tomorrow. History plays a vital role in the nations of the world because it not only tells us about our past, but it determines where we are going in the future. Not everyone is interested in history, but it is vitally important to learn about it in order to understand the power and balance of culture, and the influence of the nations throughout the millennia. We must conclude that history makes an impact on political powers, and the balance of those powers that still effect us today.

God knows about the nations of the world and who will rise in power next and He has always been in control of those nations throughout the earth. He has a plan and it can be clearly seen in the historical pages of His book, the Bible. He knows the choices these leaders will make, and based on that information he predestines it to happen. There has always been one nation, group of nations, or a people that were in the forefront and used by God to dispense His righteousness or His judgment. In the past, He has used Israel, Babylon, the Roman Empire, Islam, the Nation of England, the

United States and the Church, just to mention a few. Therefore, there is a formula that emerges from the chaos and brutality of man's sin and warfare.

The formula is this: ***The best way to know what God is going to do in the future is to find out what He has done in the past.***

In other words, you have to be a student of the Bible and its history to understand God's method of operation. You must derive a sense of His goals for humanity and His brand of morality for the world. God is developing His plan and He is lining up the nations as if they were set on a large chessboard. He is moving the pieces. He is in command. In the end time, He will speak His resounding Word as if the biblical Battle of Armageddon was a game of chess and He will yell, "Checkmate". At this time, the nations will be in a stalemate and God will have had His way. There will be a Battle of Armageddon. Christ will have returned!

In Revelation 16:14-16 we read that the evil spirits will *"go out to the kings of the earth and of the whole world, to gather them to the battle of that great day of God Almighty. Behold, I am coming as a thief. Blessed is he who watches, and keeps his garments, lest he walk naked and they see his shame. And they gathered them together to the place called in Hebrew, Armageddon."*

EYE OF GOD

Meanwhile God has been working out His plan for the ages through the global shifts of power. His eye was on the world as He detailed one purpose, one nation, and one plan. There is a definite history of global power shifts, and the center of that power is coming back to Europe and God's focus will be on the Middle East. Israel and the Arab world will be involved. All the nations of the world and the current and former super powers of the world will be involved.

All of this is happening under the watchful eye of God. His influence will help create the entire scenario, while the nations of the world move within the power of their own self-will. God determines who is in power, the length of time they exist, and even their boundaries.

The Bible says in Daniel 2:21 that God *"removes kings, and sets up kings."*

Psalm 75:6-7 says, *"For exaltation comes neither from the east nor from the west nor from the south. But God is the Judge: He puts down one, and exalts another."*

Acts 17:26 says, *"From one man he made every nation of men, that they should inhabit the whole earth; and determined the times set for them and the exact places where they should live."*

This scripture is an indication that God is in control of the political and historical events of this world. This is in spite of the power struggles of the leaders of the nations of this world. It is also in spite of these two horrendous facts found in II Corinthians 4:4 and Ephesians 2:2.

The Devil is the *"god of this world"* and the *"prince of the power of the air."*

The Devil indeed has power in this world and influences the affairs of man, but to a lesser degree. The earth still belongs to God and God is still in control of its destiny. We live for His Glory!

Psalm 24:1 says, *"The earth is the Lord's and the fullness thereof; the world, and they that dwell therein."*

God has the ultimate upper hand in every matter including His predetermined plan for the ages. God knows how He wants His creation, the ultimate love of His creative genius, to conclude.

Isaiah 46:10-11 speaks of God's ability as *"Declaring the end from the beginning and from ancient times the things that are not yet done, saying, my counsel shall stand, and I will do all my pleasure. Calling a bird of prey from the east, the man who executes my counsel, from a far country. Indeed I have spoken it; I will also bring it to pass. I have purposed it; I will also do it."*

What those verses say is that God as an eternal being who does not change, can speak His will from so deep within the past, that His eternal word becomes His will that can reach far into the future even before any predicted event actually takes place. His eternity that has no beginning and no end places Him above the confines and limitations of time. Those verses also show us that God was intent on saving Israel despite her selfish ways.

God has always been affected by the will of man and He takes man's will into consideration. He bypasses man's will if necessary when man is disobedient as Israel was, and calls in His instruments of judgment to accomplish His will. Those instruments of judgment could be an enemy nation described in that chapter as a ravenous bird and as a man to execute God's counsel.

We can see God's foreknowledge at work in which He knows everything that will happen in the future, including man's willful decisions that God uses to execute His counsel. It is God's judgment of the prideful form of man's war machinery. It is also His predestination at work in which He locks in a predetermined plan in response to man's actions that is teamed together with His own counsel. It is a masterful mix of the will of God and the will of man as God's overall plan is linked with the steps of man.

Therefore, we cannot blame evil things on God, as willful and prideful man becomes a victim to the principle of action and reaction. It is more than random circumstances as man acts out his sin and God reacts in judgment. God does not cause bad things to happen but predestines everything as man becomes consumed by his own personal decisions outside of the will of God. If we follow God, He will show that His love is with us when difficult things happen to us.

His foreknowledge of events determines his predestination as in the case of salvation mentioned in Romans.

Romans 8:29 says, *"For whom He foreknew, He also predestined to be conformed to the image of His Son, that He might be the firstborn among many brethren."*

God and man reaching a decision together and in accordance to His will are similar to a husband and wife who are pictured in the Bible to be one flesh, have their own set of individual wills, yet are supposed to reach decisions in agreement. Just as they go through the decision-making process that unites them in marriage and direction for their lives, so God and man both contribute to God's will. As a wife submits to her husband and as a husband loves his wife and both can understand God's will for their lives, so God and man determine the will of God as he submits to God. A decision together would satisfy the spirit of man that has come to know God and the Spirit of God that brings the wife and the husband closer to each other and to God. According to the Apostle Paul in Ephesians 5:32-33, the beauty of that kind of relationship is comparable to the mystery of Christ's love for the Church. Therefore, the will of God and the will of man are supposed to work hand in hand as indicated in God's Word.

Romans 12:2 says, *"And do not be conformed to this world, but be transformed by the renewing of your mind, that you may prove what is that good and acceptable and perfect will of God."*

James 4:13-15 says, *"Come now, you who say, "Today or tomorrow we will go to such and such a city, spend a year there, buy and sell, and make a profit"; whereas you do not know what will happen tomorrow. For what is your life? It is even a vapor that appears for a little time and then vanishes away. Instead you ought to say, "If the Lord wills, we shall live and do this or that."*

MIGHTY KINGDOMS OF OLD

There has always been one super power nation, or as previously mentioned two or three super powers that have vied for world dominance. The conflicts have always been east versus west or north versus south. It's always one nation interested in another nation's culture, wealth, or technology. They may have a severe disagreement with them over that culture or some territorial boundary, or they may simply be fearful of its army or weapons, as nations and cultures would rise and collapse. It has happened many times in history, as history has a tendency to repeat itself. Man doesn't seem to learn, or he hasn't been able to understand God's plan.

Major global power shifts can be seen as long ago as the earliest civilization. Each of the major super power nations of old are seen as persecutors of the nation of Israel, a design by God because of Israel's disobedience. Egypt was a major power in the early days of the cradle of civilization and kept Israel in captivity for 400 years before releasing them to become a nation of their own. Assyria eventually challenged Egypt's emergence as one of the vast superpowers in the Middle East. The great Egyptians of the south lost their powerful position as power shifted to that great Assyrian nation in the North. Then Assyria invaded Israel and brought the northern peoples of that land captive to Assyria.

It was more than likely at this time that the powers of India and China began to grow in the East. With the spreading of the great civilizations of people in that part of the world, God was already beginning to prepare vast armies of the east for His final plan for the ages thousands of years later, as power started shifting toward that region of the world. Remember that God being a God of eternity sees and makes His plans far into the future as if it's only a blink of an eye and as if a thousand years are as a day to Him.

The book of Daniel whose events took place nearly 600 years before the time of Jesus Christ, describes the next four mighty kingdoms in the Middle Eastern and Western civilizations that would lead the world up into the time of Christ's birth. They were the powerful kingdoms of Babylon, Medes and Persians, Greece, and Rome.

King Nebuchadnezzar of Babylon had a dream of a mighty man-like image with a head of gold, chest and arms of silver, stomach and thighs of brass, legs of iron, and feet of iron and clay. He couldn't even remember the dream much less know what it meant. Daniel was called in and he interpreted the Dream that was about those four kingdoms.

In Daniel 2: 38-43, Daniel speaks to the king of Babylon and says this, *"You are that head of gold. After you, another kingdom will rise, inferior to yours. Next, a third kingdom, one of bronze, will rule over the whole earth. Finally, there will be a fourth kingdom, strong as iron—for iron breaks and smashes everything—and as iron breaks things to pieces, so it will crush and break all the others. Just as you saw that the feet and toes were partly of baked clay and partly of iron, so this will be a divided kingdom; yet it will have some of the strength of iron in it, even as you saw iron mixed with clay. As the toes were partly iron and partly clay, so this kingdom will be partly strong and partly brittle. And just as you saw the iron mixed with baked clay, so the people will be a mixture and will not remain united, any more than iron mixes with clay."*

That dream shows us that Babylon, as the head of Gold was the most powerful and influential nation of all time. During that time, Nebuchadnezzar's reign had most of the known world in his grip. The Medes and Persians depicted by the chest and arms of silver would follow but their kingdom was inferior and less influential. They encompassed approximately the same territory but they weren't as morally strong as their predecessor. The Greek nation shown as the trunk of the stature of brass was a weaker kingdom both politically and morally. The reign of Alexander the Great was short lived and Greece peaked at the time of his death. He died at a young age and his nation was divided after his death. Finally, the Romans, as the legs of iron, would be morally still weaker than the previous three but their war machine and influence would be massive. Each kingdom was of diminishing moral standing and political cohesiveness, making each kingdom inferior to its predecessor leading to their collapse.

The final kingdom, shown as feet of iron mixed with clay, will be the weakest of all and will be a collaboration of ten nations brought together as one, symbolized by the ten toes. It is a future power in which the people will be of one kingdom but will not remain united in that final ten-nation kingdom of power, as clay does not mix with iron. It is not a New Kingdom but an outgrowth of the previous kingdom of iron. The introduction of a foreign substance of clay mixed with the iron does not blend well with any of the other materials. It is symbolic of the marriage of two distinct cultural elements, the strong will of an autocratic kingdom and its mixture with the cultures of the people.

This is what eventually creates disunity in the nations of the world. That disunity fits in with the strong yet weak democracies of today, a political enigma of powerful nations whose core is weakened by the will of the people and the rights they espouse. These democracies are being encouraged by the United States and will play into the hands of the last day's dilemma and used by the one opposed to Jesus Christ during the Great Tribulation. He is called the Antichrist. Such will be the nations of the last days in part, before Jesus Christ returns to the earth.

KINGDOM DETAILS

We need to understand these four mighty kingdoms in more detail. Babylon or Mesopotamia, the area of the Garden of Eden and modern day Iraq, rose as an uncontested superpower. Their power was in the known part of the north within the same region as Assyria. Babylon became a vast superior power as seen by the head of Gold. They also were a nation that persecuted Israel and eventually invaded them and carried its people from the tribe of Judah into captivity.

Stemming from Genesis chapter ten, Babylon as an early super power has taken on mystical proportions throughout history. Developing from the earliest civilization, its varied forms of religious and social systems have made an unmistakable impact on each of the succeeding nations from that time until now. Satan got to the core of civilization with his anti-god spirit of rebellion to influence the religious and social powers of the world and he began with Babylon. Babylon and its power are recorded in Genesis, the first book of the Bible. It can also be seen as Mystery Babylon in Revelation, the last book of the Bible.

Traces of Babylon's earthly and worldly power was left unchallenged by God and allowed to flourish when it was drawn deeper into cultic and devilish practices, and has intrigued generations of nations. God used this nation in his plan to create havoc with His disobedient people, and its system will be used by God to bring a disobedient world to its knees as God continues to use the powerful shifts of the nations.

Mystery Babylon in Revelation 17 was well understood by John who wrote the book of Revelation during the days of the Roman Empire. Even though he couldn't clearly see the meaning of the specifics of his prophecy, he saw Mystery Babylon as a power that was still taking form while he was living and that it had created a powerful impact from the birth of civilization until the time of his writing. The influence of this mystery was still unfolding and it was going to take centuries for it to materialize within the coming global powers until the last days.

Babylon remained strong for years and it was a power that Egypt and Assyria feared. The Persians who also persecuted Israel during the time of Esther, eventually challenged Babylon and ended that nation's physical power as a major player in that part of the world. However, Babylon's evil social and religious influence was still seen within the nations of the world and throughout the centuries.

Greece, under the leadership of Alexander the Great, eventually superceded the Persians and brought the center of power to Europe. His armies were mighty and powerful and swept from the west to the east. When his empire was divided after his death, one of his successors invaded Israel and made a mockery of Jerusalem's religious rites by sacrificing a pig on their altar at Jerusalem. The political might of Greece eventually subsided, but their culture had a powerful impact on other cultures worldwide. Greece was a sophisticated nation but eventually was weakened and declined to a Roman Province status.

Greek was the prestigious language of Jesus' day and its powerful influence on the world scene had everyone wanting to speak Greek. It was fashionable!

Today, it is the English language that is the culturally important language to speak. Many people seem to know how to speak it just like the Greek language at the time of Jesus. This of course, can make English one of the major languages of the world in the end time, and more than likely a major language that the Antichrist will be able to speak.

After the Greek Empire came the mighty Roman Empire and the battle for dominance throughout the centuries since. The power that was shifted toward Europe came under their control and became the greatest, most powerful nation up to that time. The weakness and eventual collapse of the Western half of the Roman Empire spun the Empire into the "Dark Ages". Power shifts eventually emerged in Europe as various nations tried to out maneuver each other. Cultural wars and skirmishes continued for centuries as more minor shifts of national powers occurred.

God in the future will eventually bring an end to these mighty nations, their influences, and their vast shifts of power from one nation to another. As recorded in Daniel chapter two, a mighty kingdom will follow these evil nations, depicted as a rock cut out of a mountain to become a great force that will last forever, and will destroy the power and influences of those nations of old. We believe that this is the Kingdom of God that He will set up, and Jesus Christ will reign as "King of kings and Lord of lords." That Kingdom of God will never end!

Daniel 2:44-45 says, *"And in the days of these kings the God of heaven will set up a kingdom which shall never be destroyed; and the kingdom shall not be left to other people; it shall break in pieces and consume all these kingdoms, and it shall stand forever. Inasmuch as you saw that the stone was cut out of the mountain without hands, and that it broke in pieces the iron, the bronze, the clay, the silver, and the gold—the great God has made known to the king what will come to pass after this. The dream is certain, and its inter-pretation is sure."*

PALESTINE PRE-OCCUPATION

With the rise of Islam some 400 plus years after the birth of Christ, nations have become pre-occupied with Palestine. In order for God to eventually heighten the drama and bring in end-time events, Islam, as a counter-religious group to the power of Christianity, was developing to bring God's timetable to a close. No one knew what was in store for the Christians and the Jews as Islam rose to the forefront. Islam's interest was to invade and conquer many nations, including the nation of Israel as they were still under the corrective hand of God.

It has been the national policy of some nations to totally annihilate the nation of Israel. The nation of Israel has no similar counter policy toward any nation. In Psalm 83, we can see the mindset of nations at that time and the willingness of those who would fight against Israel and attempt to destroy them. It speaks prophetically as well because we see how Israel has been viewed for thousands of years. Today, we are not sure which nations may be included or excluded in that prophetic Psalm, but some of those nations are now under the jurisdiction of the Arab world that include the nations of Jordan, Lebanon, Syria, and Iraq. It describes the agenda of those nations.

Psalm 83:4 says, *"Come, and let us cut them off from being a nation; that the name of Israel may be no more in remembrance"*.

There are a number of scriptures that indicate that the Jews will return to the land of Israel from the many other nations where they were scattered. They have been persecuted throughout their history but from their land in Palestine where they reside today, they will flee into a wilderness area in the last days in order to encounter God. One of these scriptures is found in Ezekiel.

Ezekiel 20:34-35 says, *"I will bring you out from the peoples and gather you out of the countries where you are scattered, with a mighty hand, with an outstretched arm, and with fury poured out. And I will bring you into the wilderness of the peoples, and there I will plead my case with you face to face."*

The drama heightens as the book of Revelation describes a woman that is symbolic of Israel who flees to the wilderness and is somehow protected from the hand of the Devil during a time of great tribulation. Corresponding with this, the book of Daniel says that a person of unique and great power whom we refer to as the Antichrist, will overthrow many countries but mentions a land area in present day Jordan that will escape his hand. Perhaps, that is where Israel or its leadership, depicted as that woman, will flee in order to hide despite the fact that Jordan has opposed them.

According to Isaiah and Daniel, the Antichrist will not be able to touch the nations of Edom, Moab, and Ammon where present day Jordan is located. They will perhaps become sympathetic toward Israel and be their protectorate as many Jews flee to the wilderness during the "Great Tribulation" that will come upon the world. The following verses reveal such action.

Revelation 12:14 says, *"But the woman (Israel) was given two wings of a great eagle, that she might fly into the wilderness to her place, where she is nourished...from the presence of the serpent."*

Daniel 11:41 *"He (Antichrist) shall also enter the Glorious Land, and many countries shall be overthrown; but these shall escape from his hand: Edom, Moab, and the prominent people of Ammon."*

Indeed, does Israel flee to their wilderness experience in the countries of Edom, Moab, and Ammon now occupied by Jordan, during the Great Tribulation so that the Antichrist won't be able to persecute them there? As far back as the book of Deuteronomy, it mentions the trouble that the Jews will have in the last days.

> Deuteronomy 4:29-31 says, *"But from there you will seek the LORD your God, and you will find Him if you seek Him with all your heart and with all your soul. When you are in tribulation, and all these things come upon you in the latter days, when you turn to the LORD your God and obey His voice (for the LORD your God is a merciful God). He will not forsake you nor destroy you, nor forget the covenant of your fathers which He swore to them."*

> Deuteronomy 31:29 says, *"...you will become utterly corrupt, and turn aside from the way which I have commanded you. And evil will befall you in the latter days, because you will do evil in the sight of the LORD, to provoke Him to anger through the work of your hands."*

The seventh chapter of the book of Revelation describes those who would be heavily persecuted and have to be protected by the seal of God on their foreheads. This mark of protection that is granted by God, is a direct literal opposite of the mark on the forehead or in the right hand placed later by the Antichrist on those who worship him. Those protected here in this chapter by God, are the Jews during the Great Tribulation as seen by the mention of the twelve tribal names of the Children of Israel in the verses that follow. These Jews have the seal of God's mark and become the true servants of God at that time and will do His work.

> Revelation 7:1-3 says, *"After this I saw four angels standing at the four corners of the earth, holding back the four winds of the earth to prevent any wind from blowing on the land or on the sea or on any tree. Then I saw another angel coming up from the east, having the seal of the living God. He called out in a loud voice to the four angels who had been given power to harm the land and the sea: 'Do not harm the land*

*or the sea or the trees until we put a seal on the foreheads of
the servants of our God.'"*

The Christian position is usually to defend Israel. They took
that position because of the Judeo-Christian association that they
have had over the centuries. It wasn't always that way. The early
Christians had an animosity toward Israel in part because of their
connection with the death of Jesus Christ. Later on, with the rise
of Islam as a bigger threat, man's answer was to enact crusades to
defend Palestine. However, God's resolve and restoration for the
Jews would come much later. Islam had been creating havoc in the
eastern part of the Roman Empire. The Christians felt they had to
defend that land and consequently, a rebirth of the Jewish/Christian
relationship took place. However, the Jewish/Christian relationship
has been on again, off again throughout the centuries. Much persecution came from early Christians and Church leaders, thinking they
were doing it for God and the cause of Christ. It centered on the
mistaken analogy that God would now bless the Church and not
Israel anymore.

What was with that land? Even Jenghiz Khan and the Mongols
from the East had their hearts set on the Middle East and stormed
through Palestine as they marched around the world. Was it that
Israel had the unfortunate position of being at the crossroads of
geography? Or as previously discussed, was it the aching of the
cradle of civilization that needed to be brought to peace? Are the
nations subconsciously trying to find a solution to the childhood of
the world? Is God doing something to bring us all to answer for the
trouble in the Middle East?

One thing we have to conclude and understand is that Jerusalem
is the place where all three of the world's major western religions
converge, Jewish, Islam, and Christianity. Jerusalem is the most
important religious city for the Jews because it has been the center
of all their religious rites since the time they were established in that
land as a nation. Jerusalem, because of Abraham is also one of the
most important religious cities for Islam besides the cities of Mecca
and Medina. Jerusalem is the historic religious city for Christianity
because of the death of Jesus Christ and the birth of the Church

there. That is the crux of the difficulty! Two major religions claim it to be their own and the third religion is forced to be the peacemaker! All three major religions are burning with passion for this city. It is no wonder that they lay such importance on that city as we see that zeal described in the writings of Psalms.

Psalm 137:5-6 says, *"If I forget thee, O Jerusalem, let my right hand forget her cunning. If I do not remember thee, let my tongue cleave to the roof of my mouth, if I prefer not Jerusalem above my chief joy."*

The only way that all of us can survive the tremendous shifts and struggles for dominance of power both politically and spiritually is with the help of God. God has to help us! If not, the world is in big trouble!

EUROPEAN WHIRLWIND

There has been a threaded connection of evil and warfare that has worked its way through the global powers that have appeared across the continents throughout the centuries, especially in Europe. From the power vested in them by the religious leaders of the day, many of the nations of the Roman Empire in Europe rose and fell. With the religious arm of the empire being very influential, the political arm rode and fought with their authority and blessing.

With a split occurred between the East and West, the unified Roman Empire had collapsed and ended in two stages. During attempts at reviving the empire, its death toll had long before sounded as Europe saw "the collapse of the last attempt of the Eastern Roman Empire to assert its authority in the West by force or arm. The hour was drawing near for a new Holy Roman Empire to arise, again claiming the Eternal City itself as its center, the abode of its spiritual head. The Papacy made a certain profession of loyalty to the Empire, as a protection to itself"(1) from threatening nations. This is when the power and position of the Bishop of Rome as the Pope came into prominence. Thus the unity between the political and religious systems of society was sealed and shows the connection between the spiritual and the physical regimes of the empire.

The rebirth of the Holy Roman Empire was led most notably by Charlemagne when Pope Leo crowned him as the Roman Emperor in 800 AD. It was during this time that England, Germany, France, and Spain had feuds with each other, but also had to fend off the rapidly growing religion of Islam. The spiritual warfare of the religious element of the empire had begun.

The Germanic division of the Holy Roman Empire was then secured when Otto I was crowned Emperor in 962 AD by Pope John XII. That was the FIRST REICH. The SECOND REICH was born in 1871 with the uniting of North and South Germany and lasted 47 years until 1918. The historic REICH'S of the Germanic branch of European power were used by God to set the world up for its climax. The political power of the world shifted toward Germany as endorsed by the religious branch of the Holy Roman Empire. It was the Germanic division of the empire that eventually sealed the awful fate of the Jews during World War II in order for God's mercy to be revealed and to re-establish the Jewish people in their land. God's wisdom, knowledge, and ways are powerful and mysterious.

There was something demonic about the collaboration of the spiritual and political Roman Empire. Clearly there was a diabolical union between the Church and the endorsements they made during the rise and fall of the European nations and their wars. Instead of the separation of church and state as some people try to make America to be, this was the unification of church and state. The seed of the Antichrist spirit was clearly planted in Europe as the Popes gave their blessings to the rebirth of those nations.

While attending the 1972 Olympics, I saw outside of the Olympic Stadium in Munich, Germany, a hill where some of the rubble of Hitler's THIRD REICH of 1933-1945 had been plowed over and buried. From the symbolism of that burial mound, a vanquished Germany has risen and will in the future, pass on a New European Union that is established out of the disaster of the old order. The spiritual and political connection established by the religious Popes and the political Emperors has not been lost. The ghosts of France and Germany's political past will haunt the spiritual powers that have been weakened by compromise. In a bizarre twist, a united Europe will rise above the past sin of the "ethnic cleansing" of Jews to become the New Europe that will be under the control of the Antichrist. He will return the continent and the world to an unprecedented persecution of the Jews and the saints of God during the Great Tribulation that is mentioned in the Bible. The Antichrist is described as a "great horn" and will make war with them according to Daniel.

Daniel 7:21 says, *"I was watching; and the...horn was making war against the saints, and prevailing against them."*

During the time of that Great Tribulation, the world will be looking for a leader to answer all the economic and social ills of society. In the near future and leading up to that time, Europe won't be seeking cabinet officers to solve the dilemmas of the world. They will be looking for a man of great stature and authority who will capture the mind and allegiance of all of Europe's people and lift them out of the economic and political quagmire into which they are sinking. I doubt if they will care if he is a god or a devil.

Daniel mentions that there will come an Antichrist who will arise from the rubble of the Kingdoms of the old Roman Empire as seen in the dreams that both Nebuchadnezzar and Daniel had. Following the kingdoms of Babylon, Media/Persia, Greece, and Rome, Daniel depicts the rise of the kingdom of the Antichrist. In chapters eight and eleven we see a description of him as it fully shows his character and intention.

Daniel 8:23-24 says, *"And in the latter time of their kingdom, when the transgressors have reached their fullness, a king shall arise, having fierce features, who understands sinister schemes. His power shall be mighty, but not by his own power; he shall destroy fearfully, and shall prosper and thrive; he shall destroy the mighty, and also the holy people."*

Daniel 11:36 *"Then the king shall do according to his own will: he shall exalt and magnify himself above every god, shall speak blasphemies against the God of gods, and shall prosper till the wrath has been accomplished; for what has been determined shall be done."*

To add to all this mysterious drama, news commentator George F. Will says that both Russian President Vladimir Putin and French President Jacques Chirac want to be the "President of or lead a superpower."(**2**). I'm sure that their nations in Europe and Asia will support those ambitions or the ambitions of their successors. That kind of goal will be the attitude of the future Antichrist. George Will then went on to say concerning the papacy, "The new Pope says that one reason he chose the name Benedict was to honor Saint Benedict, the sixth-century founder of a monastic order important to the conversion of Europe. The Pope wants the name Benedict to be a strong reminder of the unrenounceable Christian roots of European civilization."(**3**). The focus of attention that is returning to Europe both politically and religiously will be there for some time to come.

The powerful nations that will arise in Europe will perhaps be just a precursor to the ten kingdoms that will arise, and that are symbolically seen in the ten toes of the vision in Daniel chapters two and seven. They either will be ten individual nations or a ten-kingdom grouping of nations led by the Antichrist. Could this massive power of Europe be a part of or give way to a greater power of ten kingdoms in the last day?

Those future kingdoms have their roots in the Euro/Asia area, and the European Union that is rising in power today could quite possibly be the embryo of those kingdoms. The power in Europe did not peak in the early centuries and has not yet peaked today. The European Union has not yet come to its full potential power as it someday will and perhaps challenge the global influence of the United States as the latest super power. Recent summits involving the economies of the world have brought together both political and celebrity star power in order to provide answers for the economies of the world. Unfortunately, it is done without acknowledging God or relying on Him. Will these world leaders and celebrities give a jump-start to powerful union that will arise in Europe in this Century?

Will the European Union become, give way to, or be a part of, a greater global group of nations as the Group of Eight (G-8) nations of Canada, France, Germany, Italy, Japan, Great Britain, Russia, and the United States are today? Just as they were at one time the G-7 and then added Russia to become the G-8, will the G-8 eventually add two more nations? Will they be the economically emerging giants of China and India to become the ten final nations as mentioned in the Bible? Will that Group of Eight (G-8) nations, who are the economic forum and strength of the political power of the world's most industrialized nations, just be a part of or lend support to the final ten kingdoms that will dominate Europe? Perhaps a group of nations could arise within the European Union possessing economic and military might that would be even more powerful than those nations themselves. Only God knows!

Should we be looking for something that is based in Europe but more global that will control the world's economy? Will these nations in the future be a broader based ten-nation consortium or groupings of worldwide nations of power along with perhaps some of the Asian and Mediterranean nations of the Arab Kingdoms? They could form a broad but shaky Euro/Asian Kingdom in the last days. In the end, because of their connection with the Middle East and the tenuous balance between the Jewish and Arab world, the G-8 powers will be forced to take sides. Because of their ideological differences, their actions will eventually draw the world to war.

In the meantime, will these nations take part in an economic restructuring of the world so that cash will not be needed? With the possible advent of a worldwide cash-less society, these G-8 nations could become, or pave the way for the dispensers of economic might and worldly justice in the last days. Because of stolen I.D. and the problems of credit card fraud, will our current experimentation with personal identification to be placed somewhere on the body be instituted soon? Will it be as a mark in the hand or in the forehead to replace credit cards to buy anything of necessity? With it's ease of implementation and tracking, will that kind of a mark make it easier in the international markets of the world? The book of Revelation says that the Antichrist will dispense such a mark!

Revelation 13:16-18 says, *"He causes all, both small and great, rich and poor, free and slave, to receive a mark on their right hand or on their foreheads. And that no one may buy or sell except one who has the mark or the name of the beast, or the number of his name. Here is wisdom. Let him who has understanding calculate the number of the beast, for it is the number of a man: His number is 666."*

Despite the fact that France and the Netherlands voted against the approval of the European Constitution in 2005, out of Europe's eventual cooperation will come either that block of nations or another group of nations that will be used by the Antichrist. We know that ten nations will rise in the last days and be used by the Antichrist as signified in the books of Daniel and Revelation. It can be seen as the ten toes of Nebuchadnezzar's image dream in Daniel chapter two and the ten horns of the Beast of Daniel's dream in Daniel chapter seven.

In that seventh chapter of Daniel, we read that Daniel had a dream similar to Nebuchadnezzar's dream of the four mighty influential kingdoms leading up to the coming of Christ's Kingdom and the last days. Daniel's dream was of four beasts that came up out of the sea that represented the same four mighty kingdoms that Nebuchadnezzar saw. He recognized the significance of the ten kingdoms of the last days in the fourth beast that He saw, which was fierce. It had ten horns as in "horns of power" representing ten associated kingdoms. From out of those ten horns came another horn that we believe to be the Antichrist, and who will have to fight against and subdue three of those ten kingdoms. Daniel describes the Antichrist's power as a horn that is greater than the rest.

It shows that with some of them it will be a forced allegiance. Democracy will come hard and that's where the delicate balance between socialistic governments and democracies will come into play. Apparently there will still be a shifting between the two ideologies as three of those horns or nations will be plucked up by the roots by being either overthrown, or soundly convinced of the alliance. The weakness of democracy and a dying socialism will perhaps give way to a powerful European autocratic rule headed up by the Antichrist.

Many expositors see this horrible fourth beast that Daniel saw as the Roman Empire. It is from the logical historical sequence of nations that have transpired over the centuries and the system of the Roman Empire that the Antichrist will eventually come. That fourth beast as I have said was the Roman Empire that followed the first three empires of Babylon, Media/Persia, and Greece. The horn of power that is depicted as the Antichrist is gruesome and horrible but a necessary evil for the last days. He rises amid the power of ten kingdoms of diabolical evil and strength.

Daniel 7:7-8 says, *"After that, in my vision at night I looked, and there before me was a fourth beast—terrifying and frightening and very powerful. It had large iron teeth; it crushed and devoured its victims and trampled underfoot whatever was left. It was different from all the former beasts, and it had ten horns. "While I was thinking about the horns, there before me was another horn, a little one, which came up among them; and three of the first horns were uprooted before it. This horn had eyes like the eyes of a man and a mouth that spoke boastfully."*

Daniel 7: 23-25 further states, *"The fourth beast is a fourth kingdom that will appear on earth. It will be different from all the other kingdoms and will devour the whole earth, trampling it down and crushing it. The ten horns are ten kings who will come from this kingdom. After them another king will arise, different from the earlier ones; he will subdue three kings. He will speak against the Most High and oppress his saints and try to change the set times and the laws. The saints will be handed over to him for a time, times and half a time"*

According to Daniel 9:27, the Antichrist will guarantee a covenant of protection to the Jews and the region for a period of seven years. The time period spoken in the above verse will be the latter half of that seven year Tribulation in which great persecution will be dealt to the saints of God. With time meaning one year, times meaning two years, and half a time meaning one half year, there will be three and one half years in which the Antichrist will be the strongest and most willful. We know that the spirit of the Antichrist has already been working in the world and is still at work today leading up to that awful event.

I John 2:18 says, *"Little children, it is the last hour; and as you have heard that the Antichrist is coming, even now many antichrists have come, by which we know that it is the last hour."*

All of those European and Asian mighty kingdoms of old had a part in the persecution of the nation of Israel throughout the centuries. God allowed them to come to power and bring correction to Israel and prepare that nation and other nations for the end times. Then he removed those powerful invading nations from the scene through global power shifts because of their own sin and disobedience. God would use the evil of those nations to dispense His will and then cast them off because of their arrogance.

An example of that is seen in the book of Isaiah when God said He would punish the nation of Assyria for their pride when they fought against Israel. They thought they accomplished that feat under their own direction and power but it was God who controlled them.

Isaiah 10:12-13 shows God saying, *"I will punish the king of Assyria for the willful pride of his heart and the haughty look in his eyes. For he says, By the strength of my hand I have done this, and by my wisdom, because I have understanding. I removed the boundaries of nations; I plundered their treasures; like a mighty one I subdued their kings.*

In Isaiah 10:15 God then answered, *"Does the ax raise itself above him who swings it, or the saw boast against him who uses it?"*

In other words is the pottery greater than the potter, and is the tool mightier than the one who wields it? By His Word we know that it is God who makes the changes and not the leaders of the nations. God is in control and He will direct the nations.

As we now know, God's Armageddon is not ready yet. The end is not yet to be. The Cradle of Civilization and its cry is not ready to be settled. Before that happens, we will see a reshaping of Europe to become a superpower in its own right whose borders will be similar to the United States. Within that superpower we will see the spiritual and political connection of all that is going on with the nations of Europe. The religious community will play a huge role in its future success.

Right now, the final global super powers of the European/Western Hemispheres are waning in power and their culture will continue to collapse in part because of their narcissism. Their self-centeredness will bear the mark of a moral decline that has brought so many empires crumbling in their dust. The weakness of the feet of Iron and Clay in Nebuchadnezzar's dream is in the mix. The population of Europe is already in a state of decay and the United States will follow suit before the Antichrist rises to offer his solutions to a dying Western Civilization. Socialism is strong in Europe, particularly in France and Germany. The struggle in the Western World between autocratic and democratic rule will be waged with fierceness by the Antichrist.

The totality of Western Civilization will be affected as we have already seen a rise in population of Arabs in Europe that will begin to change the face of the Western World. There are over 6 million Muslims in France alone. "Europe's Muslims gather in bleak enclaves with their compatriots, isolated from their host population and bitter in outlook...the danger to the United States is that Jihad recruits carry European Union passports and are therefore entitled to visa-free travel into the United States."(4). With eerie similarity to the "burning of Atlanta" during the Civil War in America, a clarion call of rioting came ringing from France in October/November 2005, "Paris is burning." Rioters created havoc as youthful Arab Muslin immigrants from Africa complained of economic woes. Automobiles and businesses were burned as millions of dollars were lost.

It used to be that the changes in Europe were geographic, but now they are demographic as Christian religions are being superseded by non-Christian religions. In the future, a declining Europe and a weakening of the United States will be ripe for the time of the Antichrist. He will move in to take advantage of a precarious political and religious situation. The power of his dictatorship will flourish with great ascendancy as he moves in to take control of the European scene within the former Roman Empire.

We are seeing more shifting of the global super powers as modern time continues to add to history. These current shifts of power are centered on what God is doing in Palestine and the rest of the Middle East. Our future is being laid out before us with predictable accuracy as God deals with the world's sin and belligerence.

THE LATEST SUPER POWER

God had to replace a weakening Europe and British Common-wealth with another superpower that He could use in the last days. Now He is dealing with that single, current global super power in the world, the United States. The United States is fodder to its enemy combatants and terrorists of the world. We are open targets and will be on the receiving end of their weapons that they will bring through our borders or from their air strikes. Mid-east terror-ists consider us their enemy for at least three major reasons. First, we are on the opposing side from them in relation to the nation of Israel. In their minds, we are not solving the Israeli/Palestinian crises. Second, they have simply wanted us out of the Middle East and off the peninsula of Arabia because they do not agree with our policies. Third, because of our degrading morals, we are care-fully and systematically acting out the "Great Satan" role that they purport us to be.

What will work against us in the fight against terrorism is that we in the United States refuse to choose security over our liberty. France and England have already accepted more security for less freedom and liberty. In having to deal with terrorism as a result of the clash in Ireland between the Catholics and the Protestants, there are closed circuit TV cameras on practically every city block in London. We in the United States need to get away from our narrow-minded view of our First Amendment rights when it comes to security. We have to admit that we must give up some of our freedoms in order to be secure, or we will continue to have problems.

Liberal thinkers are the biggest proponents of the view that freedom must take precedence over security. They mention the founders of our nation when they make any comparison. They usually cite 18ᵗʰ Century logic saying that our forefathers like Benjamin Franklin, John Adams, or Thomas Jefferson would not place security above freedom. Freedom not being sacrificed for security was fine in the age of small arms fire but none of them had to live in global warfare, or in the days of 21ˢᵗ Century terrorism. The words of Benjamin Franklin are quoted who said, "They that can give up essential liberty to obtain a little temporary safety deserve neither liberty or safety." They shorten that quote and take it out of context because in the Revolutionary War and in the war against terrorism, we're not talking about "a little temporary safety." In Franklin's day it was cultural survival, and today it encompasses a major battle for cultural superiority. They forget the fact that Franklin was in favor of fighting for the security of America in order to preserve freedom. He signed The Declaration of Independence that said, "We mutually pledge to each other our Lives, our Fortunes, and our sacred Honor." Benjamin Franklin also said, "We must indeed all hang together, or, most assuredly, we shall all hang separately." Without a doubt, Franklin and others were willing to risk their liberty for security.

Freedom will be lost through a lack of security. In the days of severe terrorism and war when in the future America is attacked consistently on the home front, the concept of freedom over liberty will be cast aside like yesterday's trash! Patrick Henry's phrase, "Give me liberty or give me death" will become a stark reality, as the fight for security will come to the forefront, but it will be too late.

The United States has won the cold war, has been the global policeman, and the undisputed super power in the world. How long will that last? I predict that the United States will lose the influence and prestige of past years due to its own moral cultural failures and economic struggles. The culture of the United States in its current state of moral decline is headed for a collapse if it does not make a course correction.

With oil at the center of its survival, America will teeter as it struggles to rid itself of its dependence on it, bringing great economic strain. As the Western World develops other technology, perhaps the United States' demand for oil from the Middle East will diminish, creating great conflict with other dependant and producing oil nations. Coupled with that dilemma are the various corporations that have fueled our economy since our country began and have moved overseas for the past several decades. The high cost of running the companies and the high cost of wages because of the various workers unions and the greed of corporate CEO's has in part contributed to this. Problems with workers pension funds, the rising cost of health care, and other economic woes have put their future in jeopardy. Industries such as American automobile manufacturing, the Airline Industry, as well as other corporations will continue to falter. Greed has taken hold of everyone from workers in manufacturing to the highest paid sports figures. We have also seen bribery, extortion, and conspiracy infiltrate the ranks of our political leaders in return for illegal favors for special interests groups who lobby them. The United States has been lulled into the belief that materialism is the answer to all of its ills but instead it will be strangled by it.

The great and mighty empires of the past in Europe and Asia have collapsed. It was due to poor management of their economy, a far-reaching over-stretched, under budgeted military, and a moral and social upheaval. Not that these nations ceased to exist, but these past kingdoms began a similar state of decline after just a couple hundred years of existence that eventually led to their total collapse of influential values and power. With all three of the above debilitating factors in place, the United States will face the same fate as its towns, cities, states, businesses, and major corporations will face financial struggles and its power diminishes in the world.

America will no longer have the super power status or the will to dominate the world. America will disintegrate and split within itself due to the over-predominance of individual rights and economic woes. The United States has faced costly natural disasters and other crises, and has financed its military beyond what it can afford. Financial dependency on other nations will lead to its peril because it has been borrowing money from foreign governments due to its many other financial obligations. Its financial troubles and ill-fated rights and freedoms of its individuals without a moral compass have been the undoing of its society. It has led to a failure of decency and character. Consequently, the low morals of the United States will be to her ruin. This is the weakness of democracy shown as the feet of iron and clay in Nebuchadnezzar's vision of Daniel chapter two.

The problem for America is that it is being drained morally, spiritually, financially, and politically. The American people have lost their will to fight in any war just as it happened to the other great empires of history. Everyone is afraid of another Vietnam. America is facing economic trouble just as Mystery Babylon will have in Revelation 17 and 18 during the Great Tribulation. Is America headed for this kind of disaster sometime in the near future?

> Revelation 18:16-17 says this about the failed economy of Mystery Babylon, *"Alas, alas, that great city that was clothed in fine linen, purple, and scarlet, and adorned with gold and precious stones and pearls! For in one hour such great riches came to nothing."*

The United States will be as ill prepared to fight in any war other than a worldwide conflict, just as historic Babylon was when God overthrew their mighty power. At home, the political uncertainty and the fear of the people are taking its toll. Signs of weakness have begun to creep into our military around the world that protects our nation and other nations as well. It is sometimes difficult to find recruits to serve in our military despite the great benefits of pay, education, and retirement. War is depicted as unpopular in the press, which makes it easy to run out of those willing to risk their lives on foreign soil for the cause of freedom.

On top of that, in 2005 the Coast Guard fleet was said to have been in a dire situation when it came to protecting our waterways and ports, because they could not replace their broken down ships, planes, and helicopters. In other wars we have had to retool our war machine, but due to the fact that we now politicize our wars, our lack will someday catch up to us. Besides our being ill prepared, is the fate of the United States to be like those in Jeremiah fifty-one when God's prophet describes the weakness of Babylon as those who will not fight anymore? Women did not fight wars in those days so Babylon's warriors are described as being like women. They would not or could not fight.

> Jeremiah 51:29-32 says, *"And the land will tremble and sorrow; For every purpose of the LORD shall be performed against Babylon, To make the land of Babylon a desolation: without inhabitant. The mighty men of Babylon have ceased fighting. They have remained in their strongholds. Their might has failed; they became like women. They have burned her dwelling places, the bars of her gate are broken. One runner will run to meet another, and one messenger to meet another, to show the king of Babylon that his city is taken on all sides; The passages are blocked, the reeds they have burned with fire, and the men of war are terrified."*

The United States is being torn apart by deep divisions that are pitting various classes against each other. The wealthy and the educated are separated from the poor and the uneducated. There is a real conflict of thought and culture that will affect our future. Our multi-cultural nation is making us more and not less divisive over racial issues. Not that there hasn't been a polarization within the United States in the past. We have had severe clashes of riots, bombings, strikes, and anarchy that has left a bleak mark in our history. It is coming now however at a critical time of a global restructuring that is closer to a sense of fatality as revealed in the Bible, and when our country has reached its peak of world wide influence and power.

There will eventually be a breakdown of America into regional areas based on cultural, political, moral, and ideological differences that will nullify its great power as in the city/states that divided Greece. The United States could become a smaller country represented by fewer stars in our flag as some states may even try to secede from the country as a whole. Factional issues will grow stronger as each of the minorities will seek the strength of their own global village within the variety of global families of the United States as vengeance over racism grips America. America could perhaps still remain one nation, but will take a medium position status within the power broker nations of the Western world similar to the nation of Russia.

As Europe rises again in greatness, the lowering in power and influence of the United States will be similar to what happened to Britain when their Commonwealth vanished in the 20th Century. Paraphrasing what Jeremiah said to Israel when they were being taken from their land into captivity in another country, "It's going to happen and there's nothing you can do about it."

The Courts of the United States, fresh by being stung by controversial decisions will be granting states more liberty in governing themselves as a push for individualism rises to the forefront. The push by the United States for democracy elsewhere will help spread the power structure of the nations across the world. Mighty powers will arise elsewhere as the world is being prepared for the Antichrist.

With the United States the one and only standing global super power, the other global super powers are ever shifting as God prepares the world for its fiery end! God's master plan is involved, as the shift of power will take place at least one more time in the last days. Europe will emerge in great power under the Antichrist in the near future to either replace or rival America as the ultimate Super Power. Does that mean that there will be no one in the United States or Europe who will be serving God and Christ? There has always been and there will always be a remnant of people to serve God in every nation.

THE NEW UNITED NATIONS

We are now a global world. What happens on one side of the world economically and militarily, affects the other side much sooner than in previous generations. With a dramatic shift of power in the end of time, what will happen to the global community of the United Nations? Will a new United Nations emerge out of the inept ability of the current one? Will it meet it's demise or move and be planted in the midst of the rising European Union that will figure in geographically and politically closer to the Middle East? It may not happen in my lifetime, but those kinds of changes will take place in one form or another. For the past 20 years I have believed and predicted that the headquarters for the United Nations will move out of the United States and re-emerge in Europe or Asia. It will continue either in its current format or totally restructured in an attempt to meet modern day needs of greater autonomy and authority in the midst of the rise of democracy in challenge to autocracy.

The United Nations was more pro-western at the conclusion of World War II. In the future because of political differences with the United States and its difficulty to carry the majority of UN funding, influential nations of the United Nations will convince that world body that its place should be closer to the center of the world's oldest civilizations. Their pro-western stance of the past will then become even more pro-European and pro-world. There will be a great shift of philosophy in that world body of nations and it will move overseas once financial hardship comes to the United States. Many of the anti-American nations in that world body will turn against her even greater.

With that kind of a change, the United Nations will eventually be in control of European, Asian, and other world powers. They will work to solve the world's problems according to their own worldview. It will become increasingly inept, as the powers of the world will seek to flex their muscles in independent fashion. All of that will be a substantial change in direction for the United Nations as Europe and Asia rise to the forefront.

The United States is only one part of that world body but the attempt by the United Nations to manage the world's problems will be greater than the attempt made by the United States to micro-manage the world in the past. Just as the United States is spread thin with Afghanistan, Iraq, Iran, North Korea, and Israel, so the United Nations will be powerless and hence unable to deal with the massive world problems of terrorism and warfare among its member nations.

The cold reality of shifting global powers similar to what the United Nations is facing is found in Jeremiah. We see the call of God in his life to establish the fact that God is in control of which nations would be built up and which nations would be torn down. God is in charge of the nations and would forgive any of them if they repented.

Jeremiah 1:10 says, *"See, I have this day set you over the nations and over the kingdoms, To root out and to pull down, to destroy and to throw down, to build and to plant."*

Jeremiah 18:7-10 says, *"The instant I speak concerning a nation and concerning a kingdom, to pluck up, to pull down, and to destroy it, if that nation against whom I have spoken turns from its evil, I will relent of the disaster that I thought to bring upon it. And the instant I speak concerning a nation and concerning a kingdom, to build and to plant it, if it does evil in My sight so that it does not obey My voice, then I will relent concerning the good with which I said I would benefit it".*

THE GREATEST WARFARE

Getting back to the power shifts of the nations of the past, the peoples of the world who were scattered at the Tower of Babel eventually formed the great civilizations of China, Africa, and Central and South America. The remaining powerful central Cradle of Civilization would be embroiled in two thousand years of warfare, crusades, and dominance by national superpowers. Christianity was being birthed to spiritually counterbalance these earthly super powers. The church became embroiled in a "spiritual warfare" against the dominance of supernatural powers over the geo-political sphere. The true warfare involving the heavens and the powers that were on the earth was in full force, thus engaging a spiritual warfare of the church with the nations of the world. The warfare that clashes in the spirit world is part of the prayers of God's people.

It wasn't just prophets like Daniel that were involved with spiritual warfare as seen in Daniel chapter ten when he was struggling with the spiritual powers of Persia. Generations of Christians since then have been involved in a spiritual warfare of prayer, and the stakes were now higher. Clashes of tremendous superpower proportions were now raging over the nations of the world. These nations were expanding, their borders were changing and the people of God were praying.

Just as there are national superpowers, and clashes involving the Church with these Tsunami types of superpower shifts, Christianity has also been clashing spiritually with the superpowers of alter-ego religions around the globe. God is at war with his archenemy, the Devil. As superpower after superpower has been at war with each other, so Christianity has been in a spiritual warfare with the religions of the world such as Islam, Hinduism, Buddhism, Atheism, and others. The Devil has tried to divert attention away from Jesus Christ the Son of God and His peaceful salvation plan. Nominal Christianity will seek peaceful religious security with the other religions of the world, continuing to develop the theme that "there are many ways to God."

Sometimes it may appear that the Devil is in charge. He creates his influence and makes his impact felt as we struggle with the principalities and powers of the air. He is involved in the great events of the world, but God is still Sovereign and in control. This is the "spiritual warfare" that so many religious and spiritual leaders write and talk about. It's not just you against me. It's something more sinister than that.

Ephesians 6:12 says, *"For we wrestle not against flesh and blood, but against principalities, against powers, against the rulers of the darkness of this world, against spiritual wickedness in high places."*

As we wrestle these powers, Christ is above them all and has them under His feet.

Ephesians 1:21-23 says that Christ is *"far above all principality and power and might and dominion, and every name that is named, not only in this age but also in that which is to come. And He put all things under His feet, and gave Him to be head over all things to the church, which is His body, the fullness of Him who fills all in all".*

Ephesians 2:5-6 goes on to say that God *"made us alive together with Christ and raised us up together, and made us sit together in the heavenly places in Christ Jesus"*.

Spiritually speaking, we as the body of Christ have been raised to be with Christ and sit with Him. That means we have authority over the Devil and every demonic power and force just as He does. Our part can clearly be seen. We are above the fray and we share in the authority that Christ has.

Christianity and Islam make up about half the world's population. We find ourselves right in the middle of this tremendous supernatural and international power struggle involving these two great religions, and all the other religions of the world. It also involves great cultural clashes dating back to the time of Abraham. Therefore, it is up to the Church to remind the evil principalities and powers that God will ultimately win the battle with the Devil and over the evil intentions of the nations of the world.

Ephesians 3:9-10 says that we are to *"make plain to everyone how God will administer the mystery of the gospel, which for ages past was kept hidden in God, who created all things. His intent is that now, through the church, the manifold wisdom of God should be made known to the rulers and authorities in the heavenly realms"*.

Those verses mean that we have an obligation to make all men see the wonderful mystery of the fellowship we have in Christ. It is up to us to make the wonderful wisdom of God known unto the principalities and powers in those heavenly places. We are to pray so they can hear us and understand God's power and love. We are to speak the name of Christ so that they will come under submission to Him. It further means that we are intently involved in a prayer struggle with these vast powers. The more we pray the stronger we become, the less influence the evil powers have over the world in us, and the more the powers of God are victorious.

That's spiritual warfare at it's finest and that's what it's all about, an epic struggle of the Kingdom of God against the kingdoms of this world. It will ultimately lead to God's plan for the end of the world. Due to man's sin and his increase of knowledge and ability, and the involvement and heightening of powers and armaments, God will bring about a culmination of His plan through the return of Christ. His Second Coming will bring about a climatic conclusion to the global power shifts of the world at Armageddon.

Matthew 16:27 says, *"For the Son of man shall come in the glory of His Father with His angels"*.

REVELATIONAL WARFARE

The warfare with Satan will be brought to its conclusion as seen in the book of Revelation when he is cast out of the heavens.

Revelation 12:9, 12 says that the Devil *"who deceives the whole world; he was cast to the earth…Woe to the inhabitants of the earth and the sea! For the devil has come down to you, having great wrath, because he knows that he has a short time."*

That is when the horrible second half of the tribulation mentioned in the book of Revelation begins leading up to the Battle of Armageddon. This is when Satan's work as the "prince of the power of the air" will come to its conclusion. Hell breaks loose on the earth when he is cast down. The worst of the worst takes place on the earth. Just as God's deepest and strongest love, peace and salvation have been seen by the peoples of this earth, so the wrath of God will be seen just as deep and just as strong. The following verses speak about that wrath to come when the bloodshed will be immense and the war will be horrible!

Revelation 14:17-20 says, *"After that, another angel came from the Temple in heaven, and he also had a sharp sickle. Then another angel, who has power to destroy the world with fire, shouted to the angel with the sickle, 'Use your sickle now to gather the clusters of grapes from the vines of the earth, for they are fully ripe for judgment.' So the angel swung his sickle on the earth and loaded the grapes into the great winepress of God's wrath. And the grapes were trodden in the winepress outside the city, and blood flowed from the winepress in a stream about 180 miles long and as high as a horse's bridle."*

The book of Revelation also talks about a number of beasts that are usually metaphors of brutality and ferociousness, and depictive of someone who is a person of great savagery. It denotes their attitude or moral character. The book of Revelation chapter 17 talks of a woman who was riding on one of these beasts who is the leader of the final kingdoms. The kingdoms of the beast eventually hate this woman, cast her off, and are successful in destroying her. The woman and this beast are vividly described as John sees them both.

Revelation 17:3-5 says, *"So he carried me away in the Spirit into the wilderness. And I saw a woman sitting on a scarlet beast which was full of names of blasphemy, having seven heads and ten horns. The woman wore purple and scarlet clothing and beautiful jewelry made of gold and precious gems and pearls. She held in her hand a gold goblet full of obscenities and the impurities of her immorality. A mysterious name was written on her forehead: Babylon the Great, Mother of All Prostitutes and Obscenities in the World."*

The symbolism of this woman having a name that is mysterious means that there is a hidden, secondary, or secret meaning behind what can clearly be seen. The word mystery usually contains a dual meaning or an undisclosed truth such as an association of some kind. In this case, this woman with a mysterious name doesn't necessarily mean a literal city somewhere in the Middle East or in another part of the world. It more than likely refers to a powerful religious movement that is a mixture of a deceptive complex order of mysterious beliefs and practices filled with apostate confusion. It would contain a variety of interdependent elements of false religions and faith not seen since the evil days of Babylon. Its political aspirations, is seen by riding on the back of a massive Beast of political power. This is the influence of religious Babylon of old over generations of nations. The association of the religious with the political is what could be the mystery as they remind us of the old European political and spiritual powers of old.

In most recent years, with the advent of the Roman Catholic Vatican Councils and Protestant Ecumenical Meetings, there has been an emphasis of unity and cooperation no matter the background of any religion. In the past, Pope John II has sought cooperation among Hindus, Buddhists, Muslims, and others. I'm sure the National Council of Churches and various International Councils of Churches would applaud this. Even the Eastern Orthodox Church and the Roman Catholic Church, from which it split, has been brought together on a number of occasions in an effort toward unity.

With the death of Pope John II in 2005, he left behind a struggling Church in the United States. He kept a tight grip on the dispensing of church doctrine and teaching which has run contrary to the more democratic style of leadership that is favored by the Catholic Church in the United States. He had maintained control over the great chasm of the liberal and conservative branches in the United States that is indicative of the cultural wars that are being waged here. His teaching and practices of dogma in the church concerning women in the priesthood, celibacy for the clergy, and lay leadership, are practices that the church will have to work out. They do not affect the masses of other Christians who have no problem with those practices. That is their Catholic teaching and dogma and enforcing them is the business of the Catholic Church.

However, the greater crossover doctrines that affect both Catholic and Protestant positions are major cultural issues such as abortion, homosexuality rights, and euthanasia. The conservative stance that the Pope and the Catholic Church has taken in regard to these issues is important on the world scene. This is in spite of the weak stance that the Catholic Church and the mainline Protestant Church has taken in the United States.

Before becoming Pope, Benedict XVI had shown no sign of flexibility when it came to some of the same issues. He stood tough against those who wanted to rewrite the fundamentals of Church dogma. He had worked hard against the acceptance of Buddhism and he had a problem with Islamic Turkey joining the European Union, which was a difficulty for the Vatican that wants to improve relations with the people of those faiths. Some of his stands would have only polarized the church, but he has mellowed and I predict that as this Pope has changed some of his harsh positions, much will change either under him or under the next Pope. The possibilities are open for a more moderate policy that will of course have a dramatic affect on both the Catholic and Protestant Churches, and the world.

For now, this newly elected Pope seems to want to continue John Paul's mission to unify all Christians and dialogue with all other religions as well. He wants to continue using the Mass Media as John Paul did and feels that the possibilities of doing so are powerful and enticing. What a way to bring about a cooperative effort of politics and religion. This Ecumenical type faith along with the political ramifications of the Beast on which the woman rides is what could all be a part of this mysterious Babylon. It is the classic "all faiths combining" that makes it so dangerous in a volatile world of great cultural shifts in the end-time. Either this Pope or one of his successors along with the totality of most religious Protestant and Eastern Religious faiths will be deceived by the Antichrist System upon which it rides.

This is a climatic time in which all the religions of the world will have definitive religious power, shift toward each other in an attempt to bring religious unity, and set the stage for a dramatic conclusion in Revelation 17 and 18. After that is when we see the demise of "Mystery Babylon," the great religious and political powers of the world. This world will discover great horror when the struggles of the nations and their overwhelming shifts of power will end in great Tribulation. Jesus Christ will intervene to set up His Kingdom on earth.

These shifts of power throughout the centuries have been to bring an end to the sin and disobedience of His chosen people as well bring God's punishment to all the nations of the world. The collapse of the nations will be ubiquitous. Leading up to that time it will be important that we as individuals keep our focus on the things of Jesus Christ and the things of God.

Colossians 3:1-2 says, *"Seek those things which are above, where Christ is, sitting at the right hand of God. Set your mind on things above, not on things on the earth."*

Since the introduction of Christianity, it took nearly 2,000 years to start to bring about the proper shift of global super powers and to bring about a climax of political super power warfare for the of end time. It is taking the same amount of time for all of spiritual warfare to be able to be brought to a climax as well. These great events had been primed to happen throughout the early centuries and up through the 19th century. I want to now bring us up and into the recent 20th century as well as explain its importance in leading us to the 2nd Coming of Christ.

CHAPTER THREE:

The Importance of War

—︎ᴍ︎—

In the beginning of recorded history, God focused on one couple in the Garden of Eden that was in the land of Mesopotamia. Then He focused on the called out family of Abraham that became a nation and indeed many nations.

> God told Abraham in Genesis 12:2-3 that *"I will make of thee a great nation, and I will bless thee, and make thy name great; and you will be a blessing. And I will bless them that bless thee, and curse him that curses thee, and in thee shall all families of the earth be blessed"*.

God was not just a cosmic spectator. His character doesn't fit Deism theology. He was involved with His created people and said that He was starting a nation chosen through Abraham. Soon He had to defend that chosen nation but then allow other nations to dominate them because of their sin. He allowed warfare to seal both their future fates. Then God used still other nations to allow His will to dominate over the evil of those sinful nations that brought retribution to His chosen people. He was angry with them for their arrogance and punished them for their disobedience.

An amazing thing is that God always works through and deals with the superpower "King of the Hill" nation of any generation. He has used Babylon, Rome, and other nations in the past and He is using the United States today. Just because God chooses one nation doesn't mean that He doesn't have a plan for other nations. God has blessed and used many nations in a positive way over the centuries to accomplish His will over and over again. He has used both the Jews and the Gentiles and has blessed those nations that honored Him!

Psalm 33:12 says *"Blessed is the nation whose God is the Lord, the people He has chosen as His own inheritance."*

GOD'S VIEW

But here's the kicker, the attention grabber, and the coup de grace! God has only one faith to offer to the people of this world, and it's His idea of what that faith is. He isn't multifaceted in His religious code of understanding that makes every religious idea acceptable to Him. No, He hates the worship of idols and He isn't the pluralistic phantom god that compromises His character and Sovereignty.

Deuteronomy 6:4 says, *"Hear, O Israel, the Lord our God is one Lord"*.

He doesn't appear within the psychic ideals of other gods, nor does He accept anything and everything of what people think of Him when it comes to honoring and worshipping Him. He is who He is and we better find out who this Sovereign Creator God is and worship Him in the Spirit and with Truth! The gods of most other religions are not the same as the Creator God of the Universe! The religions that reject God in the form of His Son are not the total faith of the Creator God because the Son of God is the Creator along with His Father. Christianity has some similarity to the beliefs of other religions such as prayer, suffering, enlightenment, and proper relationships with others. These other religions will need to come to a decisive conclusion about Jesus Christ being the Son of God.

In speaking of Jesus, Colossians 1:15-17 says that He, *"is the image of the invisible God, the firstborn of every creature. For by him were all things created, that are in heaven, and that are in earth, visible and invisible, whether they be thrones, or dominions, or principalities, or powers: all things were created by him, and for him: And he is before all things, and by him all things consist."*

We can see that the Father and His Son are in control of all the powers of the world. As mentioned in the previous chapter, Daniel chapter two speaks about God's authority over the nations.

Daniel 2:21 says about God, *"He removes kings and raises up kings"*.

Because He does, He is intimately involved with the policies of nations to accomplish His will. His will has an ultimate end and that end is found in the book of Revelation. When one reads the book of Revelation, many truths about how God will end the world are found in its pages. In Revelation chapter four we can see what is called the Four Horsemen of the Apocalypse. They represent the Antichrist, war, famine, and death. That's what God is sending to the world in the last days during the Great Tribulation, and that's only the beginning.

BACK TO THE FUTURE

To believe all of that depends on how you view the writing of the book of Revelation. There are various views of this Book. The Historical view says that Revelation is currently being fulfilled throughout the 2,000 years of church history. The Preterist view, which means that the prophecies of the Apocalypse are in the past and have been already fulfilled, says that Revelation was fulfilled shortly after it's writing of approximately 100 AD. The Spiritual view involves symbolism representing various spiritual lessons and principles with little or no literal interpretation. Those views see no meaning in applying Revelation to today's global and political situations. Another view of the book of Revelation is Futuristic. This view says that the majority of Revelation is yet in our future and that the events will literally happen. This is the best view as the Bible's message in each generation has always been replete with prophetic messages of the future.

God not only has a plan for the future, but He has shared it with His people. The Bible is filled with prophecies in both the Old and New Testaments of what God was going to do in the future. In order for us to understand that future, God has revealed it through His prophets.

Amos 3:7 says, *"God will do nothing except He reveals His secret unto His servants the prophets."*

The prophets had keen political prophetic insight and their finger was on the pulse of God's heartbeat. Many biblical books carry prophetic words with great implications about the future of the nations of the world. It is not unusual then to have a book like Revelation that has so many futuristic thoughts in it.

WAR IS NECESSARY

War may be necessary, but it is horrendous, and its consequences are terrible! It makes conflict inevitable, and suffering inescapable. The collapse of the world's societies at Armageddon will have a lot to do with the culture of war and man's insatiable infatuation with its enticement of destruction and its power to annihilate. The component of war is sinister and has been far-reaching into practically all of our nations with disastrous results. In war, everyone loses. Those who survive it are never quite the same. It can lead to the collapse of any culture that is fascinated by it and uses it to further their selfish means. War is a spiritual disease that cannot be eliminated without God's help. It is an evil result of man's sin that is so degrading, pervasive, and merciless in all of society. War is an empty shell.

Before and after Christ there were wars in Asia for control of the Mesopotamia area and wars for control of the Mediterranean. Many years later, there were the great wars over the European Continent such as the 100 years war for control of France. In the 6,000 plus years of world history there have been very few years where there has not been a war being waged somewhere in the world. There has been an increase of war as well, as man has generally not listened to God and has never listened to God. Even though God has always had a nation, a people, or a remnant that followed Him, He has always had to deal with a sinful, disobedient world. It is easy to discover that war is necessary and has always been necessary. It is war that will eventually lead the world to Armageddon.

God has therefore allowed a culture of war to exist and has used it throughout history by involving man's evil ways in order to move the nations of the world into proper alignment before the end of time. War was also there to deal with man's sin. Many warmongering men of the past were evil bullies who wanted attention, but were only insignificantly biting at the heels of history as footnotes in a distant past. God allowed them to be used by Satan to ferment disobedience, disorder, and chaos in the world as a means of punishment. In the past, nations and religions were being started and revolutionized, as attention was shifted to the powers of the Western World in order to prolong God's timing and prepare the world for the end time.

With the nation of Israel set-aside after the crucifixion of Christ for the time being because of their disobedience, God was dealing with Gentile nations to accomplish His plan. God could no longer work through Israel and the reason is clear as stated in Romans. Israel had lost their purpose and direction. They had fallen out of God's favor but not without the promise that they were also to be restored in the future!

Romans 11:11-12 says, *"I say then, have they stumbled that they should fall? Certainly not! But through their fall, to provoke them to jealousy, salvation has come to the Gentiles. Now if their fall is riches for the world, and their failure riches for the Gentiles, how much more their fullness!"*

Romans 11:25-26 declares, *"blindness in part is happened to Israel, until the fullness of the Gentiles be come in...Israel will be saved..."*

Those verses make it clear that God also had a plan of salvation for the non-Jewish people of the world too. Many people have come to God as He has been using the nations of the world to accomplish His glory. God began using the Gentile nations because Israel His centerpiece was no longer able to accomplish His goals for a needy and dying world. Jesus gave Israel ample warning about what was to happen to Jerusalem.

In Luke 19:43-44 we read, *"For days will come upon you when your enemies will build an embankment around you, surround you and close you in on every side, and level you, and your children within you, to the ground. And they will not leave in you one stone upon another, because you did not know the time of your visitation."*

Many of those other nations that He then used to correct Israel were despicable in His sight but God used them anyway. The root of sin was still deep within and waiting for the tempter's snare as evil and war were standing at their door. In later years, the only redeeming quality for those nations was that the Church was born and influenced them to serve Him even though these nations would vacillate in and out of obedience.

God's Word makes it clear that man is inherently evil due to His fall into sin in the Garden of Eden. Since that time, man has generated one warfare act after another beginning with murder, until war became such a multiplied act that it became second nature to him. War began to easily spread like wildfire. National power and the prestige of warring nations began inflicting agonizing death on nations globally leading to a collapse of one culture after another over the centuries.

GOD OF WAR OR PEACE?

War was always a last resort with God. He never instigates it but uses it because of the disobedience of His people. Given the fact that God was using first the nation of Israel and then these other nations in their acts of war, we must come to an astonishing conclusion:

"God doesn't encourage evil but He uses evil to bring about His plans for humanity. He hates and punishes sin, but many times works through sin and it's evil intention, to accomplish His desire and will for the world."

Some people may call God a "God of war." The questions often asked are "does God hide His face during war and overlook the worst atrocities of man?" and, "how can a God of love allow the killing of innocent women and children?" Did He hide His face and dare not look at the Jewish Holocaust during World War II? If He uses sin and evil, doesn't try to stop war, and appears to hide His face from the worst of it, does that make Him a God of war? If some would say that He is a God of war then we must also conclude that He is a God of peace.

As far as I'm concerned God hates war, but as you carefully read the Bible, you can see that He has both prompted the use of armies, and He has instilled the element of peace in the lives of people everywhere. God uses both the good that is in man as well as his evil behavior. He has used not only godly men and good kings, but also lying prophets, prostitutes, and evil dictators. God can take the evil that man does and turn it into good. *That is the beauty and mystery of His character that reveals both His love and His justice.* It is His love that dispenses His justice and it is His justice that dispenses His love.

PEACE

God is a peacemaker. We read in the Bible that one of God's blessings is that He gives His people the attribute of peace. Many verses in the Bible speak about that peace but here are just a few.

Psalm 29:11 says, *"The LORD will give strength to His people; the LORD will bless His people with peace"*.

In Isaiah 26:3 we read, *"You will keep him in perfect peace, whose mind is stayed on You, because he trusts in You"*.

The Apostle Paul writes in II Corinthians 13:11 *"Be of good comfort, be of one mind, live in peace; and the God of love and peace will be with you"*.

Then again in Philippians 4:7 he writes, *"And the peace of God, which surpasses all understanding, will guard your hearts and minds through Christ Jesus"*.

In Jeremiah 29:11-13 it says to the captives of Israel in Babylon, *"I know the thoughts that I think toward you, says the LORD, thoughts of peace and not of evil, to give you a future and a hope. Then you will call upon me and go and pray to me, and I will listen to you. And you will seek me and find me, when you search for me with all your heart."*

God's future blessings of peace are also found in the scriptural passages of Isaiah and Micah that declare a future time when all of earth's hostilities and war will cease. God will bring his own brand of justice and peace to a world that is weary and ravaged by tribulation and sorrow as He reverses the collapse of societies. We believe that there will be a future time of millennial rest and peace for the world.

Isaiah 2:2-4 says, *"Now it shall come to pass in the latter days that the mountain of the LORD'S house shall be established on the top of the mountains, and shall be exalted above the hills; and all nations shall flow to it. Many people shall come and say, "Come, and let us go up to the mountain of the LORD, to the house of the God of Jacob; He will teach us His ways, and we shall walk in His paths." For out of Zion shall go forth the law and the word of the LORD from Jerusalem. He shall judge between the nations, and rebuke many people; they shall beat their swords into plowshares, and their spears into pruning hooks; Nation shall not lift up sword against nation, neither shall they learn war anymore."*

In the New Testament, Christ Himself declared the peace that He was transmitting to His followers. He wants us to live in peace with one another.

In John 14:27 Jesus said, *"Peace I leave with you, My peace I give to you; not as the world gives do I give to you. Let not your heart be troubled, neither let it be afraid"*.

Also in John 16:33 He said, *"These things I have spoken to you, that in Me you may have peace. In the world you will have tribulation; but be of good cheer, I have overcome the world."*

Those are comforting words about peace but the hidden message in the words of Jesus was that the world was full of trouble as well. The unfortunate thing is that man's sin, and his thirst for war comes ahead of his desire for peace. Force and might are used by the armies of the world, instead of peace, and God allows it. Throughout the Bible we see that sometimes God may use an individual, an army, or a nation to bring together His plan. However, we must come to understand this absolutely essential conclusion that sometimes even when force is necessary and allowed by God, peace is the ultimate goal.

Psalm 46:9-10 says, *"He makes wars cease to the end of the earth; He breaks the bow and cuts the spear in two; He burns the chariot in the fire. Be still, and know that I am God; I will be exalted among the nations, I will be exalted in the earth!"*

Before force and after force, God is a God of peace. We as His people must pursue peace even in time of war! Without the peace of Christ the world will fail miserably!

WAR

When God does use armies, He brings the disobedient into submission and His own people into obedience. Continually, He brought an army against his own nation as well as against other nations for correction and instruction. In a number of scriptures God said He was sending an army against His own people Israel and against other nations as well.

Deuteronomy 28:49-50 says, *"The LORD will bring a nation against you from afar, from the end of the earth, as swift as the eagle flies, a nation whose language you will not understand, a nation of fierce countenance, which does not respect the elderly nor show favor to the young."*

In Jeremiah 5:15 and 17 we read about that army. It says, *"Behold, I will bring a nation against you from afar, O house of Israel, says the LORD, It is a mighty nation, it is an ancient nation, a nation whose language you do not know, nor can you understand what they say. And they shall eat up your harvest and your bread, which your sons and daughters should eat. They shall eat up your flocks and your herds; they shall eat up your vines and your fig trees; they shall destroy your fortified cities, in which you trust, with the sword".*

Jeremiah 50:31 says this about Babylon because they have inflicted so much horror on other nations, *"Behold, I am against you, O most haughty one! says the Lord GOD of hosts; For your day has come, the time that I will punish you."*

Ezekiel 23:24 says this to Samaria and Jerusalem, *"And they shall come against you with chariots, wagons, and war-horses, with a horde of people. They shall array against you Buckler, shield, and helmet all around. I will delegate judgment to them, and they shall judge you according to their judgments."*

Ezekiel 26:3 says this about Tyre, *"Therefore thus says the Lord GOD: Behold, I am against you, O Tyre, and will cause many nations to come up against you, as the sea causes its waves to come up."*

Also, throughout the Old Testament, numerous times the phrase "the day of the Lord" was used to reveal God's judgment against those who do evil. It was used against His people Israel. Habakkuk, a prophet to Judah mentions the invading Babylonians as a "bitter and nasty nation" that would come "for violence". God brought judgment to Israel by allowing armies to inflict His justice.

One thing for sure, God uses war to raise up one nation to balance the power of another nation, so that the goals of man's power of warfare will not supercede God's own power over the affairs of man and over His authority in war. To conclude our understanding of a God of war, Psalm 76 speaks about the implements of war and the judgment of God through war, and how He uses the worst that is in man for His glory.

Psalm 76:10 says, *"Surely the wrath of man shall praise You; the remainder of wrath shall You restrain and gird and arm Yourself with it."*

RELIGIOUS WARS

You can read in various books or articles and hear on the news broadcasts that the wars and conflicts that take place in our world today have nothing to do with religious wars. They are usually cited as cultural and factional hatreds or differences between various civilizations that are brought about by leaders who are compelled by vengeance, greed, or power. Most people don't want to associate religion with war.

While their hatreds and differences are a part of the problem, I personally believe that these wars are also embedded deep within their cultural religions! These wars are connected to something inbred deep within the soul of man that makes him a lost and searching soul in society. Yes, it is connected to his civilization, his thinking, and what his culture taught him, but deep within man is an intrinsic faith that tells him that he has to reach for something higher and greater that he is. His religion forms the basis of what he is and what he believes he thinks he can accomplish, and because of his sin he mistakenly does it through war. That doesn't make war right, neither can we derive any sense out of war most of the time. Sometimes man has just simply lost his way with God, or he may not even believe that there is a God. The sad thing is that we know what God says about man's sin and the lack of peace.

Isaiah 48:22 says it perfectly, *"There is no peace, says the LORD, for the wicked"*.

For those who think that the physical wars that are waged in this world are not religious wars, only have to reference the surrender of Japan at the end of World War II. At the time, their Emperor Hirohito was regarded as a god but the United States demanded that they no longer regard him as such. "In 1947 a new constitution took effect. The Emperor became largely a symbolic head of state."(1). The Japanese had no choice in the matter. Hirohito publicly renounced his status as a god as Japan changed their view of him according to the demands of the United States. It was a difficult adjustment period for them.

There are many other instances of wars that are related to reli-gious ideology such as the Sunni's and the Shiite's who have clashed over Islamic principles. It was the religious ideology difference of Islam and Hinduism that split East and West Pakistan from India. Sectarian violence accompanied the partition of those nations. In 1970 East Pakistan then became Bangladesh in a Civil War and proclaimed independence in 1971.

"We're familiar with sweeping military campaigns in the Middle East and North Africa in the name of Islam. In the name of Christ, Crusaders marched to take land back that was previously under Christendom. In 16th and 17th Century Europe (1550-1650), wars between Protestant and Catholic rulers brought much blood-shed. There have been czarist pogroms against the Jews—often with religious justification. Mohandas K. Gandhi was killed by a militant Hindu in 1948; Sri Lanka's prime minister was assassinated by a Buddhist monk in 1959. In our day, we've seen Catholics and Protestants clashing in Northern Ireland. In India, we've seen Hindus and Muslims fighting one another. Buddhists and Hindus have been fighting in Sri Lanka. We've seen the Ayatollah Khomeini calling for the death of Salman Rushdie because of his *Satanic Verses.*"(**2**).

The terrorists who struck on 9-11 carried out their attacks in the name of their God Allah! Osama bin Laden thanked God and gave Him glory for the bombings in videotapes released after the attack. Our up to date war with them was started by them as a religious war. The extreme Muslim terrorists believe that the United States is the "Great Satan" and that they must engage us in war in the name of their god Allah. That attack had all the makings of a religious cultural clash between Christianity and Islam.

It's amazing, but I would say just about all wars and the final wars leading up to the great battle of Armageddon are religious wars, meaning they usually have a religious principle behind them. One side may believe in God and the other side may not. Even the cold war beginning in the 1940's until the 1980's pitted atheistic Communism against the religiously influenced United States of America. All along, God has been trying to engage himself in the affairs of man with peace, but man's refusal to listen to God consistently brings him war. Consequently, man is at war because of his lack of peace with God.

Right or wrong, we use war to justify that we speak for God and carry out His business through those wars! God has allowed war because of two reasons: First, we are created with "free choice" and have an evil nature as well as a good nature in us and God has let us choose whether or not to conduct war. Second, God has a plan for the consummation of the ages and everything will conclude in the end of time, bringing man's sinful and destructive ways to an end by the authority of God. He will use war to bring about that conclusion.

Looking ahead to the Battle of Armageddon, Revelation 17:12-14 says that the kingdoms and the armies of the world that are gathered with the Antichrist will fight against Jesus Christ.

Revelation 17:14 says they *"shall make war with the Lamb (Christ), and the Lamb shall overcome them"*.

Revelation 19:19-21 says that the Antichrist figure *"and the kings of the earth, and their armies, gathered together to make war against him (Christ) that sat on the horse, and against his army. Then the beast was captured, and with him the false prophet who worked signs in his presence, by which he deceived those who received the mark of the beast and those who worshiped his image. These two were cast alive into the lake of fire burning with brimstone. And the rest were killed with the sword which proceeded from the mouth of Him who sat on the horse. And all the birds were filled with their flesh."*

That makes it a religious war because they are fighting against Christ and how He will impose His will on the world! When Christ returns, there will be a religious war like never before. Then everyone will pay homage to Him as Messiah.

Philippians 2:10-11 says, *"At the name of Jesus every knee should bow, of those in heaven, and of those on earth, and of those under the earth, and that every tongue should confess that Jesus Christ is Lord, to the glory of God the Father."*

For those who do not feel right about fighting in a war, under the United States Constitution conscientious objectors have the right not to fight in any war. If someone doesn't want to raise a weapon against another individual, then that's their prerogative. They can be assured however of this one thing, the Battle of Armageddon is coming and all must eventually submit to the authority of the Lord Jesus Christ and His victory in war.

One thing that the Bible says about that is that those who are fearful and faint hearted do not have to go to war. Moses made it very clear during the call to any battle.

Deuteronomy 20:8 says, *"Then the officers shall add, is any man afraid or fainthearted? Let him go home so that his brothers will not become disheartened too."*

EARLY WARS OF AMERICA

War is not pretty; it is ugly! Soldiers have been maimed and continue to suffer because of war. Not only have we lost multiplied thousands of soldiers during all the wars the United States has fought, but hundreds of thousands of civilians lost their lives during the Civil War, World War I, World War II, Korean, and Vietnam wars.

Even to begin The United States of America, it took a war, the Revolutionary War! We would never have become the land of the free and the home of the brave without a war. It was the rockets red glare and the bombs bursting in air that started it all for us as our nation's founding fathers pledged their lives, their fortunes, and their sacred honor. With the founding of our country came the spirit of revolution, just as it has permeated every generation in the past. We are no different than any other nation that has wanted to leave its mark in history through military power. However, God was birthing the United States so He could use our nation in future wars to prepare for the end time.

The early wars of the Republic then came which helped to solidify our position in the world and strengthen our culture and ethics as a nation. Those wars were namely, the War of 1812 which was a left-over skirmish from the Revolutionary War that cast England off our backs permanently, and the Civil War that freed us from the scourge of slavery and kept our nation unified. Prior to the Civil War, the slavery compromises of 1820 and 1850 were not good enough. According to Abraham Lincoln, the Civil War became a punishment from God because of slavery. Those early wars did help make the United States a powerful nation that God would use through warfare in the generations to follow.

The United States was brought into being as part of the tremendous powers of the Western World to balance the powers of Asia and the powers of the East. All this was brought about in time for 20th Century warfare so that God's further plans for the Middle East could be unveiled. God was then ready to use another superpower nation to replace those declining European powers of the Western World, and that superpower was the United States.

20ᵗʰ CENTURY WARFARE

All of Europe's thousands of years of struggle cleared the way for a grand shift of power once again as the world raced toward the decisive wars of the 20ᵗʰ Century. There were a number of border skirmishes and wars in Europe's early history, but in the history of war, the 20ᵗʰ Century's wars began to set the final stages in God's eternal plan. They were all necessary wars waged by sinful man, to help wrap up God's plans for the conclusion of the ages. Since the beginning of the 20ᵗʰ Century, a plan was unfolding to get the Jews back to Israel and set the stage for a face to face conflict with the Arab world. Israel, who had been the absentee owners of 1900 years of occupied land found themselves once again at the crossroads of the most important piece of real estate in the world.

The two world wars of the 20ᵗʰ Century were nothing short of a miracle in re-establishing Israel back in the land that was taken from their ancestors. World War I began to allow the Jews to begin to return to Israel and World War II helped establish the State of Israel. The Korean Conflict kept the eastern powers from advancing any further until the time of Armageddon when they will make their appearance. The Vietnam War destabilized the superpower USSR and brought them into closer relationship with European powers until their advancement with those nations into Israel at Armageddon according to Ezekiel chapters 38-39.

The Iraqi wars of the 20ᵗʰ century and now the 21ˢᵗ Century have begun so that the European and Asian governments might rise in ascendancy after the United States loses it's sole superpower status. The Iraqi wars are also for the beginning of a worldwide place-ment of democracy to clash with autocratic governments around the world. That will end up being a short time of divisiveness in the Antichrist kingdom as the Bible indicates that three nations will oppose him. The current Iraqi war, like Vietnam, is an unpopular war but is a part of the broader picture of wars in the end time. Those who oppose the Iraqi war haven't a clue as to what God is doing with this war either. It has taken all the wars of the 20th Century to set the stage for the Jews to return to their land and keep the nations under control until God is ready to move them into position for the Battle of Armageddon.

God has allowed these wars and has shifted the power of these nations to prepare them for the end time, and again it's all happened through 20th Century warfare. The 20th Century was a key century to prepare for the consummation of the ages and the 21st Century will do more to bring the world closer to the return of Jesus Christ.

THE WAR TO END ALL WARS

World War I was an important war in the development of God's plan for the end time. That war began with the assassination of Austrian Archduke Francis Ferdinand and his wife Sophie. The system of alliances in Europe brought many nations into the conflict. The Arabs who had been occupying Palestine for over 1200 years had to be moved out of Palestine because God was ready to bring the Jewish people back in as promised in the Bible. That war took the land of Israel back from the Islamic Ottoman Turks and put it into the hands of the British Commonwealth. God remembered the Jews by using the nation of Britain with a plan He had for them after nearly 1900 years of being scattered around the world with no homeland. To believe any different and to say that it is a mistake for the Jews to be in Israel is to conclude that God is not in control of the situation. It would be like saying that somehow man has wrested control of that land and his will has taken precedence over the will of God. Unthinkable!

Before the end of WWI, in 1917, British Lord Balfour's letter of Declaration supported the idea that the Jews could have a homeland in Palestine among non-Jewish communities in Palestine. This was a strategic move to help safeguard Britain's interests in Palestine, but it also allowed the Jews to return to Israel over a period of years. God had begun His modern day plan of winding His prophetic clock down toward the end of time.

I recently read that "nowhere in the Bible does it mention that Israel would return to their land a second time". Well, I have news that says just the opposite.

> Isaiah 11:10-11 says just that, *"And in that day there shall be a Root of Jesse, Who shall stand as a banner to the people; For the Gentiles shall seek Him, And His resting place shall be glorious." And it shall come to pass in that day, that the Lord shall set his hand again the second time to recover the remnant of his people."*

The first time took place after that writing and after the 70 years of captivity of Israel a little over 400 years BC. The second time was in 1948, about 1900 years after their land and temple was destroyed by the Romans. That entire eleventh chapter of Isaiah deals with a future time for Israel, the return to their land, and a time of future Millennial rest for their land that does not fit within any of its historic past. The Millennium is yet for the future. What a great fulfillment of biblical prophecy that will be.

THE SECOND WAR

At the end of World War I, the Treaty of Versailles upset the Germans and kept the path open to war again. There was a general German displeasure and unhappiness at the end of World War I because of the overwhelming war debt reparations in which they were burdened.

In the United States, the history of war opposition was prevalent before World War II until Pearl Harbor. There were many pacifists at that time that wanted America to stay out of the European conflict. Even after Pearl Harbor, one vote kept the declaration of war from being unanimous in Congress. World War II, which was actually an extension of World War I, became a critical war because the formation of the nation of Israel was its result as the world was brought closer in God's end-time plan.

Adolf Hitler, the one I call the mad man of Munich because he attempted his first rise to power there, brought unspeakable horrors to the Jews. After he became Germany's unquestioned leader, millions of Jews were mass-murdered during the short leadership of that demonic, delusional, maniacal dictator. To Hitler, Israel was a laboratory for the insidious discrimination and elimination of the Jews.

Hitler's 1,000 year THIRD REICH lasted a mere 12 years, in which he killed more than 10 million people, with anywhere from 3 to 6 million being Jews. He led a despicable "final solution" to the problem of peoples that were not a part of his pure race. It involved a horrible tyranny against the Jews, Gypsies, and homosexuals that led to their incredible deaths. His appointed leaders led an execution and purposeful mass murder, of women, children and the massacre of multiplied civilians, outside the theater of war.

Hitler's killing scheme incensed the world and brought international interest and sympathy to the Jews at the end of the war, so that the United Nations was ready to help them create a Zionist State. The United Nations, which was more pro-western at the time, didn't know it but they were being moved by the hand of God to accomplish this. In 1947 the United Nations voted to partition Palestine and when the British officially withdrew their forces in May of 1948, the Jews proclaimed the State of Israel on their own. Thus, Israel was born. The world helped them create their own nation that they hadn't had in 1900 years. Christians and Jews around the world had been praying that this would happen. This was more of God's clock winding down as the nations of the world raced toward the end of time.

At first, the main players of World War II were Winston Churchill and Adolf Hitler. Then God brought Franklin D. Roosevelt into the picture and used the military might and ingenuity of the United States for His purpose. Roosevelt and Hitler both arrived on the world scene in 1933 and both left the world scene in 1945. Hitler was made Chancellor of Germany on January 30th, 1933 and assumed full dictatorial powers the following year. Roosevelt was inaugurated as President of the United States on March 4th, 1933. These two all-powerful leaders along with the likes of Churchill, Benito Mussolini, and Joseph Stalin, brought the world to near disaster as this gargantuan war was waged from sea to sea. It was an amazing godly coincidence and timing that brought both Roosevelt and Hitler, these two giant men to power the same year. As leaders of the Allies and Axis Powers respectively, they waged a critical war to insure the rebirth of Israel, then died and left that power also in the same year. Roosevelt died on April 12th, 1945, serving nearly 12 years and 1 and ½ months. Hitler committed suicide on April 30th, 1945, serving 12 years and 3 months. That's a difference of less than 2 months. They were both used by God and as the saying goes, they were "here today and gone tomorrow." The synchronization of their power during their life spans remind me of the brevity of life and how we must live in absolute certainty of God's will.

> James 4:14-15 says, *"Why you do not even know what will happen tomorrow. What is your life? You are a mist that appears for a little while and then vanishes. Instead, you ought to say, if it is the Lord's will, we will live and do this or that."*

Roosevelt's unusual four-year term Presidency and President Harry Truman's no-nonsense "buck stops here" approach was delicately timed by God to direct this war and bring it to its conclusion. The head to head combat with Germany and Japan began in order to begin to prepare the world for an end-time move. The end-time move was that God wanted one more giant piece of the puzzle to be put in place, namely the nation of Israel to be established in Palestine. That happened just 3 years after Roosevelt and Hitler were gone.

Japan was used to involve the United States in World War II and that war was used to help determine the future fate of many of the nations of the world. Even though Japan was dealt a fatal blow at that time, that Far Eastern part of the world will be dealt with in the future. Through World War II, God was dealing with the role of government in the final days and its place in the world, and how He would use it in the end of time for His plans and purposes. It was a cosmic cultural clash of good as opposed to evil that practically engulfed the entire world. Remember that God uses both the good and the evil of man.

WHAT DID KOREA DO?

The Korean conflict was another important war because God was keeping the Far Eastern Communist nations of China and North Korea at bay. China was involved in many wars over the centuries, including one with Japan in the 20th Century. With Communism being established in that part of the world after World War II, their aggression needed to be contained until the biblical timing of their appearance at Armageddon. At the end of World War II, China backed the Communist North Koreans and the United States backed the free South Koreans. The Korean Conflict was to stop their advantage in the Far East. It became part of a pre-emptive condition of war because the Far East will be part of a much larger war at a future time. The eastern nations will arise again in the last days, and will march into the Battle of Armageddon. During the Korean War, God used the United States to hold the Communists back and keep the lines of these two vastly different ideologies separate for the time being. North Korea's secretive regime has brutalized the dissidents of their nation as they heard of the freedoms outside their borders.

A later time will come that is mentioned in the Bible, which says that an army from the East will invade Israel. This vast, robust army, from the most populated region of the world, may include China that is expanding in a great way economically. It may include North Korea, with potential nuclear weapons and long-range missiles capable of reaching the United States. It may also include India, a burgeoning nation of the future. God is dealing with atheistic Communism and the Eastern Religious nations of the Far East to prepare them for the end of time.

Interesting news has developed in recent years concerning India and China. "India and China has agreed to form a 'strategic partnership,' creating a diplomatic bond between Asia's two emerging powers that would tie together nearly one-third of the world's population. The agreement reflects a major shift in relations between the two nuclear countries, whose ties have long been defined by mutual suspicion. Also, it is another step in a charmed offensive by Beijing, which is trying to build ties with is neighbors and ensure regional stability for economic growth."(**3**)

Corporations in the United States are making bold moves to invest in China and helping it to become a powerhouse in the economic world. As a free market-producing neophyte, China is interested in the great American economy and their capitalistic system of financial strength. It has made dramatic moves to purchase United States' bonds and other interests. It could be a threat to our national security for someone of a different ideology to control any of our economic interests. This step and others similar to it could help deplete the United States' economic power, and strategically put its military at risk. This will shift the world's economic power back to Europe in time for the rise of the Antichrist. It will also bring greater economic power to the Far East nations as they rise in power in the last days.

Will the two countries of China and India not only form a bridge for economic purposes to strengthen their position in the world, but also turn into an even greater formidable offensive alliance for military might in the last days? Will they partner with Korea and other nations of that region as a mighty army that comes from the East to invade Israel in the last days? What roles will the nation of Japan play, if any?

Pray for China as missionaries are now saying that a mighty sweeping revival is taking place there as millions of Chinese now know Christ and believe in Him as their Savior. What was once a group of 2 million Christians a few decades ago, has exploded to over 100 million as the Chinese are being converted by the droves as God is preparing that land for the end of time. God always had and will always have a remnant of people in any nation who will serve Him regardless of its politics.

During the sounding of the 6th Trumpet judgment and the pouring out of the 6th Bowl judgment on the earth in the book of Revelation, we see an amazingly powerful army that comes from the East.

In Revelation 9:14-16 a voice in heaven is heard, *"Saying to the sixth angel which had the trumpet, Loose the four angels which are bound in the great river Euphrates. And the four angels were loosed, which were prepared for an hour, and a day, and a month, and a year, for to slay the third part of men. And the number of the army of the horsemen were two hundred thousand thousand: and I heard the number of them."*

> Revelation 16:12 says that the Euphrates River will be dried up at the Battle of Armageddon *"that the way of the kings of the east might be prepared"*.

This army will number 200 million and will march through the dried up Euphrates River! God will move the great peoples of the East in His time when they will appear in Armageddon. The advance of this massive army means that perhaps the East may use a marching military beside their nuclear capability, or they may be restricted by treaty. Today, China and North Korea have, and are boasting of developing nuclear weapons. With thousands of nuclear weapons scattered around the world, we now surmise that this will be part of the agony when God's judgments of unspeakable horror will fall on the earth. The nuclear arsenal of North Korea may be developing stronger, and soon for that future time.

The Korean conflict held Korea and China in check until then and God used the American military to do so. That conflict may be the forgotten war but veterans who fought there, can rest assure that God used them for a future plan that is far beyond their wildest imagination or understanding. The impact of that war is still being felt today. The conflict with North Korea today is going to eventually expand into a last day scenario that will prepare that part of the world and the total world, for its brutal and fiery military end.

Revelation chapter six mentions that one quarter of the earth will die in war and hunger. Chapter eight says that a great mountain burning with fire was cast into the sea. In the same chapter it describes a great star that fell from heaven, burning like a lamp. Much of the earth's trees, grass, and water will be polluted, no doubt with these potentially devastating nuclear weapons. In addition, it says in chapter nine that one third of the population will die at the hands of demonic tormentors. It sounds like great horror will fall on the peoples of the world in the last time during the Great Tribulation.

Could this be God's mighty power that does all this or could it be an exchange of nuclear, biological, or chemical weapons?

THE SHORT COLD WAR

Since World War II, there not only was the Korean Conflict, but there was the continued Cold War intense rivalry going on between the United States and the Soviet Union with their competing political ideologies. It didn't last long. Just "one generation" of 46 years, from 1945 until the collapse of the Berlin Wall in 1989, and the dissolution of the Soviet Union in 1991. God dealt with Communist Russia.

In 1961, President John F. Kennedy and Premier Nikita Khrushchev had a meeting with each other in Vienna. They both had the opportunity as leaders of their respective countries to exchange their own world-views with each other. Khrushchev was an intimidating force and Kennedy came away from the meeting upset with his performance at the summit. Kennedy thought that nothing was gained from the meeting because their world-views were so different.

The paranoia that Khrushchev had because of East Berliners escaping into West Berlin prompted him to construct the Berlin Wall. All this was part of the dilemma and tension in 1961-1962. It helped set the stage for the Cuban missile crisis, when Russia attempted to place missiles on the tiny island of Cuba just 90 miles from the United States coast. Kennedy wanted to prove he wasn't a pushover and Khrushchev wanted to further prove to the younger President that he was a force to be reckoned with in the world. In a stare-down of nuclear power, Kennedy and Khrushchev were determined that their wills were going to prevail over the other.

The purpose of this gigantic struggle was to keep Cuba's flirtation with Communism under check and isolated in the Western World for now. Fidel Castro was caught in the middle, and now all these decades later, Castro's brand of Communism is part of a dying breed in the world and he has become an aberration in the Western Hemisphere. This is despite the support of other Communist leaders of the region in such countries as Venezuela and Bolivia who may rise in notoriety once Castro is gone. Once Castro and his henchmen are gone, relations between the United States and Cuba will eventually improve.

During the Cuban missile crisis, Kennedy thought for sure that there would be a nuclear exchange. There was a war of words and plenty of saber rattling but Kennedy won the stare-down and prevailed as Khrushchev backed off. It was a global chess match that caused Khrushchev to blink first and finally send the Russian missiles back home from their trip to Cuba. The crisis was averted. Kennedy was assassinated the next year and Khrushchev lost his job the year after that because of those in the Soviet Union leadership who thought he was too weak in that particular international crisis. These two men who appeared briefly on the national scene as part of the Cold War Crisis were used by God to bring about international changes in the 20th Century for the future consummation of time. It was another culture clash of two ideologies with near disastrous results.

I clearly remember this intriguing event because I was doing my preparatory work for ministry, and along with all of my friends, we were glued to the television set as much as possible. We witnessed a monumental event that began to change the course of history. Changes were in the works, but God wasn't ready for the end-time to transpire yet. There was much more to be done.

What transpired between Kennedy and Khrushchev as part of the Cold War, was designed by God to help dismantle the Soviet Union. That stand off which was less than 20 years after the end of World War II, was the beginning of the end of Communist Russia. It was the beginning of change for a nation that was to break apart within 30 years. The Cold War reached its climax during the Vietnam era when the United States became the alter ego for South Vietnam and the Soviet Union for North Vietnam. In this extended confrontation, the Soviet Union became totally drained of their financial resources after decades of armament buildup in a race against the United States. Their people were starving but their arms flourished. We haven't seen the end of Communism in either the Western or Eastern Hemispheres, but Christ will nullify that great ideology at the Battle of Armageddon.

RUSHING RUSSIANS

In order for the Soviet Union to continue to defend their Cold War position, they along with China spent billions in Vietnam. This war, as well as their involvement with Afghanistan, financially drained the Soviet Union and helped lead to its demise. The Berlin Wall that Nikita Khrushchev built lasted less than 30 years. Within 15 years after the end of the Vietnam War, the Berlin Wall was remarkably dismantled in 1989. The Soviet Union collapsed in 1991, and after a mere 74 years of Communist rule, her Republics were spun off from her. This collapse of the Soviet Union is an important event for end-time prophecy.

Russia's President Vladimir Putin recently said that the collapse of the Soviet Union was "the greatest geopolitical catastrophe of the century." His political understanding gave no spiritual insight to the ramifications of massive changes in the former Soviet Union and how its collapse has affected the entire world before the end of time. His opposition to democratic reform in the former Soviet satellite states is because he is still hanging on to the idea of authoritarian rule, but it's too late for him to oppose what God is doing to set up those end-time events.

Two major international leaders who died after the turn of the 21st Century, President Ronald Reagan and The Roman Catholic Pope, John Paul II, had a powerful impact that helped bring about the collapse of Communism. Both of these men made historic visits to Europe in the 1980's that helped bring freedom and democracy to the forefront, and place the seal of death on the coffin of Communism in the Soviet Union. With their powerful rhetoric and peaceful demeanor and presence, they became the catalysts of change for the world. These two little stones became an avalanche of rock on the world stage. No one can forget Reagan's famous words, "Mr. Gorbachev, tear down this wall."

The historic and nation-altering change of the Soviet Union brought them in line with the events found in Jeremiah 6 and Ezekiel 38-39, that will transpire in later times. These chapters indicate what we believe to be Russia, but described in Ezekiel as Gog, the land of Magog, seem to eventually join forces with European armies and invade Israel in the last days. Many Christians have said that this invasion was the Soviet Union coming in her strength at the beginning of a seven-year time of Tribulation for the world, when Israel was dwelling in safety. Now with the collapse of the Soviet Union, we know that Russia is weaker and her dependency is on others. Therefore her invasion of Israel at the beginning of the Tribulation is out of the question. I cannot see Russia joining forces to attack Israel at the beginning of this time period, given these circumstances. I have always felt that this invasion was part of the Battle of Armageddon at the end of the Tribulation. All the armies of the world will come together for warfare because of Israel and will eventually fight against Christ.

In that 38th chapter of Ezekiel verses two through six, it mentions these attacking armies. We know them to be the sons of Japheth, who was a son of Noah, whose descendants lived in the Northern Nations as described in Genesis chapter ten. Etymologically, these nations seem to include Russia, and armies from the European and Asian nations of Germany, Greece, Iran, Iraq, Armenia, and Turkey among others.

Jeremiah 6:22-23 says, *"Thus says the LORD: Behold, a people comes from the North Country, and a great nation will be raised from the farthest parts of the earth. They will lay hold on bow and spear; they are cruel and have no mercy; their voice roars like the sea; and they ride on horses, as men of war set in array against you, O daughter of Zion."*

Ezekiel 38:4, 7-9 says, *"I will turn you around, put hooks into your jaws, and lead you out, with all your army, horses, and horsemen, all splendidly clothed, a great company with bucklers and shields, all of them handling swords. Prepare yourself and be ready, you and all your companies that are gathered about you; and be a guard for them. After many days you will be visited. In the latter years you will come into the land of those brought back from the sword and gathered from many people on the mountains of Israel, which had long been desolate; they were brought out of the nations, and now all of them dwell safely. You will ascend, coming like a storm, covering the land like a cloud, you and all your troops and many peoples with you."*

In the latter part of the first millennia A.D, Russia was a country that became converted to God when the daughter-in-law of the first ruler in Russia carried the gospel back to that land from the Eastern Roman Empire. A number of years later, Russia was defeated in two desperate wars with the Byzantine Bulgarians that also helped bring Christianity to Russia. The Russian Orthodox Church was born and when the Eastern Roman Empire fell, the center of Christianity in the east shifted to Russia, "The Third Rome." It was so named third in line following the Western and then the Eastern Roman Church after the Roman Empire collapsed.

When Peter the Great became Czar of Russia in 1689, he had always been interested in Europe so he turned his eyes and heart there to bring its influence back to his homeland of Russia. He attempted to westernize his nation and build its military might. He tried to bring European ideas to Russia by imitating the west. He attempted to revolutionize Russia's social and political systems along western lines.

The Russian Orthodox Church was not entrenched deeply enough nor was it strong enough in the spiritual sense to guarantee the safety of the Russian Government from revolutionaries. In time the Czars became cold, indifferent and filled with corruption and God had to deal with this massive nation. The reforms brought back to Russia by Vladimir Lenin and Leon Trotsky from decades of religious, political, and social ideological upheavals in Europe, was Karl Marx's social and political philosophy. Again, we see a colossal clash of culture as changes of ideology had demolished Russia's hierarchy. God's punishment upon Russia was the Bolshevik Revolution in 1917, and it spun Russia back to her own personal "Dark Ages" for 74 years under Communism. Russia was to falter through Communism as a superpower and bring massive persecution of its people, but God used them in war to help defeat the German dictator Adolf Hitler who was crazed with anti-Semitism. After its collapse because of atheism and with its loss of the Eastern Block countries of the Soviet

Union, Russia has shifted its political center back toward Europe in time for God's timetable for the future.

There has always seemed to be a mysterious connection between Europe and Asia with the exchange of social ideals, and even war, such as the invasions of Napoleon and Adolf Hitler. Just as it's heart turned to Europe in the 17th Century, Russia's fate today is sealed as their dependency has now shifted toward Europe, the North Atlantic Treaty Organization (NATO), and the new alliance with the European Union and eventually all of Euro/Asia. Russia is no longer that giant of a bear and no longer that tyrannical power of the Joseph Stalin era when he massacred millions. Russia is not to be appeased as in World War II when in order to keep them in the war they would be given about half of Europe when the war was over. The Soviet Union went broke, bankrupt, depleted, kaput – end of story. Her influence will continue to be powerful but in line with the nations of Euro/Asia and with the G-8 nations.

There is a bit of irony connected with the fact that Russia turned to Communism. The very nation that will one day be part of an invasion force against Israel, had turned into an anti-god Communist state the very same year of the British Balfour Declaration of 1917 that allowed the Jews to return to their homeland to worship their God. One of the goals of Soviet Communism after that time was to eliminate any symbolism of Judaism in the Soviet Union. Now the symbol of the Communist Hammer and Sickle that attempted to strike its fatal, final blows on Judaism is gone entirely, forever collapsed! God has a sense of humor!

VICTORLESS VIETNAM WAR

I know that I am going to be criticized for this next remark, but the Vietnam War of the 1960's and 1970's was an absolutely essential war for the end-times as well and was a major event in the plan of God. In regard to the United States, it's been said that they lost the Vietnam War in 1974, but clearly there was a purpose in that war that was designed by God. Win or lose, the United States was there to help dismantle the Soviet Union. Vietnam was only the pawn in something that was happening of a much bigger consequence, and that was the collapse of the Soviet Union. I place the blame of the loss of that war squarely on the shoulders of an era of protest and dissatisfaction in the United States during the 1960's and 1970's and on the shoulders of the politicians who made it a political war. The politicians were too weak and caved into the masses of hysteria. That's the weakness of the democratic system. It mingles governmental power with the will of people as seen in the iron and clay vision of Nebuchadnezzar in Daniel chapter two, of which there is no mixture or cohesiveness. As evil as a strong autocratic rule is, it is far greater in strength in the short run and will not break apart as the iron and clay mixture of democracy will. The ineptness of democracy caters to the will of the people and the rights they espouse. This is what will help bring the weakness in the kingdoms of the world before the return of Jesus Christ. Today, that weakness is what will help bring about the collapse of the United States.

What a shame about the protestors who became a whole generation that was caught in the middle of the "greatest generation" from World War II and the current generation of brave soldiers, families, and supporters of our country in the current struggle against terrorism. We have protestors today who have protested at military shows, and at least one American City has not allowed the Navy to dock in their ports because of the Iraqi war. They have acted presumptuously and condescendingly toward the President and the Congress. That is a shame! I'm not sure we'll have another "greatest generation" but I trust that this generation would honor the memory of that generation and have nothing to do with protesting war to the point of destroying troop morale as the generation of the 60's and 70's. Had the protestors of that time not been there the outcome would have been the same anyway, namely the dismantling of the Soviet Union. It's too bad the protesters didn't understand that! The protestors were on the wrong side of which Super Power was going to come out of Vietnam the strongest. God was dealing with the United States as well but its fate is yet to be uncovered at a future time.

The evil of the 1960's and 1970's was not just the protestors. That was only the tip of the iceberg as God used their dissension. Beneath those waters of protest was the move of atheism, secularism, humanism, greed, and self-ism that fueled the anti-war movement and the cultural change that we have seen in America in the past 40 years.

THE MISSING GENERATION

Tom Brokaw, the author of the best selling book "The Greatest Generation," seemed to be disappointed that President Lyndon Johnson was not totally honest with the American people about the Vietnam War. I loved reading his book, but his sentiment is indicative of those who could never see the larger picture of a political purpose, particularly in light of the Bible, one of the oldest historical writings. His view represents the feelings of the antiwar protestors.

When in view of what God was trying to do in moving Russia toward the European Union bloc of nations, unbeknownst to them the protestors were really fighting against what God was trying to accomplish. God had His way anyhow. You would think our pullout and failed policy in Vietnam would have kept the Soviet Union strong to dominate the world scene and would have been a feather in the cap of the protestors. No, the protestors couldn't see what was designed by God that America's strength was to expose the Soviet Union's weakness.

A handful of Vietnam veterans have spoken out against the war but they don't understand the bigger picture either. In calling the Vietnam War illegal and immoral, they couldn't see the forest for the trees. The protestors accomplished their narrow objectives but missed the broader importance of the war. The Soviet Union eventually fell anyway, and the protestors could not envision the bigger picture. They couldn't see what God was trying to do. They could only see what they perceived as their political agenda. It was only what concerned them and the confused agenda of the Universities and College secularists and atheists who taught them. They were bedded down with inept evolutionary professors whose intellectualism and dark rhetoric blinded their eyes and fostered a delusion to seal their minds. By not knowing what God was trying to do, they were open to the wickedness of the work of Satan as seen in Thessalonians just before the Second Coming of Christ.

II Thessalonians 2:10-11 talks about those *"with all deceivableness of unrighteousness in them that perish; because they received not the love of the truth, that they might be saved. And for this cause God shall send them strong delusion, that they should believe a lie"*.

Their support was the teachings of atheism and secularism that caused them to misunderstand a broader picture, hence the only thing they knew to do was protest. They were deluded with a mixture of anti-establishment and ultra-liberalism that penetrated and over-exposed their minds with atheistic thought. It has helped to lead America down the road to cultural collapse as each generation since that time has produced increasing levels of moral decline. Today, the battle is with the aftermath of their misguided intentions that has brought about a generation that is nearly socialistic and clearly unstable. Because of the sins of the United States, they became part of God's plan to expose America's weak underbelly. It was a two-edged sword. Like the Crucifixion of Jesus Christ when Judas betrayed Him, you see in scripture that it had to be done but you would hate to be a partner of the one who did it.

In Mark 14:21 it says about the death of Jesus, *"The Son of Man indeed goes just as it is written of Him, but woe to that man by whom the Son of Man is betrayed! It would have been good for that man if he had never been born."*

It's possible to fight against the will of God even when you think your cause to be a legitimate one. It is better to give in to the will of God. Some may view my approach as resignation or fatalistic in not resisting certain evils. However, you need to pray about and understand what God may be trying to work out in His Divine plan and make sure that you are not resisting it as in the Vietnam protests.

In the book of Acts the religious leaders of the day tried to prevent the Apostles, another group of religious leaders from spreading the story of Christianity. The potential to fight against God's plan was there but for that one time, sane minds prevailed. They ended up persecuting the Apostles and setting them free.

Acts 5:38-39 says about the Apostles, *"...I say to you, keep away from these men and let them alone; for if this plan or this work is of men, it will come to nothing. <u>But if it is of God, you cannot overthrow it—lest</u> <u>you even be found to fight against God</u>. And they agreed with him, and when they had called for the apostles and beaten them, they commanded that they should not speak in the name of Jesus, and let them go."*

To paraphrase the title of Tom Brokaw's book, I call the Vietnam era of protestors the "missing generation." On the one hand, they felt that this country owed them something as they enjoyed such benefits as grants for college education, while on the other hand, they felt it was their duty to go out and protest against its war. Apparently, they had to come of age and find themselves in regards to the Vietnam War, the feminist movement, free love, abortion, drugs, protest, and pacifism. They were involved with sit-ins, they burned their bras, their draft cards, and they burned American flags. Ironically, they spoke against the establishment, yet they studied in our colleges and universities enabling them to become a part of the establishment. They thought they were going to change things. Their idea of changing things and then eventually become part of the establishment they detested, made them just as big of hypocrites as they accused the United States of being in regards to the war in Vietnam.

The college students were the prime candidates for protesting particularly when President Johnson moved to the lottery system in the draft during the Vietnam War. Johnson attempted to use others for the wartime effort and not just the poor and disenfranchised, because it posed Civil Rights problems for him. Johnson was under pressure to deal with those Civil Rights issues; therefore the change to include the well to do college kids in this country in the war effort was quite profound. The end result was that college students would be drafted too, so they protested.

The protestors misapplied the meaning of the 1st Amendment that gives "the right of the people peaceably to assemble, and to petition the Government for a redress of grievances". I'm all for that even if you disagree with war, but their protests led to violence that changed the psychological direction of our country. They were protesting against a war that God was using to help dismantle a huge nation that occupied one third of the worlds land area. That generation of protestors didn't understand it! They just didn't get it! As the "missing generation," they could not decipher any political understanding that carried a broader geopolitical meaning for our country and for the world. They were missing the foresight and the spirituality to know what God was doing.

According to the First Amendment, of course we have a right as "people peaceably to assemble" such as the Civil Rights movement when Martin Luther King Jr. attempted non-violent reform. Respectfully speaking against injustice on any level is always appropriate such as the causes against segregation, abortion, and speaking in favor of justice for farmers, workers, and the poor. Such was not the case in the protesting era of the 60's and 70's when they protested against the war. War is an injustice as well but God had no plan to overthrow the United States at that time. Apparently, the protesters did not understand the principle of authority based on government, neither the principle of justice to punish any one that does evil. They protested against the United States and against both of these principles that are found in Romans and in I Peter.

Romans 13:1-2, 4 tell us... *"there is no authority except from God, and the authorities that exist are appointed by God. Therefore whoever resists the authority resists the ordinance of God...For he is God's minister to you for good. But if you do evil, be afraid; for he does not bear the sword in vain; for he is God's minister, an avenger to execute wrath on him who practices evil."*

I Peter 2:13-15 says, *"Therefore submit yourselves to every ordinance of man for the Lord's sake, whether to the king as supreme, or to governors, as to those who are sent by him for the punishment of evildoers and for the praise of those who do good. For this is the will of God, that by doing good you may put to silence the ignorance of foolish men."*

The protestors of that time were so adamant that they caused confusion in the rest of the country. This made the heart of the American public to become callous toward those who served in Vietnam. It obliterated troop morale. It weakened the resolve of the United States and helped determine its future fate as a super power. In their confusion, hardness, and delusion because of the protests, the American people couldn't even acknowledge the veterans of that era. Consequently the Vietnam Veterans were never given the proper financial help, respect, and welcome back home. Thankfully, a Vietnam memorial was finally erected for the Vietnam Veterans in Washington, D.C. and the Vietnam Veterans now have a rightful place in our history.

Men of other past wars have paid a heavy emotional, physical, and mental price. The Vietnam Veterans, similar to the Civil War Veterans who also fought in a divided nation, bore a distinctive scar throughout their lives because of a divisive war that damaged the military conscience of the nation. One consolation for the Vietnam Veterans is that they played an important role that helped move the mighty nation of Russia so that they would fall in line with the prophetic plan of God before Armageddon.

In 2005, the Prime Minister of Vietnam was interviewed on television and thanked all the anti-war protestors in the United States that helped end the war. He wants a closer relationship with the United States government. Here is a Communist who along with the protestors, knew nothing of what the Bible says about the armies of the North and the East that will be involved in the Battle of Armageddon. He knew nothing about how God used the Vietnam War to help break the back of Communism in Russia. He didn't understand that Russia would align itself more with Europe, and how armies coming from Asia could also include his country. He and the protestors were both in the dark and lost in their own ignorance.

No thanks can be given to Jane Fonda during that era. Otherwise known as Hanoi Jane, Miss Fonda made a feeble attempt a few years back at admitting her wrong during the Vietnam War, but not too many believed her or forgave her. Now, years after her famous 1972 incident of sitting on an enemy aircraft gun, laughing and appearing to have a good time, she now expresses remorse for that decision.

She said she would go to her grave regretting that incident. In an interview with NBC News in 2005, they said that she didn't apologize, but that she said her visit to Hanoi was her largest "lapse of judgment." At the time she was thumbing her nose at the government and some say it was a betrayal and treason. Thankfully and hopefully her ideals have somewhat changed, but it's too bad that we have to talk about this so many years after the fact. I wonder where her politics have been between then and now! Apparently in the same place because it seems to be deja vu as she pretty much feels the same way about the war in Iraq. Notice that she has pulled back from any front-page headlines of her opposition to the Iraq war. I'm sure she's had enough of the "poster girl" image of anti-Americanism from the Vietnam War that she didn't want her reputation soiled anymore.

One thing that was disgraceful and happened to Jane Fonda after she came to talk to the press again, was that a veteran of Vietnam came up to her and spit in her face at a book signing. He said that he spit in her face because she has spit in the faces of veterans for years. I can understand the resentment of the veteran, but no matter how many people disagree with her, politeness and respect is still the order of the day. There is no call for spitting on someone, pies in the face, or eggs thrown at a speaker as some have done in the past. There is no call for disrespecting, interrupting, or making a mockery of politicians and other lecturers as they are speaking.

In the social, political, academic, and religious realm there have been influential individuals such as Jane Fonda who refused to listen to the judgment of their peers that were trying to give them wise counsel. Their counselors would try to steer them from the mistakes of believing, doing, or teaching the wrong things, but they would get themselves into harmful situations anyway. This has happened with religious teachers many times in the past. They would then try and make amends years later but in the meantime, they've done irreparable harm to countless thousands of innocents. An apology of course is always accepted, but even if they repent and cry with tears, there are some things that one cannot repent of. That means that you're forgiven, but you can't go back and undo, change, or reform what you messed up, which is usually a part of repentance.

There are a number of situations in the Bible that could not be changed even after a person felt sorry, but I'll mention only two. After Judas sold Jesus for 30 pieces of silver that led to His crucifixion on the cross, he repented or regretted his betrayal but He could not change what he had done.

Matthew 27:3-5 says, *"Then Judas, which had betrayed him, when he saw that he was condemned, repented himself, and brought again the thirty pieces of silver to the chief priests and elders, saying, I have sinned in that I have betrayed the innocent blood. And they said, What is that to us, see to that yourself. And he cast down the pieces of silver in the temple, and departed, and went and hanged himself."*

Another time was when Esau sold his birthright to his brother Jacob and lost the "first place right" of his inheritance in the Old Testament. The following verse in Hebrews means that he couldn't undo what he had already done. It tells of Esau's horrible plight. He could not get his birthright and blessing back that was rightfully his. There was no going back to change what he did. He lost the right to possess the better share of his father Isaac's inheritance. This is one of the saddest verses in the Bible.

Hebrews 12:16-17 says *"he found no place of repentance though he sought it carefully with tears"*.

Of course, when there are things that you either can or cannot make right, God forgives anyway. You can still be a blessing to others no matter how terrible your situation! That is the beauty of the grace of God!

WHAT HAVE WE DONE/WHAT ARE WE DOING?

It may be our right to question our leaders but never to disrespect and resist them as some of them did during the 60's and 70's. That's why I am not a protestor or an activist against the government. I'm in favor of "peaceable assembly", but I'm not in favor of protesting, or activism, and there's a fine line between the two. One is a positive, non-violent, peaceful approach and the other is a negative, arrogant, destructive approach.

I know that all is not right in any government, including the United States. I am also aware that scandals have been a part of many of the presidential administrations in the history of the United States. There was one while George Washington was president and it continued on into the John Adams administration. History records the near impeachment of Andrew Johnson. There was the construction company and the whiskey ring scandals of the Ulysses Grant administration, and then the Teapot Dome scandal during the Warren Harding administration. We are all familiar with the Watergate, Iran-Contra, and Whitewater scandals of the Richard Nixon, Ronald Reagan, and William Clinton administrations.

It seems to me that ever since those years of protest in the 60's and 70's, we have had a great disrespect for the leaders of our nation, particularly our presidents. That includes the "deep throat" revelation in 2005 of the former Nixon Administration official Mark Felt, when he worked for the Federal Bureau of Investigation. Many say that Felt saved the country, but here is a man who leaked information to reporters Bob Woodward and Tom Berstein rather than going to the proper authorities. Some would argue that he had no one to go to. Wrong! Since Nixon was a Republican, Felt could have gone to the Democratic leaders in Congress who were already starting to get involved with the investigation and were going to be involved in the impeachment process anyway and could have sought the protection of anonymity and immunity. If he had waited just a little longer he would have had the likes of Special Prosecutor Archibald Cox, who was fired by Nixon and Attorney General Elliot Richardson who resigned in protest, and they would have rallied to his side. Something would have happened. The whole point is, Felt did the right thing the wrong way and he said the right things to the wrong people. We didn't need the likes of Bob Woodward and Tom Berstein and the liberal press to be the "confessional booth" for the nation.

While the President, the Congress, and the Judiciary were all involved in the Watergate Scandal, the Yom Kippur war was being waged in the Middle East. Leonid Brezhnev and Aleksei Kosygin of the Soviet Union backed the Egyptian and Syrian forces, while the United States of America backed the Israeli forces. This was a dangerous time that could have led to world war, all while we were trying to rid ourselves of a President whose scandal was deemed greater than other Presidents whose administrations were also filled with scandal. After the resignation of Nixon and by the time we got to William Clinton, I think the country had enough of impeachment, or has it?

Because of all that, you can see what America has consistently done to our recent Presidents. We practically crucified Lyndon Johnson because of the Vietnam War. We forced Nixon to resign because of Watergate. We rejected Gerald Ford because he pardoned Nixon. We laughed at the ineptness of Jimmy Carter and rejected his administration as he tried to stare down the Ayatollah of Iran. We tried to catch Ronald Reagan with the "weapons for hostage" deal. We were concerned about "the economy stupid", as if our personal economy was so badly affected, so we threw George H.W. Bush out of office after one term. We impeached William Clinton and nearly booted him out office.

In the George W. Bush administration, we've impaled him because of the Iraqi war, and went after top advisors who supposedly leaked information about a Central Intelligence Agency agent. As scandalous fate would have it, the testimonial words of Bob Woodward were a part of this uproar as well. What else are we going to do to President Bush? Will we impeach him because of his National Security Agency spy program that is designed against terrorism and that certain individuals had leaked information about? Will it be over some other issue?

What will we do to any Presidents who follow George W. Bush? Is more impeachment a part of America's future? The press, the critics, and anyone's opponent tries to raise questions and put doubt in the publics mind in order to change the course of political direction in their favor. While many of our past political leaders were not guiltless, our response to them has shown the hypocrisy of our ways and how desperately we need God. There is a real visceral political hated in America and for the foreseeable future we cannot undo what we have done. What a mess!

10 WISE MEN

It's a strange political world trying to stay ahead of those who are out to destroy reputations. Our leaders are constantly being questioned and criticized no matter what they do or don't do. When anyone disagrees with those in authority or with someone of an opposing view on a talk show, all they need to do is get in front of a camera and ask theoretical questions for diversion and confusion. This usually happens when they disagree with someone else's position and want to avoid a question or skirt around one that is asked of them. Their motive is to try to avoid the truth in what their opponent may be saying, or they will try not to come to any compromise. They do this by attempting to send the opposing person into a tailspin in their debate in order to sidestep the issue in question and avoid being pinned down when they don't want to admit their opponent is right. It's as if they carry a chip on their shoulder and dare their opponent to conversationally knock it off. A political game is usually played, as truth can never be the goal or outcome in our society that is continually focused on relativism and political correctness. They question every answer that is given by asking their opponent every question imaginable from every conceivable angle. No matter what answer is given, they will then question the answer given in order to tear down their opponent's viewpoint. They do not follow debate strategies so they never get to the truth. This is also done when someone's character or motive is in question, or when being a witness of a questionable event, or when testifying in court. They speak in hyperbolic terms and then ask or raise more confusing questions then what 10 wise men can even answer. It's dumbfounding!

Are we really searching for truth? When Jesus stood before Pilate and was asked whether or not He was a King, He made an astounding statement about truth that is recorded in John 18. That was when Pilate asked Him a classic question.

John 18:37-38 says, *"Jesus answered, you say rightly that I am a King. For this cause I was born, and for this cause I have come into the world, that I should bear witness to the truth. Everyone who is of the truth hears my voice." Pilate said to Him, "What is truth?"*

Jesus came to bear record to the truth. When Pilate asked his infamous question, he nullified what understanding of truth he could have had. He was already biased and could only conclude that he found no fault with Jesus. He did not come to the truth as to what Jesus stood for and what He was about to do.

What are we doing to ourselves and to America? Is it disrespectful, and are we helping to send our country down a media-filled drain of disaster? Are there right ways and wrong ways to change leadership? I believe a change of leadership can be made if it is done the correct way. If not, we are in for utter chaos and that is what we have done over the last 30 years and that is where we are heading right now as this has contributed to the constitutional crises we face today. All of this shows the weakness of democracy as seen in the dream of Nebuchadnezzar found in Daniel chapter two where societies are given over to the will of the people, and the rights they espouse, as the nations begin to unravel.

There are seven basic requirements for an effective appeal to someone who is in leadership. They are based on solid biblical principles. (**4**)

[1] We must be in right standing. We must immediately come under the jurisdiction of the proper authorities.

[2] We must have the right motives. There can be no selfishness or ulterior motives.

[3] We must appeal at the appropriate time. That depends on our relationship to our authorities.

[4] We must give accurate information. Correct information about ourselves and the accuracy of our information about another party.

[5] We must have the right attitudes. This will affect the merits of our information.

[6] We must use the appropriate words. It can be very easy for our words to be misunderstood.

[7] We must display the right response if our appeal is rejected. A gracious response is appropriate whether our appeal is accepted or rejected.

Is that what we do to our leaders? Do we follow the basic rules of respect and decency and try to remove someone the proper way, by going to the right people in authority with the right motives? Are we resisting leadership just because we are a willful people and we want our own way? This is democracy in its weakest form! The wars of the world and the dissension of America will bring God's plans to the forefront as we see the collapse of western ideals to prepare for the Antichrist.

THREE VIEWS

There are three ways of looking at the events of this world throughout the centuries and very few look at this world as God does. First there is the political view that sees your own nation from your political perspective and interest. Second there is the geopolitical view that views your nation as it fits in with the interest of some of the other nations. Third there is the solar political view that sees all the nations of the world and how they fit in with history, the changing events that have brought on that history, and the future that is unfolding with a certain plan for winding down that history.

The first view would be like riding in an airplane a few thousand feet in the air and seeing a lot of the landscape, but being unable to relate it to other lands and nations. You rise above the clouds and the view is nice in the atmosphere, but you don't see much of the world. You cannot fathom the connection of lands and oceans. Protestors, self-interest groups, most politicians and theologians see the world that way. They know we have to have proper relations with other nations for peace and prosperity, but they neither make the spiritual connection to God, nor see the interconnecting of His plan throughout the centuries.

The second view is like rising in a space shuttle far above the clouds and earth's atmosphere and seeing the breathtaking views as seen on television. You can visualize the relationship of nations and see the lines of demarcation of oceans and land. You see the earth's orb and pass over the various continents, and the world becomes smaller and the struggles we pass through become meaningless. Many astronauts have come to grips with their faith while in space. They may pray or read a scripture or meditate. Their connection with God becomes enormous. There are a few privileged politicians and theologians who understand this concept and they feel that they have been put on this earth for a purpose. They will bring God into their lives regardless of the peer pressure to do just the opposite. They somewhat see the broader picture as God sees it.

The third view is much greater and would be like riding a space capsule to the moon and back. You see all of the earth as God sees it. You see the bright blue of the earth, the clouds, the oceans, and the landmass from hundreds of thousands of miles out in space. You begin to understand the vastness of a Creator God and His universe, and not an evolutionary process. You come to grips with the idea of a God given master plan that has something to do with all the nations of the world and the entire universe. You realize that there isn't much time left because the plan of the ages is winding down and God will soon return to rescue the world from its own destruction.

This third view is given to those who have read history and see a disobedient world that has known little peace. That person inquires of God as to what He is trying to accomplish through all this. Is there a master plan? Will God bring things to a close? How much longer can the world stand the violence? Will the nations of the world and their leaders acknowledge that there is a God? Will they try to find His plan for their lives and the lives of their nations? Very few politicians and theologians will explore these concepts and ideas. Not many individuals see it that way.

What we need to do is pray internationally because God always seems to send revival to people globally, giving nations opportunity at one time or another to follow Him. Revival seems to come to the nations in cycles over the years as remnants of those various nations and continents seem to return to God. Most continents and nations seem to have that opportunity just like the Holy Spirit is doing in the African nations of Uganda and Ethiopia today. In the midst of times of war, God prepares any nation for what lies ahead in difficulty or persecution. He would then send revival to their land. They would become powerful, but unfortunately return to their sin and fall into spiritual despair and separation from God.

Over the centuries there has been a rise in powers in Europe, the Middle East, and Asia. All those conflicts have been connected with Israel's wars over the centuries and who it is that should occupy the land of Palestine! The wars of all the millennia have been to discharge God's overall will in bringing many of His obedient creation to heaven with Him. The nations of the world will have to pass through Armageddon and all the wars throughout the centuries will have to find their conclusion there. The God of war, who will impose His peace and justice at that battle, will then be revealed as the God of peace. Hallelujah!

CHAPTER FOUR:

Why the war on terrorism will lead to Armageddon.

—⚌—

This chapter deals with the role of the United States and other countries in their global war against terrorism. We are not the only countries that are facing terror as a powerful frontline of terrorism has developed in Europe and has spread to North America. However, God generally deals with and uses the Super Power nations of any generation, to bring about international change to the world scene.

The United States is continually threatened by some of the illegal immigrants who may be involved with terrorism and who are attempting to gain entrance through our porous borders. There is a real danger of terrorism coming to the United States as terrorists are looking for ways to enter our country by assuming a false identity. They are willing to bring weapons to either use against us or sell them to others that can. It is easy for foreigners to enter our country and learn at our universities and then terrorize us through their easy access. Some home grown terrorist groups within our country are connected with terrorist groups from around the world. They wish nothing but to find some soft spot in our defense systems to deliver a fatal blow to the culture of America. This weakness along with the protests and legislation to ensure easy immigration will not go away. Our open borders with both Canada and Mexico are one of the biggest threats to the security of America. Terrorists will try to find their way through to inflict the most damaging blow to America as possible, hitting our major ports or cities.

Terrorist groups that have been halted in other parts of the world won't be deterred from making attempts in the United States. The real dilemma is that our intelligence has failed us in the past and I'm afraid it will fail us again in the future. America will come under attack again and there will be no appeasement with the terrorists. Those connected with terrorism have not only brought terror to New York City, but have been caught in the state of California as well as in other areas of our country.

WHAT IS TERRORISM?

The word terrorism in the dictionary is defined as "the calculated use of violence (or threat of violence) against civilians in order to attain goals that are political or religious or ideological in nature; this is done through intimidation or coercion or instilling fear". It is an incredulously evil ideology that will spread mercilessly, being very difficult to protect against.

Terrorism is sometimes well organized and other times simply scattered indiscriminately. It is used to intimidate leaders of the state, disrupt the economies of the industrial nations, and it is intended to sabotage and bring down governments. It has been used against populations of enemy nations and against their leaders in a psychological way. Government leaders have been assassinated or kidnapped, including Presidents, Kings, Prime Ministers, and Diplomats. Even if an attempt at terrorism fails, terrorists want to invoke fear in the lives of citizens. That happened in a foiled attempt to simultaneously explode 10 airliners flying from Great Britain to America in August of 2006.

Terrorism is profound and has been used powerfully throughout the history of the world. It has been with us for centuries and is a pattern well established even in the days of the Bible. It can be seen in the war of the five kings against the four kings in the book of Genesis chapter 14. In that instance, Abraham had to intervene after his nephew Lot was taken prisoner by the five kings.

Terrorism involved God's people when they were being thwarted from re-entering Palestine under God's direction with the promise that the land that the people of Canaan had occupied would be theirs. It was seen in the powerful nations of the world that persecuted the nation of Israel. Egypt enslaved Israel for 400 years. Assyria captured the Northern Kingdom of Israel and brought them into their land, never again to be organized as a nation again. Babylon captured the Southern Kingdom of Israel, brought them to Babylon and held them in captivity for 70 years. The Persians persecuted Israel in the book of Esther with the wickedness of Haman. Greece invaded and occupied the land of Israel and desecrated the Temple of Jerusalem. Rome destroyed Jerusalem in 70 AD and they never were a nation again until 1948. Rome then tried to stem the tide of the growing sect of Christianity. Many of the Emperors did all they could to kill and imprison the Christians, until the Emperor Constantine who supposedly was converted to Christianity. Later, the Mongols and the Muslims used terrorism as they fought for victory in their battles as they marched through the continents. The nations of the European Continent struggled with wars for a couple of centuries as the God of eternity watched and waited patiently for the conclusion of His timetable for the world's powers.

In the past, many of these terrorists were isolated and their acts of terrorism were localized and it sometimes took years for the overthrow of governments or officials. With modern day powerful weapons and instant communication their dastardly deeds can be affected much easier, and more profoundly serious and deadly, hitting anywhere it creates the most damage.

Even though some terrorists may seek a truce, the frightening thing is that it will continue to become worse, more common, and uncontrollable. When one terrorist group is contained another will rise in its place. The Devil will jump at the chance to use this anarchy for his benefit and to continue to create havoc in the world. He will equip his henchmen of demonic activity to create confusion, hate, and chaos in the world. He will soon discover that he hasn't much time left. His attack is particularly against any nations that are the most powerful at the time. Today, those nations include the United States, Great Britain, and others.

Suicidal or homicidal bombings, germ warfare, chemical, and biological warfare will continue to increase along with the nuclear threat. All of this will more than likely be used during the end time that is mentioned in the book of Revelation. The Devil also wants to create chasms between the nations, so that he can rally them together for the final onslaught against Jesus Christ during the Battle of Armageddon. The Devil figures that he can divide and conquer.

20th CENTURY TERRORISM

There are many acts of terrorism that can be cited as taking place in the 20th Century as small groups of terrorists have learned how to cripple a super power. Some of the terrorist attacks given below can be found on various terrorist web sites (1) and are as follows:

In 1964, the purpose of the Palestine Liberation Organization (PLO) was to create a Palestinian State through proper diplomatic channels, but there were some that were part of that group who resorted to violence.

In 1967 the Israeli army conquered Jerusalem and other key areas of Israel in a war that took 6 days.

In 1979 there was the take over of the United States Embassy in Iran when 52 American hostages were held for 444 days. It cost President Carter his job.

In 1983 there were the bombings of the United States Embassy and the Marine barracks in which over 300 hundred were killed.

1988 marked the bombing of the Pan Am jet over Lockerbie, Scotland in which 270 were killed, including 189 Americans.

In 1993 there was the first bombing of the World Trade Center. Six people were killed in what was a pre-shadow of the nightmare that was to come just eight years later.

Between 1992 and 1995, some of the worst genocidal activities occurred in Bosnia-Herzegovina. Over 200,000 deaths occurred in cultural fighting and ethnic cleansing. In the town of Srebrenica, 8,000 men and young boys were systematically slaughtered. It was the worst mass murder of civilians in Europe since the end of World War II.

1998 marked the bombing of two United States Embassies, in Tanzania and Nairobi. Over 200 people were killed in those attacks.

In the year 2000 we saw the attack on the USS Cole in Yemen. 17 servicemen were killed.

Then the big one happened on September 11, 2001. An act occurred that caught the United States off guard. Four airplanes were hijacked in the United States as 19 hijackers turned them into weapons of mass destruction. One crashed in Pennsylvania and 45 were killed. One crashed into the Pentagon and 43 were killed. Two crashed into the World Trade Center in which 2,800 were killed. Ten of the 19 hijackers on board those planes passed through Iran and many of them came from Saudi Arabia. The collapse of the twin towers is a symbol of the future collapse of American culture. God is sending a message to America.

Outside the United States in Madrid, Spain in March of 2004, four trains were bombed as nearly 200 individuals were killed. The whole political process of Spain was turned on its heels as the elections were influenced by this act of terrorism. The Pro-American government that supported the war in Iraq lost the election and the Spanish troops were brought back home to Spain. The terrorists were successful in influencing government policy.

In September of 2004, another incident of terrorism happened in Russia. Twelve hundred people in a school were taken hostage for three days and 300 of them were killed by terrorists as mothers and fathers mourned the loss of their little ones.

On July 7, 2005, the day when the G-8 Summit of the Industrialized Nations was to begin, there were the barbaric bombings of the subways and buses in London. At the time when their Summit in Scotland was to discuss changes in the climate, and the impoverished in Africa with their health issues, six or seven nearly simultaneous coordinated terrorists attacks were delivered. They inflicted casualties with over 50 people killed and over 700 injured through multiple explosions. A Jihad cell related to Al Qaeda has claimed responsibility for these acts of depravity. Another attack of terrorism was made on July 21st in an attempt to deal a double death-blow within two weeks as a botched bombing attempt was made in

London again. This time no one was killed in that failed attempt. Unfortunately, the police did kill one innocent man when they thought he was trying to run from them. In the midst of the seriousness of terrorist threats all of us must give unquestioned cooperation in order to uncover the vile acts of modern day terrorism.

The G-8 leaders who attended that summit are united to fight against terrorism. This continued struggle will broaden, then perhaps temporarily subside as antiterrorism gains a foothold, but then re-ignite in a different form into a worldwide conflict that will conclude at Armageddon.

In July 2005 and April 2006, a series of bombings in Egypt killed at least 88 people and 24 people respectively in an attempt to rattle the government. There are some that try to tie terrorism in directly with those who side with the United States' war in Iraq, but Egypt is not even involved in the war in Iraq. That attack shows that terrorism is an across the board pattern and attempt by terrorist groups to disrupt governments regardless of their political ideology.

November 9, 2005 showed us the destructive force of three suicide bombers that hit hotels in Amman, Jordan. 57 people were killed and hundreds more were injured. This was done to punish Jordan and the United States because of their political ties with each other.

In July of 2006, eight explosions occurred on seven commuter trains in Bombay, (Mumbai) India, killing nearly 200 people as bombs were placed on luggage racks above people's heads. Train bombings are easy targets to hit in any nation.

Terrorist groups are active all around the world. It is nothing new as cells continue to spring up and operate with swiftness and great vengeance. These cells are known to be in South America, on the continent of Africa, in Europe, the Middle East, and in Asia. Some of the better-known terrorist groups are Al Qaeda, Hamas, Hezbollah, and the Palestine Islamic Jihad. The question that needs to be answered is, "How many terrorist operations are there in the United States and how soon before they make a major and destructive impact on our society?"

Imitator terrorist cells have spawned off of Al Qaeda as if they were being franchised around the world like McDonald's restaurants or 7-11 convenience stores. There is no military solution that can be established to fight these cells. The war with terrorism could possibly escalate as a war starting with the extreme leaders of Islam and the western world, and particularly the United States because we are the remaining super power that is supportive of Israel.

It is truly astounding to realize that all of this terrorism is a result of sin in the world. It is something that will be a part in gathering the world to Armageddon in the last days as the sparks fly, and international war develops. Terrorism is just one of the stepping stones to the greater gathering of nations for this last great battle.

The scourge of terrorism is on the increase. It is always a step ahead of its victims because of the element of surprise. It can strike without a warning or at a moment's notice when people least expect it as they go about their daily routine. It places a psychological imprint of fear on the minds of victim countries so that there is a real scare of traveling or being in crowds. Acts of terror can strike against airports, airliners, power plants, chemical plants, water supplies, federal buildings, sports arenas, or anywhere the public gathers. The United States needs to be alert and guard it's national monuments such as the Statue of Liberty, the Washington Monument, and the Lincoln and Jefferson Memorials. I believe terrorists will attempt to strike at the symbolic heart of America as well as try to inflict as much bodily harm as well.

These and other acts of terrorism continue to make the world more volatile as the culture of terror is spread worldwide. Acts of mass murder continue to plague the nations around the world as the war on terrorism in part has the world on a path to the Battle of Armageddon.

I WAS TERRIFIED BY TERORISTS

Modern day terrorism got its biggest boost in a most shocking and powerful form just five short years after the Arab/Israeli conflict of 1967. That was in Munich, Germany at the site of the 1972 Summer Olympics when terrorists entered the Olympic village and killed Israeli athletes and hostages at the airport as they attempted to flee. Yasir Arafat was supportive of and behind that murderous plot. I was at those fateful games in 1972 and I shall never forget them. I was helping lead a group of approximately 150 High School students when the news came to us where we were staying in our dormitory a few miles from the Olympic site. We were told that athletes in the Olympic Village were killed. We went to the stadium that day and found out that the games were cancelled.

We went back to our dorm but later that night I returned to the Olympic site because we couldn't locate a couple of our students. Thankfully, we found them right away. But while I was there at the Olympic site, I saw the police cars zooming through the streets and a dozen or so ambulances all lined up in a row waiting for the inevitable to happen. I felt the terror as the helicopters flew over my head waiting to pick up the terrorists and athletes. They were heading for the airport where more hostages and the terrorists were eventually killed. Before the games were reopened for the final few days, I attended the moratorium service in the stadium. There in the stadium, the tension seemed so heavy that I felt that one could cut the atmosphere with a knife. That was the beginning of modern day terrorism because it was the first time that we were able to see it through instant communication. The world has never been the same since.

I have attended only two Olympics in my lifetime, but this was one that was forever etched in my mind of all the ones in sports history. I was as close to the peril of terrorism as possible without being directly involved. Since that time, there has been a terror tie to the Olympics and the authorities must be alert at all future Olympic games.

That wasn't the only act of terrorism I was able to get close to. While I was in Munich, I visited Dachau Concentration Camp, the first Concentration Camp that Adolf Hitler established. Everyone with me walked through the camp in utter silence out of respect for those who died there. I saw the gas chambers, the brick ovens, and the field of death. I walked past the foundations of the dormitory style buildings that housed the suffering and dying. I was incensed as I saw what was left of the atrocities of Hitler's "Final Solution." I realized that terror could be easily brought to the surface in the future by some mad, hungry leader who could be just as evil as

Hitler. Hitler was not the Antichrist as some of the people of that day thought. He certainly did come in the spirit of the Antichrist as mentioned in the Bible. True, he was evil and diabolical, but the real Antichrist is yet for a future time.

A JUST WAR ON TERRORISM?

As far as the war in Iraq is concerned, Senator Edward Kennedy has totally disagreed with it. He said that Iraq is President Bush's Vietnam and that the Bush administration has misled the nation into a quagmire. He said that we were a part of the problem and not the solution.

In comparing Iraq to Vietnam with such derogatory words, he spoke against his own brother's policy about Vietnam. Robert McNamara, Secretary of Defense at the time, now says that had he lived, John Kennedy would have done things different in Vietnam than Lyndon Johnson. I think however that if Kennedy had lived and been elected a second term through 1968, it would more than likely have been Senator Kennedy's own brother who would have been mired in Vietnam instead of Johnson. Senator Kennedy would have to make the comparison of Bush's policy with his own brother's policy. He said about Vietnam that "we lost our national purpose in Vietnam and we cannot allow history to repeat itself". Without thinking, Senator Kennedy was hypothetically speaking about what was his own brother's policy that he inherited and passed on to Johnson. The Senator from Massachusetts speaks from a frozen time warp and is wrong, dead wrong! He cannot see how war, right or wrong, and whether he would agree with it or not, will eventually lead to Armageddon.

Senator Robert Byrd called the Iraqi war "pernicious by this administration". He called the war in Afghanistan and the war in Iraq, two separate wars. Liberals of Wilson, Truman, and the Kennedy eras would have applauded the freedoms for Iraq instead of continuing to criticize the current administration. Senator's Kennedy and Byrd disagree with the Bush Administration over how the war on terrorism has been carried out. They should drop their pride and now agree with the fact that Saddam Hussein has been ousted from power. Our country is polarized and a culture of war power struggle is being waged between these two positions as Vietnam is forever burned on our minds. America may never again rise to greatness and sustain its defense as in World War II.

I've been asked if the war in Iraq was a just or righteous war. My ministerial colleagues cite reasons why we should not enter into war unless the reasons are just. They have stated their opposition to the role of the United States in any unjust war. To be passive in regard to war is OK, but you can't pick and choose which wars you will support for a superpower in a modern day when war continues to threaten and then break out on any front. My answer to my colleagues is "from a human standpoint, no war is just and no war is righteous." However, as previously stated war is inevitable and will play a huge role in the end of time. I realize that there have been justifiable reasons given for a "just war" and as to when a nation should enter war. I'm sure that there's truth in those reasons, but in my opinion all wars are a result of man's failure, sin, and disobedience to God.

God will bring his punishment how and when it is least expected, through terrorism and war! God's punishment will include what He is going to excise upon the United States. The United States will not escape the judgment of God. As in the Bible, God will even use enemy acts of war and terrorism to bring His people to their knees. This would be for the moral crisis and failures that America has committed. Peace will be elusive.

We may seek peace but I Thessalonians 5:3 says, *"For when they shall say, Peace and safety; then sudden destruction cometh upon them, as travail upon a woman with child; and they shall not escape"*.

Much of the terrorist's acts in recent years are against a people who have been targeted for annihilation, and over a strip of land that was given by God to the nation of Israel in the book of Genesis. Not only are the Jews targeted but any nation or people who side with them, including the United States. Make no mistake about it, Israel was disobedient many times and twice removed from their land through captivity and disbursement. That opened up the door for their fellow Middle Easterners to come in and occupy the land, many of whom were their sworn enemies. Now, they cannot get along because of their religious, cultural, and national differences. They will not get along until God interrupts their plans and straightens out the whole mess. Whew!

WORLD WAR III

Since September 11, 2001, the United States has been in a state of quasi World War III against terrorism due to the tremendous spiritual and religious struggle that is in the world today. With the United States being the lone superpower, its war on terrorism is but the beginning of a war, and series of wars, that will engulf the entire world and eventually lead us to Armageddon. As I mentioned in the previous chapter, we are involved in a religious war. Everyone tries not to make religion the centerpiece of this conflict with terrorism, but this World War, as in most other wars is all about religion and how religion conducts its wars. It's all a spiritual warfare that spills over into the physical battlefield involving the nations of the world.

When the terrorists who were flying jets into the World Trade Center, the Pentagon, and into the field in Pennsylvania, they invoked the name of Allah. They were all anticipating a place in heaven with women as their reward. To them it was religious, make no mistake about it! The terrorist's war is so religious to them that they call the United States the great Satan, and its people, infidels. They are at war with us in part, because of the morally degrading way that we are living. We refuse to acknowledge God, admit our sin, and confess it to God. If the United States or other economically important nations suffer another major attack, a global recession could result. That is what the terrorists are after.

In these wars of terror, the terrorists invoke the name of God and speak of His rewards to them for their acts of violence. Wars have been marshaled in the name of religion since time immemorial because we are a spiritual people. Right or wrong, nations employ the strongest method available to prove that God is on their side. Unfortunately, that method is war!

The current fight against terrorism is an indication that these wars are continuing and it has now become a global condition that threatens the very existence of our cultures on every continent. Terrorism may not continue in the same manner as before. It may take on a new form that will widen to far greater than local terrorist acts and become something that no one was able to predict or envision. Terrorism is only a side issue as war breaks out and rears its ugly head and warlords take over a particular nation, or war may come through the current nations and leaders themselves. Great jealousies can break out as well in the form of great conflicts over territory, cultures, and ideology. All out war will be the broader issue as it widens and engulfs great regions and continents. This current war on terrorism as in all wars is a condition of man's fallen nature. War that is conducted in man to man combat is only a by-product of our spirit to spirit conflict that we have with the enemy of our souls.

BURNING BUSH

In Exodus chapter three, Moses had an experience at a burning bush in the desert of Midian. His burning bush experience was to help birth a new nation. It was a bold geo-political move at the time.

Exodus 3:2-5 says, *"And the Angel of the LORD appeared to him in a flame of fire from the midst of a bush. So he looked, and Behold, the bush was burning with fire, but the bush was not consumed. Then Moses said, 'I will now turn aside and see this great sight, why the bush does not burn.' So when the LORD saw that he turned aside to look, God called to him from the midst of the bush and said, 'Moses, Moses!' And he said, 'Here I am.' Then He said, 'Do not draw near this place. Take your sandals off your feet, for the place where you stand is holy ground."*

Moses was fixated at that burning bush. He was also intimidated because of his encounter with God and that he lacked the wherewithal to do what God was asking him to do. There was something

that burned deep within him as he heard the voice of God. God called him and gave him signs to let him know that he was to be the leader that would help deliver the children of Israel from bondage. Moses was at a crossroads and had a decision to make, but he accepted the call and the rest is history.

What in the world does George W. Bush have to do with all of this? Both he and his father, President George Herbert Walker Bush seem to have had their "burning bush" experience as they both were involved with Iraq and its rebirth. President Bush's dogged determination seems to be afire with a burning passion. He has been preoccupied with Iraq because he and the United States are involved in a warfare that dates back to the very beginning of civilization. God is using the United States to prepare for something bigger and far greater than anyone can imagine for the end of time and something far greater than the war plans of George W. Bush could foresee. Exactly what that is, many are not totally sure yet. One thing for certain, Afghanistan and Osama Bin Laden are only a small part of a gigantic puzzle of the war on terrorism. They were there only to pull on the heartstrings of the world to ready the powers of Europe and Asia. It will more than likely involve and affect many other nations of the Middle East such as Saudi Arabia, Iran, Egypt, Jordan, and as we have seen in Lebanon.

There is something very interesting about Iraq, because Iraq is the place where everything began. That territory has been a "key" strategic landmass for some period of time. Israel is the nation most mentioned in the Bible but the area of Iraq is second to it. There are other names used in place of the Iraqi name, but none the less, it is the same territory. The other names mentioned in the Bible for Iraq and circulated through various e-mails are "Babylon, Land of Shinar, and Mesopotamia. The Garden of Eden was in Iraq. Noah built the ark in Iraq. Abraham was originally from Southern Iraq. The Tower of Babel was in Iraq. Jonah preached in Nineveh, which is in Iraq. Daniel was in the lion's den in Iraq. The three Hebrew children were in the fiery furnace in Iraq. The events that took place in the book of Esther were in Iraq. The Wise Men were from Iraq."(**2**). No other nation, except Israel, has more history and prophecy in the Bible than does the land area of Iraq. Many of the Bible's occurrences and events happened in that land and today those events may be part of an open door for change in that part of the world that lead to end-time events recorded in the Bible.

The reason for the involvement of the United States in Iraq is becoming more evident as time goes on. We are involved there with terrorism because, as already mentioned, a shift in the balance of geopolitical power in Europe and the Middle East is taking place again. It is helping to determine the future balance of powers for that region of the world. Iran is flexing its military muscle and other Middle East nations will do the same. God will soon deal with the United States as their number one nemesis. The political might of Europe and the Middle East Mediterranean countries is sure to be riled, and they will rise again to supercede the might and power of the United States.

At first we thought it important that America demolish the weapons of mass destruction that Saddam Hussein had. Well, he apparently had none or we're not sure what types of weapons he had, even though both Democrats and Republicans thought he did and voted to go to war with Iraq. Rumor has it that there were weapons of mass destruction but were moved to Syria before the United Nations weapons inspectors made their investigation. Who knows?

Even though Saddam Hussein may not have had ties with Al-Qaeda, he had ties with terrorism, being a terrorist himself. That leads us to believe that it has just been a blame game to say that President Bush misled the nation into war with the intelligence that he had, when apparently all of the intelligence was misleading. Even though the President may have had more information than others may have had, it makes no difference when it was all faulty intelligence. Scary isn't it?

Protestors of the war in Iraq today speak out of both sides of their mouth when they say that they are for the troops but against the war. That's like saying "I'm in love with my wife but I'm against our marriage." It is very difficult to portray both ideas. As a left-over struggle from the Vietnam era that has come back to haunt us, leaders in Congress have had bitter shouting matches as they have called for the troops to come home from Iraq. It will be very difficult for America to ever be involved in any sustained war in the future, other than a world war with its culture on the line. This we owe in part to John Kerry, Jimmy Carter, John Murtha, Cindy Sheehan, Michael Berg, Michael Moore, and others. They as well as the New York Times and Amnesty International are clueless as to what God is doing in the Middle East. Some who oppose the Iraq war say that agreeing with the President would be treasonable and unpatriotic and would be following him blindly.

The protestors of the war in Iraq are making the same mistake as the Vietnam protestors, not realizing the shift of power from the United States to Europe. It is horribly unfortunate for those who have lost a child in Iraq and may now oppose the war, but America's involvement in Iraq is a part of God's plan. To emphasize this very important point again, God is shifting the balance of the Middle East nations and the nations of Europe as well, to prepare the world for the Second Coming of Jesus Christ.

Just as God used the United States in Vietnam to deal with Russia, God is using the Iraq war to deal with the United States. God will have His way, as America grows culturally and militarily weaker and pays for its sins through war. With their involvement in that war, the United States is not off the hook. America is being drained morally, spiritually, politically and financially which will have a long-range effect on our standing in the world. America's sin will come to the forefront. Financially, we will be drained either through entitlement programs or through war. It matters not if you stand with Democratic issues or Republican issues and it matters not which party carries the majority in government. Even a grass-roots or political antiwar movement in America won't change the world's race toward Armageddon. Antiwar antics will only lessen our interest in war and allow another superpower to emerge.

Some people say that Iraq had nothing to do with the war on terrorism, they never attacked us, and we preemptively struck at them first as a pretext to war. During World War II, Italy and Germany never attacked America either but we bombed them and invaded them. The reason we did that was because they were connected to the Axis with Japan, who did attack us, and declarations of war followed. Other Presidents have used a pretext to involve us in other wars in places like Korea, Vietnam, and in Bosnia. Declarations of war or not, most people cannot see the broader picture of the connection of Iraq and many of the other Middle Eastern nations.

Many cannot see what God will be doing in that part of the world in the end time. In particular, the religion of Islam runs a loosely held together thread of loyalty and commitment throughout the Arab world. With a religious and emotional connection embedded in Islam, its radical wing leads the way, with terrorism as its needle. The religion of Islam relates directly to their national cause because when you fight against an Islamic nation, you fight against Allah.

In the midst of the cries for Bush's head, and the complaints from the liberal quarter that Bush had bungled everything, came the insurgency of democracy for the Middle East. I thought, democracy, how appropriate. The United States foreign policy of democracy and freedom is rational, decent, and humane for the world. Democracy is not the cure-all answer for long-term stability in the world but it is on the march, and America is leading the way. Waves of democracy are sweeping over Eastern Europe, the Middle East, and parts of Asia. Peace will seem to reign in the world. Democracy has become the dream of some Iraqi's, and now those in other countries such as Georgia, Belarus, Ukraine and the Baltic States believe that it's not such a bad idea. Those former republics of the Soviet Union that are embracing democracy are doing so, much to the chagrin of the current day President of Russia.

Iraq may stand or fall as a nation despite our involvement there and despite the apparent successful elections in 2005. Democracy is a two-edged sword that can bring both good and bad, and as it turns out, Iraq could implode or become a democracy unfavorable to the United States. It is possible that we will end up with an Iraq that is more counterproductive to the policy we wanted to establish there. Also, democracy may or may not work in Iraq and we may or may not win or complete our mission of war there, but it has opened the door for freedom and democracy for other Middle Eastern nations.

There is a wave of extraordinary optimism for democracy all over the Middle East. It will make changes to the face of the Middle East forever, as America does not have a monopoly on democracy. God is preparing that part of the world for His plans. Those plans will either help bring a weakened form of democracy to that region, or the Islamic nations will form a new solidarity in response to the aggressiveness of the United States and the Western World. Either way, it is to create a new resolve in those Middle East countries and pave the way for the Antichrist. With terrorism grating at the heart of the Arab world, it will bring horrible unrest and at best a unified divisiveness.

Not many want to admit that there is a connection between Islamic Jihad and the nation of Iraq. Politicians say the two are not connected but the fact that terrorists are pouring into Iraq to help fight against the United States is proof that Jihad and terrorism are connected to many of those Islamic nations in one way or another. No matter where President Bush would have involved us in war against terrorism, the terrorists would have gone there to help fight their Jihad. If Bush would not have gone into Iraq and centered the war only in Afghanistan, all of the insurgent terrorists would have flocked into Afghanistan where they are currently fighting anyway. Instead, they descended upon Iraq. Had Bush invaded Syria or Iran, the terrorist insurgency would have taken place there. If Bush had invaded Egypt or Saudi Arabia, the terrorist insurgents would have gone there. It wouldn't have made a difference. The focus will continue to be the Middle East. The whole region is volatile and even if the war in Afghanistan and Iraq goes away, we can be sure that trouble will arise in other Middle East countries such as Iran or Syria. The Western World will continue to be trapped in a Middle East quagmire with a questionable future for that part of the world until the Antichrist appears during the great Tribulation.

The politicians had to show disagreement and zero in on something that they had no foresight for so they politicized all other theaters of war. They have tried to make Afghanistan a more accepted war. In addition, they wanted to be sure not to criticize the military. Criticizing the military would be a politically disastrous mistake. That's quite a difference from the 60's and 70's when criticizing the military was more fashionable.

President Vladimir Putin of Russia called the war in Iraq "Bush's mistake." President George Bush and Prime Minister Tony Blair did admit to mistakes during the Iraqi War but stopped short of calling the entire war a mistake. God would rather use our obedience, but

He does use our sins, our mistakes, our failures, and turns them to triumph. He works with the mistakes of the world. It matters not if we consider President Bush to be right or wrong, the more important thing to consider is "what is God trying to do?" He is a sovereign God and just as He has used other wars in the past to deal with man's sin, He is using this one as well. God is using the Iraqi war to accomplish His purpose for Israel, the Church, the Middle East, and for the world, in bringing His plans to a climax. In the overall plan of God for the end time, it matters not if the United States is considered liberators or occupiers, God's will and what He is doing are the overriding principles.

When President Bush's term as President is over, future Presidents will continue to be involved with the Middle East. It may not be Iraq because another President may totally reverse the current policy, but be sure of the legitimate biblical idea that the Middle East will be strategic for the world until Jesus Christ returns. Other Presidents will have to make similar and critical decisions as the world races toward Armageddon. Once our involvement in the war in Iraq is over and our troops are home, terrorism won't be about Iraq, it will involve the world even as it is doing so now, as terrorism moves from local skirmishes and bombings and leads the world to all out global warfare.

The involvement of the United States in Iraq has made the Middle East take a critical turn so that the end-time events will unfold. The European Continent and the rest of the Asian Continent will become more involved in the Middle East as well as the influence and power of the United States lessens in that part of the world. To add to the grave situation, world leaders who side with Israel need to concern themselves with assassination attempts and kidnappings for ransom that would be made on their life.

With or without the war in Iraq, the war with terrorism is here to stay and the United States is a target. That's because the war with terrorism has been on the rise since the 1972 Olympic killings and will continue to be on the rise. Just as I know that those Olympic killings were terrifying because I was there, so the terrorism that is striking all over the world is equally terrifying. At first, the war on terror is centered in Iraq and Afghanistan. That is where America has engaged them and they have engaged us. We took the war to them after 9-11 and it doesn't matter where that is because their brand of terrorism can strike anywhere in the world. Whether or not we should have been in Iraq is a moot point now because other Middle East countries will eventually become involved as the war on terror fans out globally.

The war against terrorism is a war without a battlefront. No one knows where to always put the troops, or where to fight. The front line in fighting against terrorism is wherever they make it to be. Fighting the war against terrorism is like shooting at a target hundreds of yards away, with a shotgun full of buckshot. It's like engaging in a war where we don't know where the enemy is and we don't know where we will engage them next and we don't know how to get back at them. It is very difficult to win a war when many are willing to kill themselves as they kill others. It is different than during World War I and World War II when there was a battlefront and there was some idea where the soldiers were, and the battle was engaged between soldiers. Instead of flushing out the enemy in a Pacific Island somewhere, we have to deal with the terrorist enemy as they strike at the middle of civilian population, killing innocent people at will. The terrorists have engaged this war against civilians as well as soldiers. It will get a lot worse before it gets better.

The bottom line is, the war with Terrorism is not about Iraq or Afghanistan. The various Islamic factions, the struggle with terrorism, and the power of the Western World will come to a spiritual climax and explode into Armageddon. God used World War I and World War II to establish the nation of Israel in the Middle East again, and the Vietnam War to remove the USSR as a Super Power. Today, God is preparing the balances of power for the event of Armageddon. Armageddon looms larger than life in our future. What leads us to Armageddon in part is the defense of the world against the brand of terrorism that will begin to engulf the world in an all out war.

The nations of Euro/Asia will have a shaky alliance of peace with the hubs of terrorism nestled in the heart of some of their own nations. In the middle of those alliances will be the radicalism of Israeli/Palestinian injustice and the difficulty of keeping that peace.

The Israeli and Arab worlds will be in unrest as the nations of Europe, Asia and the Far Eastern lands will disagree with some of the western world's infatuation with the nation of Israel. Most of the western world will cave in to the demands of censure over the nation of Israel and the division of their land and authority.

There will be a tremendous power struggle at the center of conflict in the Middle East as members of the Arab nations even become divided against themselves. The war in Iraq and the unstable situation in Iran and other Middle East countries will perhaps make the Middle East more unsettled because of their differences with the policies of the Western world and with Christianity. The whole region will become a powder keg as the various nations take sides on both sides of the political spectrum. The Arab nations will struggle among themselves, with Israel at the heart of everyone's disagreements. There will be no easy panacea as the United States and all the nations of the world will be drawn into war to settle the score. Jesus Christ will then return to the earth and interrupt their plans.

Of course leading up to all of that is the fact that not all nations are rising to embrace democracy. Iran is one nation that may or may not do so. There are some Iranians who want regime change in order to rid that nation of the power of the Mullahs or Imams in politics, so another change for Iran may be coming. They also want nuclear weapons, as they become an even greater threat than Iraq. A nuclear Iran is not acceptable by most stable and democratic governments but it may be difficult to keep Iran as a nuclear free country. They will continue to be a nuclear threat in the future, adding fuel to the fire of that already tormented region of the Middle East.

Five countries have the legitimate right to own nuclear weapons according to the Nuclear Non-Proliferation Treaty and they are the United States, France, Russia, England, and China. It is believed that other countries have obtained nuclear weapons such as India and Pakistan and Israel is widely believed to have them. Still others such as North Korea and Iran either have them or are attempting to develop them. All of this weaponry will be part of the horror of Armageddon. A still further problem is that after the collapse of the Soviet Union some of its nuclear weapons may have fallen into the hands of rogue nations.

As mentioned in chapter two, democracy is one of the weakest forms of government in the world and could easily play into the hands of the Antichrist. The rise of the Antichrist would be a little more difficult if the powers of the Middle East were all dictatorships. As already stated, democracy is being formed in Iraq, and will perhaps be formed in other Middle East countries in preparation for the rise of the Antichrist. Iran and other countries may feel the pull toward democracy. India seems committed to it and other nations in various parts of the world may do the same. It seems necessary for them to be formed because the leaders of those countries will give their allegiance a lot easier to the Antichrist under a democracy rather than a dictatorship. They will do exactly that, as indicated in the book of Revelation. The struggle will then be between this sweeping new democracy and the past autocratic form of government.

Revelation 17:12-14 says, *"The ten horns which you saw are ten kings who have received no kingdom as yet, but they receive authority for one hour as kings with the beast. These are of one mind, and they will give their power and authority to the beast. These will make war with the Lamb, and the Lamb will overcome them, for He is Lord of lords and King of kings; and those who are with Him are called, chosen, and faithful."*

THE MAJORS

With the war on terrorism involving the three major religions of the Western world, it is important to discover one vast important difference. The Jews of course follow Judaism, the Arab culture follows Islam, and the Western culture follows Christianity. All three of those religions have had to encounter Jesus. The Jews rejected Jesus as the Messiah. Islam believes in Jesus and accepted Him as a prophet and in addition, they believe that He is returning to the earth. Christianity has promoted Jesus as deity, the Son of God, and the Savior of the world. Everyone has to answer which idealism is right. It is worthy to note that the God of Islam and the God of

Christianity are completely different in some terms of character and attributes.

There are those who call Islam a religion of peace. To the average Muslim they are a religion of peace, but according to the Koran and the radical Muslims, they are at war with all others who do not follow Allah and Mohammed's teachings. It is especially true if they feel they are defending themselves or their religious way of life. There are some isolated voices in the Muslim world that may be condemning terrorism, but as long as there are extremists in any religion in which there is no one to control their warlike nature, there will be terrorism.

Proof of that can be seen when much of the Islamic world was disturbed at a publishing of an unflattering cartoon of the Prophet Mohammed in a Danish newspaper in 2006, insinuating a connection of Islam to suicide bombings. Rather than express their displeasure calmly, some infuriated Muslims incited riots in numerous nations in the Western world inflicting damage to embassies and Christian sites. The somewhat fractured relationship of Islam always brings them forcefully together when something like this happens. It makes for an explosive powder keg and shows the sensitive balance that is increasingly hard to maintain in a worldwide situation that will continue to become a giant rift between East and West. In the United States, Islam will grow exponentially.

There is an erratic Islamic insurgence in our world. The double-edged sword of terrorism both feeds off the lack of freedom and democracy and strikes at the heart of freedom and democracy. The Islamic terrorists and other terrorists have used disillusioned and disenfranchised youth to strike out of their lack of freedom. They are compelled as freedom fighters but they don't want freedom of choice for the nations. It is an enigma.

Islam has a powerful grip on the world and it is in continual conflict with Israel and Christianity, but some of its teaching has an inherent flaw. As much as they say that they are a religion of peace and as much as we would like to believe they are, there are too many quotes in the Koran that indicate the opposite. Jihad seems to be a term that can be used to cover many other aspects of Muslim living. However, the bottom line answer to any discussion about war and peace always ends up for some Muslims with the word Jihad, meaning war. That's what makes it so powerful for the radical Islamic. Without the peaceful message and solution offered by Christ, the answer will always be Jihad! That's the inherent flaw.

That inherent flaw is found in the contradictory statements about both peace and Jihad in the basic principles of Islam and it's Koran. There are enough terrorists who are taking the message of Jihad literally, and without Christ, it makes Jihad a very easy thing for them to do. In the Koran we read such statements as found in Surah 2:190-193, *"Fight in the way of Allah against those who fight against you, but begin not hostilities. And slay them wherever you find them, and drive them out of the places whence they drove you out, for persecution is worse than slaughter…But if they desist, then lo! Allah is forgiving, merciful. And fight them until persecution is no more, and religion is for Allah…"*

In Surah 2:216 we read, *"Warfare is ordained for you."* In Surah 9:36 and 41 it says, *"Wage war on all the idolaters as they are waging war on all of you. Go forth, light-armed and heavy-armed, and strive with your wealth and your lives in the way of Allah!"* In Surah 9:73 it says, *"O Prophet! Strive against the unbelievers and the hypocrites! Be harsh with them."* In Surah 9:111 we read, *"They shall fight in the way of Allah and shall slay and be slain."*

As we read the Old Testament, the Jewish religion could have been a religion of war because of the many calls for war in it's past. One of the reasons they did not become a religion of war is because the Jews were decimated widely across the globe and they had no lasting global power as a nation. Christianity didn't become a religion of war either, because it brought a balance to the Old Testament with a new faith that was tempered by the peace concept introduced by Jesus Christ the Messiah. Islam as a powerful force in many nations of the world has been reduced to a religion that extremism and terrorism easily feeds on and survives in. The reason is that it has not accepted Christ's peaceful and redemptive role.

There has been a rise of Islamic and Arab power. That was because the Jews had become a people in the center of the rejection of Christ. It was also because the disunited world of Christianity had drifted from its strength of obedience to become spiritually divided.

With the Jews missing the Messiah and Christianity in a lukewarm state within the Old Western Roman Empire, it left the door wide open for Islam to come in the 7th Century. This was God's counter balance to prepare for the end of time as all of religion drifted away from its center of truth. If it wasn't for Charles Martel who stopped the Islamic march in Western Europe in 732 AD, the West could have come under the heavy influence of Islam. God had enough so He stopped the Islamic move westward. He will bring Islam, the western and eastern world, and the Jews into the picture in the end of time at the Battle of Armageddon.

The conflict over the continued existence of the world and its cultures will continue at a feverish pace. It is a clash of civilizations and extremism at its worst. Terrorism will come forth in the world as another form of war as the ten kingdom nations of Euro/Asia will seek to end it. They will war against other nations of the world who are not a part of their alliance. We find that both the Jew and the Arab are central to the war on terror, and the final war that brings all nations to the Battle of Armageddon. Who are the Jews and who are the Arabs and how does Christianity fit into the picture? Will God bring the Iraqi war, future wars, terrorism, and the divisions of Islam, Christianity, and other world religions to a head in a spiritual warfare to eventually end at Armageddon? How will God use their differences in the end of time and how does their view of Jesus Christ affect things?

WHO KILLED CHRIST?

What does the Crucifixion of Christ have to do with the war on terrorism and how it leads the world to Armageddon? That's just it, it seems as if that act had compounded the problem of the Jewish controversy that has been at the center of anti-Semitism for centuries. Judaism, Islam, and other religions differ over the impact and validity of the Crucifixion of Christ. That makes their worldview, particularly of Islam, far different than the view of Christianity. That puts the Crucifixion of Jesus at the center of an already difficult problem. Well, of course, there was a problem before Jesus concerning the land and who was going to be in control of that land.

Since then however, Jesus has been in the center of it for centuries and is still in the center of it now.

The Jews could have been the kingpins, the barons of the land but they rejected the Christ. They could have influenced the world and stayed in their land. There would have been no question as to the rightful owners of the land. The Arabs are actually in a "one-upmanship" position because they have accepted Jesus as one of their prophets. We might not be having this war on terrorism had the life and teachings of Jesus been accepted by the Jews and extended by the Arabs.

After all, John 1:11 says, *"He came unto His own, and His own received Him not."*

Some people ask the question "Are all Jews going to hell?" If we want to nationalize salvation by asking that question, why not ask if all Russians, Chinese, Italians, French, or Germans are going to hell? Aren't Russia and China anti-god nations? Therefore, the question should not be asked whether all Jews are going to hell. Entrance into heaven or hell is not based on a national heritage belief system, but on individual decisions. A number of Jews and Arabs believe, and have in the past believed in Jesus Christ as Savior. All individuals no matter their nationality must come to their own personal decision about Jesus, whose name means "Jehovah is salvation," an equivalent of the Jewish God "Jehovah."

Then there are those who claim that the Jews are to blame for the death of Jesus Christ. Actually, aren't we all to blame for the death of Christ? It was your sin and mine, and all the sin of the entire civilization since time began, that put Him on that cross. In the same chapter where Peter accuses Israel for the crucifixion of Christ, he says the Jews weren't the only ones involved. The leaders of that time, and we ourselves are all to blame; the entire world and the generations that followed. We can see by the following scripture that it wasn't only the Jews.

Acts 4:26-27 says, *"The kings of the earth stood up, and the rulers were gathered together against the Lord, and against*

His Christ. For of a truth against thy holy child Jesus, whom thou hast anointed, both Herod, and Pontius Pilate, with the Gentiles, and the people of Israel, were gathered together."

How is it possible that there are those to be blamed for the death of Christ who were not even born yet? How can you blame those who were born in the centuries after the death of Christ during the Christian Era and place the responsibility for Christ's death on their shoulders? It happens through a process that we don't believe in today which is "guilt by association." We are actually blamed through a type of ancestral association of the sinful nature that is birthed in us before we are born. We are guilty by the process of sin and the nature of its association with our conception and birth.

What I mean by that can be seen in the story found in Hebrews chapter seven. It talks about Abraham paying tithes to Melchizedek the Priest after meeting him. It was said of Levi, the great grandson of Abraham who wasn't even born yet, that he also paid tithes through Abraham his great grandfather, when Abraham and Melchizedek met. In other words, he symbolically paid tithes to Melchizedek before he was born because of his ancestral association with Abraham. That's a picture of how we can be associated with sin through birth and also associated with the Crucifixion of Christ.

Beside all the guilt and blame that was placed on the world for the death of Christ, one reads further in Acts chapter four, that God designed Christ's death. Other scriptures support that thought.

Acts 4:28 says that God's Sovereign plan was *"to do whatsoever thy hand and thy counsel determined before to be done."*

Revelation 13:8 speaks of Jesus as *"the Lamb slain from the foundation of the world"*.

I Corinthians 2:7 says that the wisdom of the preaching of Christ was *"ordained before the world unto our glory."*

The Crucifixion of Christ was the design of God, planned even before He formed the worlds. In other words, it was another one of God's mysteries that involved the evil of man to accomplish God's purpose that became our salvation. Can you imagine being on the wrong side of God's plan? Christ needed to be crucified, but would you want to be one of the ones that helped to do it?

The Jews have paid a price for their part in the murderous plan to do away with Christ; they lost their land for the next 1900 years. The nations of the world also paid a price for their part in the murderous plot to do away with Christ. They have been involved with multiplied centuries of war, confusion, hatred, heresy, and violence that were there before the death of Christ. All of that evil has continued to increase exponentially in the span of time since then.

Satan was behind this murderous plot to crucify Christ but little did he know what spiritual freedom it brought to the entire world. Poor Satan, he didn't understand. He was always saying and doing the wrong thing. One could say, "He was created with a cleft foot in his mouth." It was his prideful sin and dissent against God that got him in trouble. In the midst of all the confusion that he brought to the world by his involvement with the death of Christ, the Church was born. Hallelujah!

God had a pre-ordained plan for the wisdom of the mystery of His salvation. The plan was well hidden. Not even the evil spiritual powers of the world could understand God's masterful plan of redemption.

In I Corinthians 2:8 it says that *"none of the princes of this world knew: for had they known it, they would not have crucified the Lord of glory"*.

Satan just didn't get it. The "princes of this world" that were deluded, included Satan. What a glorious shame! Satan did not know God's plan. The murderous plot by Satan to have Jesus crucified was actually a blessing of salvation in disguise. God's Kingdom took on spiritual proportions instead of earthly territories. Jesus Christ declared that the real temples were within the heart of men and women. There would be no more physical battles, torture, and chaos in order to be a part of God's Kingdom. Martyrdom may not have been elusive for some but it certainly wasn't a prerequisite for everyone joining Christ's Kingdom.

That's the mystery of God, a hidden, secondary, secret, or associated meaning behind what can clearly be seen, a kingdom within the heart, within the kingdoms of this world. As we will discover in the last chapter, the mysteries of God can contain a dual meaning or an undisclosed truth to be known only when we see God. It is now up to us to try and understand what those mysteries are.

ARE THE JEWS, JEWS?

God has His sights set on the Middle East and He won't let anything happen that He isn't aware of. Just as God has used all nations of the world through the ages, including the Islamic Arab world, so God is now using the establishment of the nation of Israel for His end-time plan. At a Jewish Conference in Jerusalem in 1897, Theodor Herzl shared his passion with the gathered delegates of his desire for Israel to be a nation again. It was a strong Zionist thought at the time. He and others had worked feverishly for the Jews to be brought back to their land. Beginning with the 20th Century, God began to bring Theodor Herzl's prophetic ideas to fruition.

The Jews are back in their land because God said He would never forget Israel. I certainly do not believe in "Replacement Theology" where the Church now receives all the promises of Israel, and that Israel is now lost in the mind of God. No, God has them there in His plan too. He has not forgotten them. We are reminded of His unmistakable promises to the nation of Israel that He would restore them to their land.

Isaiah 41:8-9 says, *"But you, Israel, are my servant, Jacob whom I have chosen, The descendants of Abraham My friend. You whom I have taken from the ends of the earth, And called from its farthest regions, And said to you, ' You are My servant, I have chosen you and have not cast you away."*

Isaiah 49:22 says, *"Thus says the Lord GOD: " Behold, I will lift My hand in an oath to the nations, And set up My standard for the peoples; They shall bring your sons in their arms, And your daughters shall be carried on their shoulders."*

Jeremiah 30:10-11 says, *"Therefore do not fear, O My servant Jacob,' says the LORD, ' Nor be dismayed, O Israel; For behold, I will save you from afar, And your seed from the land of their captivity. Jacob shall return, have rest and be quiet, and no one shall make him afraid. For I am with you,' says the LORD, 'to save you; though I make a full end of all nations where I have scattered you, yet I will not make a complete end of you. But I will correct you in justice, and will not let you go altogether unpunished."*

Jeremiah 31:8-10 says, *"Behold, I will bring them from the north country, And gather them from the ends of the earth, Among them the blind and the lame, The woman with child And the one who labors with child, together; A great throng shall return there. They shall come with weeping, and with supplications I will lead them. I will cause them to walk by the rivers of waters, In a straight way in which they shall not stumble; for I am a Father to Israel, and Ephraim is My first-born. Hear the word of the LORD, O nations, And declare it in the isles afar off, and say, ' He who scattered Israel will gather him, And keep him as a shepherd does his flock."*

Jeremiah 31:35-37 says, *"Thus says the LORD, who gives the sun for a light by day, the ordinances of the moon and the stars for a light by night, who disturbs the sea, and its waves roar (The LORD of hosts is His name). "If those ordinances depart from before Me, says the LORD, then the seed of Israel shall also cease From being a nation before Me forever." Thus says the LORD: "If heaven above can be measured, and the foundations of the earth searched out beneath, I will also cast off all the seed of Israel for all that they have done, says the LORD."*

Ezekiel 39:25-27 says, *"Therefore thus says the Lord GOD: 'Now I will bring back the captives of Jacob, and have mercy on the whole house of Israel; and I will be jealous for My holy name. After they have borne their shame, and all their unfaithfulness in which they were unfaithful to me, when they dwelt safely in their own land and no one made them afraid. When I have brought them back from the peoples and gathered them out of their enemies' lands, and I am hallowed in them in the sight of many nations."*

Zephaniah 3:17, 20 says, *"The LORD your God in your midst, The Mighty One, will save; He will rejoice over you with gladness, He will quiet you with His love, He will rejoice over you with singing." At that time I will bring you back, Even at the time I gather you; For I will give you fame and praise Among all the peoples of the earth, When I return your captives before your eyes," Says the LORD."*

What do the Jews have to do with the war on terrorism that leads to the Battle of Armageddon? The Jews are and have always been a people that are in the center and forefront of terrorism. The antagonism toward them and their place in the center of controversial nations will lead the world to the brink of disaster before Jesus Christ returns.

Not only are they the targets of terrorism but they have been the targets of terrorism longer than any other nation in history. Terrorism has been brought on many nations and peoples for centuries of course, but nothing has been as long enduring and so consistent and blatant as what has plagued the Jews. Not only are they targeted but anyone who stands with them and for them are targeted as well. Standing with Israel and being a target hasn't always been the case but this new twist to the terrorism tale is the most recent rise in terrorism. All of these compounded reasons that has brought terrorism to the nations is what will bring the world to the end as designed by God.

The Jews were told of the persecution and terrorism against them numerous times. As long as 1500 years before the birth of Christ they were told of what the other nations would think of them. What is revealed about them and the evil that they must endure just doesn't quit and won't quit until Jesus Christ returns. Israel has been looked down upon and has drawn suspicions and jealousies for centuries. There past times of persecution is patently described for us in the following verses.

> Deuteronomy 28:37 says, *"And you shall become an astonishment, a proverb, and a byword, among all nations."*

> Jeremiah 29:18-19 says, *"And I will pursue them with the sword, with famine, and with pestilence; and I will deliver them to trouble among all the kingdoms of the earth—to be a curse, an astonishment, a hissing, and a reproach among all the nations where I have driven them. Because they have not heeded my words, says the LORD, which I sent to them by My servants the prophets."*

> Jeremiah 30:7 says, *"Alas! For that day is great, so that none is like it; and it is the time of Jacob's trouble, but he shall be saved out of it."*

Their night of terror turned into 70 years of being captive in a strange land about 600 years before the birth of Christ. Later, their terror continued for another 1900 years after Christ's death on the cross. They were ignored by the Church, picked for annihilation by Adolf Hitler, and hated by their half brothers, the Arabs.

There have been ethnic cleansings in the history of the world that's for sure, but never has there been a nation like Israel that has been targeted for annihilation. No one has known the slaughter of their own people like the Jews. No one has known it for such a sustained period of time, practically over the lifetime of their nation. Never has that happened. The history of that pattern of persecution and enslavement dates back to several hundreds of years before the time of Christ, to over three or four thousand years ago.

In America, the African/Americans had slavery and segregation but never were they targeted for elimination, as were the Jews. Their treatment was horrible and atrocious. The Dutch and the English brought them to America, as some of their African brothers sold them. They were tortured, brutalized, and murdered. Unfortunately, the southern whites of America treated them as a commodity, and wanted to keep them alive and working. The horrible thing was that in the process, many lost their lives. That happened either in transport to America, were killed when they were trying to escape, or, when whites thought they weren't useful anymore. How horrible!

If the Jews are in the center of the conflict of terrorism, what shall we do with them? As a matter of fact what shall we do with the Arabs? And how does the war on terrorism lead to Armageddon? Let's try and answer some of these questions!

God has plans as to what He is going to do with the nation of Israel and with the Arab states. God has given promises in Genesis 12 through 25 concerning land to the nation of Israel, and to the Arab world for their land. We can see that in Genesis, God gave a blessing to Abraham that would be passed on to all his children and that included both the Jews and the Arabs.

Genesis 12:1-3 says, *"Now the LORD had said to Abram: Get out of your country, from your family and from your father's house, to a land that I will show you. I will make you a great nation; I will bless you and make your name great; and you shall be a blessing. I will bless those who bless you, and I will curse him who curses you; and in you all the families of the earth shall be blessed."*

In Genesis 13:14-17 we read, *"And the LORD said to Abram, after Lot had separated from him: Lift your eyes now and look from the place where you are—northward, southward, eastward, and westward; for all the land which you see I give to you and your descendants forever. And I will make your descendants as the dust of the earth so that if a man could number the dust of the earth, then your descendants also could be numbered. Arise, walk in the land through its length and its width, for I give it to you."*

In Genesis 15:18-21, God specifically told Abraham the land area that his family would occupy. That blessing would be given to him and would cover the entire land area between the river in Egypt to the Euphrates River in Mesopotamia.

When God further stated His blessing to Abraham in Genesis 17:1-8, he was told that his wife Sarah was going to have a child named Isaac. All of that blessing would fall upon him, and not on his son Ishmael whom he had with Hagar. Abraham then inquired of God about an important burden that was on his heart. He wanted Ishmael to be blessed, but God's plan was different.

In Genesis 17:18 Abraham said, *"If only Ishmael might live under your blessing!"*

God's answer to him in verse 19 was, *"Yes, but your wife Sarah will bear you a son, and you will call him Isaac. I will establish my covenant with him as an everlasting covenant for his descendants after him".*

There are those who say that the present Jews who are occupying the land of Israel are not descendants of Abraham therefore they have no right to the land. In other words, they are not who they think they are. They are not real Jews. The claim is that throughout the centuries, conversion, proselytism, and with the introduction of mixed bloodlines, there's no way to prove or find the exact proper descendants of Abraham. However, over the centuries they have retained their nationality and their distinction that has identified them as a race of people. The fact remains, proper lineage or not, it wasn't always the bloodline that mattered to God. Weren't there people who became Jews not because of blood, but because they believed in Jehovah God? And isn't conversion an accepted spiritual behavior ideal in the eyes of God, as it was in the case of Rahab and Ruth in the Bible. They were not originally Jewish but became part of the proper Jewish lineage by inclusion. Today, the Jews are there for either secular or religious reasons. What shall we do, remove them from the land of Israel? No! They are planted there as the key that brings terrorism and war to its knees, until it surrenders to the authority of Jesus Christ. He will return to the earth, and engage the world's armies at the Battle of Armageddon!

ARE ARABS WHO THEY SAY THEY ARE?

In regard to the Arabs, there are those who say that not all present day Arabs are descendants of Abraham either, so their rights are lost also. With so many Arab/Islamic nations that have changed or have been occupied over the years, it is difficult to prove their heritage. Shall we then make an attempt to displace all the Arabs in the world? Is all of that an excuse and does that make Bible prophecy irrelevant?

Does that mean that Ishmael and his descendants, the Arabs, were left out in the cold with no land and no blessing? Absolutely not! The biggest unfortunate thing is that they got involved in the Islamic religion that accepts only half the truth about Jesus Christ. Many have now accepted Christ, but for the most part they have been kept from the great freedoms and blessings of the western world. It is the freedom of Christianity that provides such great spiritual and physical blessings. Islam does believe in Jesus as a prophet but not as God.

Two brothers who converted from Islam to Christianity said, "The generally accepted Muslim view affirms that Jesus did not die, but that Allah raised him to himself (Surah 4:148-149). According to Islam, since Jesus, a human as was Adam, has not died, his ministry cannot be complete. Tradition explains that he will appear to all just before the final judgment. He then will battle the Antichrist, defeat him, confess Islam, kill all pigs, break all crosses, and establish a thousand years of righteousness." (**3**).

In the mean time, the Arabs wealth in the world of oil is what gives them their financial base that will financially support their part of the world's war at Armageddon. It was God's design for the Arabs to be in their land. God has allowed them to be blessed in the land that He originally gave them through Ishmael.

God told Ishmael's mother Hagar in Genesis 16:10-12, *"And the angel of the LORD said unto her, I will multiply thy seed exceedingly, that it shall not be numbered for multitude. And the angel of the LORD said unto her, Behold, thou [art] with child, and shalt bear a son, and shalt call his name Ishmael; because the LORD hath heard thy affliction".*

Also in Genesis 17:20 it says, *"And as for Ishmael, I have heard thee: Behold, I have blessed him, and will make him fruitful, and will multiply him exceedingly; twelve princes shall he beget, and I will make him a great nation".*

And finally in Genesis 25:16, 18 we read, *"These are the sons of Ishmael, and these are their names, by their towns, and by their castles; twelve princes according to their nations. And they dwelt from Havilah unto Shur, that is before Egypt, as thou goest toward Assyria."*

JEW AND ARAB OCCUPANCY

All of the questions of opposition with regard to the Jews and Arabs occupying their land because of their lack of proper lineal descent, are too complex to prove one way or the other. While so many may question the legitimacy of their being in their respective lands, they are in the mean time dealing with animosity, jealousy, and bitter hatred toward each other. For centuries this has divided them over their land, and their religion. Terrorism will continue to be at the heart and soul of the struggle of these two great Semitic peoples.

Therefore, shall we call Israel and the Arabs illegitimate pretenders of the occupancy of the Middle East? I do know that the whole situation is a timepiece in the plan of God, legitimate ancestral lines or not. In the book of Genesis, there were promises made to both these vast peoples of the Middle East. There has to be something to that.

Islam believes who Abraham was and they make their lineal connection with him and his promises. If they truly implored the God of Abraham, Isaac, and Jacob as Israel does, then they need to go back in time and investigate the stories of Abraham, Isaac, and Jacob in the Old Testament – not just the Koran. The Old Testament is a vastly older historical book than the Koran and a bridge could be built to the Old Testament that could make a difference for both these peoples. The Jews also need to look backward in time and understand where they have been disobedient. They need to look at the character of their faith to find out what they as a religious people have missed and how they can get along with their Arab neighbors.

Regarding the Bible, "If the Islamic peoples of the world, especially the Arabs, were to carefully read these passages, it might allow them to sit down and negotiate peace in the Middle East with the Jewish people. However, the Word of God reveals that the Middle East will not find true peace until the Prince of Peace returns to set up His kingdom on earth."(4). Of course, the Prince of Peace is Jesus Christ!

As far as ancestral lines are concerned, I do know that the northern tribes of Israel were mixed with other nations during their dispersion some 600 years before the time of Christ. Then they returned to Israel and were called the Samaritans during the days of Jesus. God was displeased with them because of their idolatry, but nevertheless, they were back in their land as a race that was mixed with the Assyrians and other peoples.

It was a mixed race Samaritan woman that Jesus met in the Gospel of John chapter four near Shiloh the place of God's "departed glory". Jesus told her that neither there, nor in Jerusalem, would they worship the Father. He was looking to a future time when there would be those who would worship God "in spirit and in truth." Jesus didn't bother to decipher anyone's lineage when he made that statement. He didn't split hairs over proper background checks, because He knew the Samaritan woman's background and it wasn't pretty. Neither did He say that the Samaritans shouldn't be occupying their land. In fact, He was always perturbed at the exactness of the religious rulers of His day who were precise keepers of the law, but showed no mercy and faith. He was looking beyond, to something more profoundly prophetic. He had his eyes on what His heavenly Father's will was. His emphasis was on worship. What a God!

Romans chapter eleven talks about the Gentiles being grafted in as branches into the tree of God's goodness and severity. Also, it says something very important about the Jews.

> Romans 11:17-23 says, *"But some of these branches from Abraham's tree, some of the Jews, have been broken off. And you Gentiles, who were branches from a wild olive tree, were grafted in. So now you also receive the blessing God has promised Abraham and his children, sharing in God's rich nourishment of his special olive tree. But you must be careful not to brag about being grafted in to replace the branches that were broken off. Remember, you are just a branch, not the root. "Well," you may say, "those branches were broken off to make room for me." Yes, but remember—those branches, the Jews, were broken off because they didn't believe God, and you are there because you do believe. Don't think highly of yourself, but fear what could happen. For if God did not spare the branches he put there in the first place, he won't spare you either. Notice how God is both kind and severe. He is severe to those who disobeyed, but kind to you as you continue to trust in his kindness. But if you stop trusting, you also will be cut off. And if the Jews turn from their unbelief, God will graft them back into the tree again. He has the power to do it."*

That means that even while God is blessing the Gentiles, He will remember the Jews, bring them back in and use them as part of His plan too. God has brought the Jews back to Israel despite some of their unproved lineage. He has a plan and it's above the exactness of the law. Their ancestral line may or may not be all confused but I believe that it's the prophetic conclusion that God is interested in reaching and not the proof of lineage. God has brought the multiplicity of Gentile lineage into salvation by ignoring their bloodlines and grafting them in. God will do the same with the Jews as He brings them back into belief. We will discover in the last chapter of this book that "all Israel shall be saved." The important fact is that God will wrap up the end-time events according to His timetable using both Jew and Gentile in His plan.

There is a lot of controversy about the land of Palestine and who the earliest occupants were. That is about the biggest part of the debate in the Arab/Israeli conflict and a part of the great scourge of terrorism they are involved in. The Jews believe that land was given to them and that they are the legitimate descendents of Abraham through Isaac. The Arabs of today lay claim to Palestine because they say that they are descendents of Ishmael, who was the son of Abraham.

In the first place, the statement that the Palestinians are descendents of Abraham cannot be conclusively proved in terms of exact lineage because of its historical complexity. Are the Palestinians actual descendents of Abraham and is their bloodline pure? Are all the Islamic Arabs of today descendents of Abraham? Who knows? Can we conclude conclusively that the Jews of today who are occupying Palestine, are the legitimate descendents of Abraham in terms of lineage? They as a people have been so badly decimated over the centuries with perhaps no exact lineage able to be proved. Are the Jews who are in Israel today pure bloodline descendents of Abraham? Who can tell? There are Jews who can probably say that they can prove their nationality. The bottom line is, both the Jews and the Arabs are lined up in their lands and God will use them in the last days.

In the second place God never went on record in the Bible, indicating He gave the land of Palestine to the Arabs. Nevertheless, ancestral proof or not, both the Jews and the Arabs are there. The complication in the matter is that the Arabs did become occupants of Palestine after God uprooted Israel from their land because of Israel's disobedience. God will have to eventually sort all that out, and He will.

There are some that would say that the Bible does not give the complete picture as far as who the first occupants of the Middle East and particularly, Palestine were. Early settlers of Palestine, not the Palestinians of today, go back long before even Israel got there and these are the people who some consider the true Arabians. Despite the criticism, Genesis does a good job of describing the various peoples and cultures that settled there after the flood. As explained in chapter one, the Bible is one of the best and most trusted historical book we have. Many other writings try but misapply the dates as to when these historical people existed. You can check the Encyclopedia Britannica and other articles that take a "best guess" when it comes to placing many of these ancient peoples in their land.

There is no doubt about it, other people occupied Palestine before the Israelite's came knocking! The Amorites, Assyrians, Babylonians, Canaanites, Egyptians, Hittites, Jebusites, Philistines, Sumerians, and many others either forcibly occupied that land at one time or another, or they were just simply there first! Many of these people who are now Arabs of Egypt, Iraq, Libya, Morocco, Jordan, Lebanon, and Syria today, will along with the people of the former Soviet Republics be a mighty but shaky alliance in that part of the world in the last days.

WHAT THE BIBLE SAYS

According to the Bible, Palestine was first occupied by the descendents of Canaan who was the progenitor of many of the people just mentioned. Canaan was a son of Ham, who was a son of Noah, the first family living there after the flood. You can read about the territory that Canaan occupied in Genesis 10:15-20. The nation of Israel was not the first inhabitants of Palestine, but of course neither were the current day Palestinians who adhere to Islam.

In Genesis 15:18-21 we can read where God then gave the land of Canaan to Abraham once He began to establish a nation through that chosen family. That land was passed on through the line of Isaac and not the line of Ishmael. In short, Isaac was to receive the land of Palestine and Ishmael was to be given other lands and territory that were greater in land area. There was a distinction made between these two half brothers. You can read about Ishmael's blessing in chapter 17, verses 20-22.

Later, when God led the children of Israel out of Egypt, he then told them that He was going to give them the land of Canaan as their heritage. You can read about it in Exodus.

Exodus 3:7-8. It says, *"And the LORD said: I have surely seen the oppression of my people who are in Egypt, and have heard their cry because of their taskmasters, for I know their sorrows. So I have come down to deliver them out of the hand of the Egyptians. And to bring them up from that land to a good and large land, to a land flowing with milk and honey, to the place of the Canaanites and the Hittites and the Amorites and the Perizzites and the Hivites and the Jebusites."*

WHY THE JEWS ARE BACK

There are many promises found in the Bible concerning the Jews and one is that God said they were going to be back in their land. Someone may say they don't believe it, or may say it was because of aggressive individuals or trickery that they are back there today. They may also say that the Jews are the Christian's "Sacred Cow" and that they are the sacrifice on the altar of Christian understanding. The Jews are more than a sacred cow they are a historic fact. The Jews have always been associated with what we now call the land of Palestine, even before they were called Jews. In the book of Genesis, God gave Palestine to Abraham, who gave it to his son Isaac. The land was later resettled under Moses and the Israelites. Before the birth of Christ, they were taken from their land and were brought back after a 70-year Diaspora. After being torn from their land after the Crucifixion of Christ, they then established statehood in 1948 after 1900 years of absenteeism. God gave the Arabs much of the Middle East, but the Jews were given the land of Canaan, or Palestine.

Man couldn't get the Jews there through the crusades, and neither did the hopes and wishes of Christians get them there. The point is they are there and it took two major wars of the 20th Century to do it. It was God who did it, and in His mysterious plan, the Arab world was meant to be there to confront them before the great and terrible battle of Armageddon. One of the scriptures that mention the return of the Jews is Jeremiah 30. This scripture is a direct reference to their first captivity before the time of Christ but the prophetic promises of God are applicable in more than one time period and usually have a dual purpose in mind.

Jeremiah 30:3 says, *"I will bring again the captivity of my people Israel and Judah, says the Lord; and I will cause them to return to the land that I gave to their fathers, and they shall possess it."*

Jeremiah 30:10-11 says, *"I will save thee from afar, and thy seed from the land of their captivity; and Jacob shall return, and shall be in rest, and be quiet, and none shall make him afraid. For I am with thee, to save thee; though I make a full end of all nations yet will I not make a full end of thee: but I will correct thee in measure, and will not leave thee altogether unpunished."*

Then there are the great prophetic chapters that clearly speak of a time that is far different than any other time for the nation of Israel. The events of Isaiah chapter eleven talk about the future Messiah and the future Millennium, and then mention the return of the Jews. Ezekiel chapter thirty-seven talks about the dried bones of Israel that shall one day live and all of Israel will become unified. These prophecies have never been fulfilled in the past history of Israel but give great prophetic insight into their future.

Isaiah 11:10-11 says, *"And in that day there shall be a Root of Jesse, Who shall stand as a banner to the people. For the Gentiles shall seek Him, and His resting-place shall be glorious. It shall come to pass in that day that the Lord shall set His hand again the second time to recover the remnant of His people who are left, from Assyria and Egypt, from Pathros and Cush, from Elam and Shinar, from Hamath and the islands of the sea."*

Ezekiel 37:10-12, 19 says, *"So I prophesied as He commanded me, and breath came into them, and they lived, and stood upon their feet, an exceedingly great army. Then He said to me, Son of man, these bones are the whole house of Israel. They indeed say, Our bones are dry, our hope is lost, and we ourselves are cut off! Therefore prophesy and say to them, Thus says the Lord GOD: Behold O My people, I will open your graves and cause you to come up from your graves, and bring you into the land of Israel. Say to them, Thus says the Lord GOD: Surely I will take the stick of Joseph, which is in the hand of Ephraim, and the tribes of Israel, his companions; and I will join them with it, with the stick of Judah, and make them one stick, and they will be one in My hand."*

Now, anyone can argue all they want as to whose land it really is and who was there first. It doesn't matter now because the Jews are there. God told Israel to occupy that land when they left Egypt, probably 1500 years before the time of Christ. Their fight and disagreement with the Palestinians will play center stage in the end of time. If one feels any different, they would have to take up their argument with God. They need to ask Him why he ripped that land away from all those other peoples and nations, and gave it to a bunch of squatters, namely Israel! That has become the center of the problem, both the Jew and the Arab try to lay legitimate claims in their own right as to who should be in Palestine.

"The Old Testament is not the only document to declare that the Jews are entitled to their Promised Land. It is fascinating to note that there are a number of passages (known as Surahs) in the Koran, as written by Mohammed that relate to the Children of Israel and her possession of the Holy Land. These passages in the Koran, though ignored by the Arabs, are intriguing in that they clearly acknowledge and affirm the right of the Jews to possess the land of Israel."(**5**)

Surah 5:20-21 of the Koran says, *"And (remember) when Moses said unto his people: O my people! Remember Allah's favor unto you, how He placed among you Prophets, and He made you kings, and gave you that (which) He gave not to any (other) of (His) creatures. O my people! Go into the Holy Land which Allah hath ordained for you. Turn not in flight, for surely ye turn back as losers."* That is a clear indication that even the Koran recognized Israel and her right to be in the land of Palestine. Another passage written in Surah

17:104 of the Koran says, *"And we said unto the Children of Israel after him: Dwell in the land; but when the promise of the Hereafter cometh to pass we shall bring you as a crowd gathered out of various nations."*

Getting back to many years ago when Israel was in their land, many nations ran roughshod over them as discussed in chapter two, including Babylon, Assyria, Persia, Greece, and Rome. When the rise of Rome came over the Middle East, that pretty much ended it for Israel for over 1900 years. I relate the loss of their land directly with their refusal to believe in Jesus as the Son of God. The Jewish people suffered for hundreds of years after their encounter with Jesus Christ and the cross.

After their refusal of Jesus Christ, there came the rise of the Empire of Islam. The civilization of the Islamic Arabs took root and their armies took over the Middle Eastern Countries of Egypt, Syria, and Palestine. They used the ideas of the great civilizations of the Greeks and Romans that they took over and sent the western world into the Dark Ages. That was a time of enlightenment for the Arab world but it didn't last long. It did last long enough to preserve it until the Western World went through their Renaissance. The Arab world didn't have enough depth of ingenuity and education to continue the upward spiral they found themselves on and they plunged into a time of Darkness themselves.

Then came the Crusades when Europe tried to win Palestine back from the Arabs. There were about eight Crusades that covered a period of approximately 175 years. Those Crusades were man's answer to the 200 plus years of crusading done by Islam but it wasn't God's timing to establish the nation of Israel yet. After that the Mongols from Mongolia came and then finally the Ottoman Empire that ruled over Palestine until World War One.

The Jews and the Islamic Arabs then seemed to somewhat get along until the 20th Century when the Jews started to come back to Palestine. The important thing now would be for them to respect each other. Then perhaps, they could occupy the land God has given each of them in peace. We cannot go back in history and unscramble the politics of countless numbers of generations. As far as Israel and the Palestinians are concerned, the bottom line is that they will have to share that land as they have done recently with the Gaza Strip and parts of the West Bank. Israel began a disengagement from those areas as part of a good will gesture after occupying them for 38 years but they are still having difficulty getting along with each other.

Trouble also started in Lebanon in 2006 with the terrorist group Hezbollah as the entire area of the Middle East seems to be an area waiting to explode, drawing neighboring nations into a regional conflict. Israel's war with Hezbollah developed fast and furious, involving captured soldiers, warplanes, and random-less rockets. It is a very troubling, escalating, and precarious situation that could eventually involve the nations who support each side of the broader Jewish/Christian/Muslim conflict. That strife dates back to the days of the Bible when even then, the Jews and Arabs were the fiercest of enemies. That conflict may not be the one that draws the world to Armageddon but one similar to it will. Jesus called conflict like that, "the beginning of sorrows."

Peace may be established temporarily between Israel and the people of Lebanon, but truly we can see that what is happening in the Middle East is only the beginning of a much wider war some day. Hezbollah is but one of the many factions that wish to continue fighting the Jewish people. God's original plan for the Jews was to occupy the land of Israel. Today, He plans to use the deep waters of strife and terrorism in Palestine of separate peoples and religions to bring about His will for the end of time.

Much has been said about Israel's disproportionate response in this situation. Any country when they feel threatened will use as much firepower as possible against their enemies. The advice I give then will only be to those who oppose someone with greater weapons than what they have. They are the words of Jesus.

Luke 14:31-32 says, "What king, going to make war against another king, does not sit down first and consider whether he is able with ten thousand to meet him who comes against him with twenty thousand? Or else, while the other is still a great way off, he sends a delegation and asks conditions of peace."

I predict that an unsettled cooperation in the area will continue to happen although I'm sure with great difficulty. The superpower nations will attempt to ensure a conclusion of safety and peace no matter who is in political power among the Jewish, Palestinian, or other peoples of the region. Compromises will continue to be made by the United States and other nations in the form of "rights" and land deals for Israel and the Palestinians. God is preparing that part of the world for many of the events that are mentioned in the book of Revelation. This will include whatever compromises to be made in order for the Jews to build a new Temple in Jerusalem, so that they may restart their centralized worship.

According to Daniel 9:27, a 7-year diplomatic agreement will be guaranteed by the Antichrist. He will allow religious and political safety for everyone in Palestine. We call that period of time, the Great Tribulation. The Antichrist then breaks that covenant half way through that agreement and begins an awful persecution of God's people. Then, mayhem and destruction ensue during the bleakest of times for the world.

All of these historical times and events were God's way of preparing His people for His plans. The end of strife, occupation and the peace among the Semitic peoples of the world will come in God's time! God's plan for the Second Coming of Christ and the long awaited millennial peace will come! The terrorism that breaks out into war among the Jews and Arabs and against the rest of the world will end with the return of Jesus Christ! The Battle of Armageddon looms in the foreground as terrorism and war become the hallmark of civilized and uncivilized humanity. We are not sure how soon Armageddon will take place as many other nations and territories will have to be politically reconfigured and put in place before that time. Much sorrow, warfare, and bloodshed will be a part of that time as Great Tribulation engulfs the world.

CHAPTER FIVE:

When Catastrophe Strikes

—⟋⟍—

A national disaster or catastrophe is not something that the average person would normally think about, but when we look back over the history of the world it is something that has happened repeatedly. With the exception of Noah's flood, the catastrophes in the past were not worldwide. They may have only been nationwide or they may have affected a small group of nations, but nevertheless, they were catastrophes.

There seems to be a connection between the downward slide of excellent moral living and the upheavals of social ills, geological tremors and other catastrophes felt around the world. God grieves because of our sin and He is willing to allow destruction to afflict us for the purpose of correction. To some, the thought of a world-wide catastrophe ending the world is out of the question. Many of us cannot collate the connection of our unacceptable moral behavior in the eyes of God and the catastrophes that come as a result of a society, that is unhealthy and reeling with incurable symptoms. Cultures seem to implode with each major catastrophe.

The Bible makes it clear that God is in control of weather patterns around the world. He has His way of stopping the works of man through nature. God is trying to get our attention through His love, but also during times of great catastrophe.

Job 37:6-7, 12-13 says, *"He says to the snow, 'fall on the earth,' and to the rain shower, 'Be a mighty downpour.' So that all men he has made may know his work, he stops every man from his labor. At his direction they swirl around over the face of the whole earth to do whatever he commands them. He brings the clouds to punish men, or to water his earth and show his love."*

POTENTIAL CATASTROPHES

We always have to be on the alert for numerous catastrophes, mishaps, and accidents caused by nuclear power plant failures, fires, explosions, shipwrecks, aircraft disasters, railroad accidents, and space accidents. Each year we are concerned with the wild fires that destroy thousands and thousands of acres and homes in the western part of the United States, and also concerned with the tornadoes of the Midwest.

Famine, war, and Aids crises of the African nations are not just a potential problem but a reality as they are facing these crises there now. Massive amounts of people are dying and it seems to only get worse. Also, the threat in 2005 and 2006 of a major flu called the "bird flu" or "Avian Flu" still has some health authorities very concerned that as an imminent danger, it would mutate into various forms and spread to humans. This could cause a major flu pandemic and would break out all around the world, including the United States.

To further add to what amounted to a scare as far as catastrophes are concerned, it has been predicted that for years to come there would be a frequency of hurricanes that would hit along the East Coast of the United States. That prediction was eerily forecast and became an omen for trouble ahead. Florida was particularly concerned because of the "four big hurricanes" that caused such devastation in 2004. These hurricanes rattled everyone's nerves and brought a disturbance to thousands of people. It was very difficult to predict the path of these hurricanes because they didn't always exactly follow the tracking lines that were projected by the computers of the meteorologists. The predictions for the next few decades is perhaps many hurricanes coming out of the Caribbean to roar toward Florida, the Gulf States or the entire Southeast, as Katrina, Rita, and Wilma tore through the Gulf in 2005. What does the future hold with hurricanes and disasters that are sure to hit the United States for decades to come?

The Caribbean is in a weather cycle pattern for perhaps the next 10-20 years because the water is warmer, causing an increase of turbulent weather for the Atlantic coast. Is this just another one of the difficulties that we have to deal with as we are preparing for the time of the end? Will conveyor belts of bad weather continue to cause the nation to be pummeled? If the threatened global warming is a reality, it will play into the hands of an end time scenario of climate changes, crop failures, drought, destructive weather patterns, flooding, and melting ice caps of biblical proportions. The warming of our world could be a warning from God as each warmer degree brings the world closer to its fiery end as predicted in the Bible. Will we see an increase of catastrophes such as earthquakes, hurricanes, tidal waves, and volcanic activity around the world as we pull further away from God? How catastrophic will many of these events be?

CATASTROPHE IN HISTORY

There have been many catastrophes in the world throughout the centuries. In ancient history, the city of Pompeii in Italy was destroyed on August 26th, 79 AD when Mount Vesuvius erupted. This happened no doubt because of their paganism, sin, and also I believe for the Roman Empire's part in the destruction of Jerusalem in 70 AD. Pompeii was 150 miles southeast of Rome, and Titus, allowed by his father the Emperor Vespasian to invade Jerusalem, had to deal with this catastrophe just two months after he became Emperor in June of 79 AD. Also, he had to deal with a fire that destroyed large sections of the city of Rome in 80 AD.

Just about the greatest catastrophe in human history was the Black plague of the 14th Century that lasted about four years. Over 23 million people died in Europe, which was about 30 percent of their population. It is believed the Black plague was devastating in Asia as well. Although reports were sketchy, it is estimated that about 35 million died in China.

In the years 1918-1920 a major flu epidemic caused nearly 20 million deaths worldwide with over 500,000 deaths in the United States alone. In major epidemics of the 20th Century in the United States, over one million have died because of polio, influenza, and Aids.

Just in the 20th Century alone there have been many great earthquakes and volcanoes of dramatic proportions. The most famous earthquake here in the United States occurred in 1906 in San Francisco when conservatively speaking, 500-700 people were killed or lost. Since that time from 1906 until the present between one and one half to two million people have died in earthquake activity around the world.

In 1964 the earthquake and tsunami in Alaska was the strongest to ever hit North America. There was a 50-foot high tidal wave that came ashore at over 400 miles per hour and killed over 100 people. In 1989 there was the earthquake that hit San Francisco during the World Series. Many were killed and injured and thousands of buildings were destroyed. Along that same area of the North American western seashore was the volcanic eruption of 1998 at Mount St Helens in the State of Washington that totally transformed the terrain in the Northwest part of the United States. In 2005 over 79,000 people died in a massive earthquake that hit the region of Pakistan.

In 1900 the deadliest hurricane and tidal wave on record in the United States hit Galveston, Texas as an estimated 6,000 to 8,000 people died. In 1928, the second deadliest hurricane ripped through southeast Florida and killed over 1800 people.

Floods, avalanches, tidal waves, drought and heat waves inducing climatic changes have claimed the lives of over four million people in the 20th Century all around the world. The worst of all 20th Century catastrophes was in China in 1931. Three million seven hundred thousand people lost their lives by disease, starvation, or drowning when the Yangtze River flooded. Major storms such as cyclones, hurricanes, typhoons, blizzards, tornadoes, drought and heat waves claimed the lives of millions more all across the globe.

The catastrophe the day after Christmas in December of 2004, occurred when an earthquake and tsunami brought devastation to a score of Southeast Asian nations with approximately 225,000 people killed and missing. With many still missing who may never be found, it proved to us that a mini-global catastrophe could happen. The 9.3 earthquake happened deep within the ocean when one of the tectonic plates beneath the surface of the earth shifted 60 feet. The earthquake would have been bad enough, but the waves of the tsunami that followed traveled anywhere from 200 miles per hour to 600 miles per hour. The quake had caused a massive displacement of water on top of the surface and beneath the surface to form the massive tsunami or tidal wave.

It came to the shoreline that is naturally up-sloped and with terrific force it hit land. Waves were estimated at anywhere from 10 feet to 90 feet high, depending on which shore and which country. The water came inland anywhere from a quarter mile to two and a half miles. Never before in modern times had a natural disaster impacted such a large area. There were three or four wave surges that came higher and higher each time. The devastation was unimaginable.

Its impact was felt around the globe. In satellite photographs the ripple effect of that tsunami was seen throughout the oceans of the world as the waters of those oceans were movably impacted by the tsunami's power. Since that December, more after shocks have hit that Southeast Asia area as a reminder of God's mighty power that controls the land and the seas.

With modern day instruments, it was recorded that the earthquake was so powerful that it affected the earth's rotation and caused it to wobble in its orbit. The massive movement of the plates in the Indonesia/Australian Fault Line caused the earthquake and then the tsunami that followed throughout Southeast Asia. And if that wasn't enough, volcanic activity since then has hit Indonesia and a 6.3 earthquake struck there in May of 2006. It is estimated that over 6,200 died in that earthquake. Then in July of 2006 a tsunami tore through Indonesia again with 6-foot high waves and claimed the lives of hundreds more. Future volcanic and earthquake activity are sure to follow.

As already mentioned, the massive hurricane Katrina hit the Gulf States in August 2005 in a disaster of biblical proportions, plowing through the states of Louisiana, Mississippi, Alabama, and Florida. The city of New Orleans became a "city of death" as its levees failed making it a logistical nightmare, as 80 percent of the city was flooded with water, turning it into a "giant bath tub." Its infrastructure collapsed in just a few short hours as it went from a popular, inhabited city into an unlivable flood washed city in crisis, filled with looters. The entire city was devastated and vacated, as the "The Big Easy" became part of the night that loomed with an eerie silence. Thousands were presumed dead as the stench of bodies was unbearable, and the entire area resembled a disaster movie with a war-torn landscape. Families, workers, and students were displaced. People lived in cars, huddled under tarps, in apartments surrounded by water and in a sports area shelter as initially, Christian and private organizations were in the best position to help. As a major United States port, commodities had to be diverted to trains and trucking, driving prices sky high and contributing further to the shaky economy of the United States. The response to disaster put in place after 9-11 initially failed. The city is still a colossal mess. It too was one of the worst natural disasters in America's history. The local, state, and federal governments were ill prepared and slow to respond. The follow-up hurricanes Rita and Wilma were of no help to New Orleans and the Texas and Florida coasts.

The earthquake in India and Pakistan in October 2005 measured 7.6 on the Richter scale. It tore through those countries and killed between 80,000 to 100,000 people and left millions homeless and living in tents and makeshift structures. Billions of dollars are needed for infrastructure reconstruction.

Other types of catastrophes have been ones that were financial in nature, similar to the stock market crash of 1929. Before the "crash," Wall Street was booming. Thousands of people had their hopes pinned on getting rich quick as an alternative to saving over their lifetime and working their 9-5 job. Money was easy and brokers in the stock market were always ready to loan money to people who wanted in. The "Roaring Twenties" was the "wave" of the day and stocks were climbing in value. Much hope was placed in scraps of paper and on a financial empire built like a house of cards. Sellers outnumbered the buyers, but by October of that year, prices fell dramatically. Everyone wanted out except for the rich investors who were buying. The economy took a tailspin into the Great Depression.

That financial boom is similar to today as thousands have their investments in stocks, bonds, portfolios, and investments of all kinds. People all across the country are deeply in debt with mortgages, but yet they trust in their retirement portfolios and pension plans. I know that our financial geniuses and men of business say that a "crash" like that could never happen again. However, we have had serious financial downturns since then and the world's economy is still tenuous at best. To complicate matters, the debt load of the United States is enormous.

The economy of the United States is intertwined with the economies and stock markets of the world. When financial failures occur all over the world, the economies of the nations will fall like dominos. The United States is trillions of dollars in debt and I predict that the creditors will some day call, impacting the lives of every average American. If a worldwide "crash" takes place today, not only will Americans be affected but also the cultures of the entire world will lay financially dormant, while someone comes up with a solution that will work for everyone. Will that someone be the Antichrist?

EARTHQUAKE INEVITABILITY

"While California has been the state most prone to serious earthquakes in recent years, there are many other fault zones in other areas of the United States. For example, geologists and seismologists have predicted a 97 percent chance of a major earthquake in the New Madrid seismic zone of the central United States (including Arkansas, Missouri, Tennessee, and Kentucky) between now and the year 2035. While earthquakes with the power of the one that hit the greater Los Angeles area in January 1994 are fairly rare, less severe earthquakes can interrupt your normal living patterns and cause substantial injury."(1). The risks for earthquakes interrupting our lives are becoming increasingly greater.

As to why the earth is subject to earthquakes, it is thought that "the world was made up of a single continent through most of geologic time" called pangaea, but broke up and floated free of each other. "According to the generally accepted plate-tectonics theory, scientists believe that the Earth's surface is broken into a number of shifting slabs or plates, which average about 50 miles in thickness. These plates move relative to one another above a hotter, deeper, more mobile zone at average rates as great as a few inches per year. Most of the world's active volcanoes are located along or near the boundaries between shifting plates and are called plate-boundary volcanoes."(**2**)

Some other estimates of these huge masses of land or chunks of gigantic slabs of rock can be as thin as only 10 miles in thickness. They cover thousands of miles of the earth's surface on both land areas and the ocean floors, and are shaped in all sorts of irregular patterns. They extend in jagged patterns around the various continents such as Eurasia, Indonesia/Australia, North and South America, Africa, and Arabia.

These plates are in a constant state of flux and it is when these plates move that we have earthquakes. Tremendous forces of energy are released from deep within the earth's core that causes a powerful movement along the fault-lines and the earth to move in the form of an earthquake. There are essentially three types of slippage of these plates that cause all the problems. Either they pull apart, rise up and overlap the other, or slip by one another. It doesn't take much slippage for the damage to be done. The earthquakes that can be caused because of the slippage of these gigantic plates can bring about devastation that is beyond the control of man.

I compare these patterns of earthen plates like the peelings on an orange. If someone were to remove the orange peel with their fingers they would have chunks of peelings taken from off the orange in their hand. If they were somehow able to paste the peelings back on the orange in a loose manner and leave them there, that is about what the tectonic plates would be like. The orange peelings would remain there but would be somewhat movable and pliable. The orange of course would be under the orange peels and represent the core of the earth.

That is the way the tectonic plates would be as they cover the magma that we know is under the earth's crusty surface. There is multiplied tons of hot liquid under the surface of the entire earth and

these plates hold it all in place. It is when these hot gases erupt that they come to the earth's surface usually through one of the volcano sites.

"The earth has some 200 million cubic miles of water, but this is but a drop in the bucket compared to its volume of semi-fluid magma (or lava). There is about 5,000 times as much magma as ocean, ton by ton."(**3**). As I have pointed out, the crust of the earth is only 10 to 50 miles thick. In the days of Noah as the earth opened up from underneath, tremendous upheavals were caused in the earth. Consequently, birth was given to the vast mountain ranges and the great volcanoes that are tied in with those mountain ranges.

"It must be kept in mind that the Earth's thin crust or skin is considered to be as flexible as a man's leather belt. The fragileness of the earth, the minute thickness of it's crust, the vastness of its internal oceans of magma, the velocity of its rotation, the flexibility of its crust, the confinement and the viscosity of the magma."(**4**). All of those conditions were the catalyst for disaster in Noah's day and they are a potential for future disasters somewhere along those fault lines where the volcanoes are most active.

CATASTROPHE ORIGINATION

I believe the tectonic plates had their origination at the time of the flood in Noah's day.

> The Bible says in Genesis 7:10-12, *"the flood came and covered the earth. When Noah was 600 years old, on the seventeenth day of the second month, the underground waters burst forth on the earth, and the rain fell in mighty torrents from the sky. The rain continued to fall for forty days and forty nights"*.

As already mentioned in this chapter, the ground was probably more of a solid mass than in the form of the tectonic plates, as we know that it is today. The underground waters and probably magma (lava) burst forth from out of the earth, as the crust of the earth must have broken apart and formed the tectonic plates. After the flood, I believe God readied the earth to fulfill the prophecies about earth-quakes that were to take place in the last days. Many of the world's cities are sitting in danger zones and our mountains and fault lines have disaster written all over them.

I quoted part of the following scripture earlier but it bears repeating because of the tremendous sign it gives us in God's Word about the end of time. The disciples had asked Jesus some all-important questions.

The Bible says in Matthew 24:3-4 and 6-8 about the last days, *"Now as He sat on the Mount of Olives, the disciples came to Him privately, saying, 'Tell us, when will these things be? And what will be the sign of your coming, and of the end of the age?' And Jesus answered and said to them: Take heed that no one deceives you. And you will hear of wars and rumors of wars. See that you are not troubled; for all these things must come to pass, but the end is not yet. For nation will rise against nation, and kingdom against kingdom. And there will be famines, pestilence's, and earthquakes in various places. All these are the beginning of sorrows."*

Small wonder! God said that in the future He was going to shake up and move the earth.

In Isaiah 13:13 it says, *"Therefore I will shake the heavens, and the earth shall remove out of her place, in the wrath of the LORD of hosts, and in the day of his fierce anger".*

In Joel 3:16 it says, *"The LORD also shall roar out of Zion, and utter his voice from Jerusalem; and the heavens and the earth shall shake: but the LORD will be the hope of his people and the strength of the children of Israel".*

In Haggai 2:6 we read, *"For thus saith the LORD of hosts; Yet once, it is a little while, and I will shake the heavens, and the earth, and the sea, and the dry land".*

Before the coming of the Lord He will begin to shake the earth, wars will explode all over the planet, and volcanoes will erupt. God has plans for this planet as He begins to deal with the disobedient people of this world.

Isaiah 24:19-21 says, *"The earth is violently broken, the earth is split open, the earth is shaken exceedingly. The earth shall reel to and fro like a drunkard, and shall totter like a hut; its transgression shall be heavy upon it, and it will fall, and not rise again. It shall come to pass in that day that the LORD will punish on high the host of exalted ones, and on the earth the kings of the earth."*

Revelation 6:14-17 says, *"Then the sky receded as a scroll when it is rolled up, and every mountain and island was moved out of its place. And the kings of the earth, the great men, the rich men, the commanders, the mighty men, every slave and every free man, hid themselves in the caves and in the rocks of the mountains. They said to the mountains and rocks, fall on us and hide us from the face of Him who sits on the throne and from the wrath of the Lamb! For the great day of His wrath has come, and who is able to stand?"*

That doesn't mean that God doesn't have any godly people in those places. He does! And there is hope for the people of God that He will be there for us in the most severe of all calamities and catastrophes.

Psalm 46:1-3 says, *"God is our refuge and strength, a very present help in trouble. Therefore we will not fear, even though the earth be removed, and though the mountains be carried into the midst of the sea; Though its waters roar and be troubled, though the mountains shake with its swelling."*

I am reminded of the story in Genesis chapter 18 when Abraham pleaded with God to spare the unrighteous cities of Sodom and Gomorrah. Abraham kept asking God if he would spare the cities, if there were enough good people there, and he kept decreasing the number each time he asked. He asked if God would spare the cities if 50 righteous people lived there, then 45, then 40, then 30, then 20, and then 10 righteous people. Each time God said that He would spare the cities if that many righteous people were there but Abraham knew it was a lost cause. There weren't even 10 righteous people there. God was going to destroy the cities. There were too many homosexuals who lived there and too many people with other sins as well. The beautiful thing about that story is that God spared Abraham's nephew Lot and some of his family members right from out of the middle of that catastrophe.

God is readying this world for the catastrophes that will go along with the wars and calamities of the time of the Great Tribulation in the last days. In the midst of all this He wants the peoples of the earth to trust Him. He wants us to believe that He has everything under His control.

CATASTROPHE IN THE BIBLE

God's sovereignty is the key ingredient in understanding catastrophes in the Bible. Throughout the Bible there have been many other instances of God bringing massive catastrophes for correction of God's people and the world. Many times when God would send a plague in the Bible, it was directed toward the Children of Israel. It usually centered on their complaints and murmuring about the leadership of Moses and Aaron, their sin of worshipping idols, or else they weren't listening to the voice of God. Many times it involved the deaths of thousands of individuals at a time.

When the Children of Israel were to be set free from Egypt under the leadership of Moses, God sent 10 plagues because of the disobedience of Pharaoh who would not let the Children of Israel leave to worship Him. The Bible says that God hardened Pharaoh's heart which sounds like poor Pharaoh had no choice in the matter and that he was doomed for destruction. In actuality, I believe he would have had a chance if he had made the right choice in the first place. Initially, when God told Moses to talk to Pharaoh, He told Moses how Pharaoh was going to react to Moses being sent from God, and then what God was going to do about it. It sheds an interesting light on Pharaoh's heart. Pharaoh was the one who to begin with, would not let God's people go. God had no choice but to harden his heart because of his stubborn refusal to release the Children of Israel. Pharaoh had already sealed his own fate. Moses was sent to Pharaoh the king of Egypt, and this is what God said was going to happen in that first visit. Notice God's prediction of Pharaoh's initial reaction.

Exodus 3:18-20 says, *"you shall say to him, "The LORD God of the Hebrews has met with us; and now, please, let us go three days' journey into the wilderness, that we may sacrifice to the LORD our God.' But I am sure that the king of Egypt will not let you go, no, not even by a mighty hand. So I will stretch out my hand and strike Egypt with all My wonders which I will do in its midst; and after that he will let you go."*

It was Pharaoh's choice whether or not he would let them go. It's just that God knew what his decision would be. After that, God sent the 10 Plagues. Some people may say that they are not miracles but just freaks of nature. Well, we know that God is in charge of both miracles and nature. Some may consider them natural disasters but I believe that the hand of God directs nature.

These plagues were devastating to the Egyptians as it disrupted their entire cultural life and livelihood, but God spared and protected the Children of Israel. Each time, Pharaoh's heart became harder and harder, and he would not let Israel go. The book of Exodus describes the plagues:

[1] The water was turned to blood and all the fish in the river died and made the river stink.
[2] They were inundated with frogs when they came into their houses, their beds, and their ovens.
[3] They were smitten with lice that were on every person and animal.
[4] There was an infestation of flies as they swarmed into everyone's houses.

[5] There was a fatal disease of their cattle and all the cattle of Egypt died.

[6] They were plagued by boils and blisters which were inflammatory sores on man and beast.

[7] Their land was smitten with thunder, fire, and hail that come upon the trees, herbs, and cattle.

[8] They were overrun by a swarm of locusts as an east wind came all day and all night and brought the locusts.

[9] Their land was covered with darkness for a period of three days.

[10] All the firstborn of the Egyptians were killed which was the worst of all, as cattle, prisoners and everyone else in Egypt, including Pharaoh's house were affected.

After that, the Children of Israel were reluctantly set free. Then Pharaoh changed his mind, his army pursued them and their final catastrophe was that they were drowned in the Red Sea. The Children of Israel made it safely to the other side.

Another one of the most striking portrayals of God's judgment on Israel is found in the book of Amos. We are not told how many people died in the catastrophes of that book but the frequency of disaster I'm sure would have been overwhelming just as it was to Pharaoh in his day. In Amos we read how God sent famine, drought, pestilence, disease, and mildew to their vineyards, and had their cities destroyed by war. The devastation to their culture was terrible and the prophet describes it as being nearly complete.

Amos 3:12 says, *"Thus says the Lord: "As a shepherd takes from the mouth of a lion two legs or a piece of an ear, So shall the children of Israel be taken out who dwell in Samaria. In the corner of a bed and on the edge of a couch!"*

Amos 5:19 describes it this way, *"As if a man did flee from a lion, and a bear met him; or went into the house, and leaned his hand on the wall, and a serpent bit him."*

It was as if the Children of Israel during the days of Amos could not escape the devastation. Each time God sent these disasters he mentioned their response and attitude toward God.

Amos 4:6, 8, 9, 10, and 11 say, *"...yet you have not returned unto me, says the Lord."* Verse 12 says, *"Prepare to meet thy God, O Israel."*

In the catastrophe of Numbers chapter 16, it tells of a man named Korah, who along with other followers, rebelled against the leadership of Moses and Aaron, the High Priest. They persuaded another 250 well known men to side with them. God was so angry that he allowed an earthquake to engulf Korah and his followers. Fire came out of heaven and devoured the other 250 men. That was a catastrophe involving an earthquake and fire. The next day the children of Israel complained to Moses and Aaron about all the men who died and the Lord sent a plague among them and another 14,700 people died.

Numbers also records an incident of idol worship when the Children of Israel committed adultery with the women of Moab. They sacrificed to false gods and worshipped them. Needless to say, God was very angry with them and 24,000 people died by a plague that God sent.

In another massive time of a plague, King David took it upon himself to conduct a census without consulting God. We read in the books of II Samuel and I Chronicles that both God and Satan were involved in this catastrophe. Satan actually provoked David to do this but God also prompted David because He was angry with Israel. God reacted with displeasure and He gave David some choices in regard to the catastrophe that was to fall on him and the Children of Israel. David's choices given by God were either 7 years of famine, 3 months of running from his enemies, or 3 days of pestilence at the hand of God. He chose to fall into God's hands for the 3 days of pestilence. The Bible says that from God's hand came a pestilence among the people and 70,000 people died.

In the Old Testament there are numerous stories where thousands were killed in battle or with disease. On a number of occasions God sent fire, pestilence, war, famine, and earthquakes to a people that were disobedient. He was a holy God and demanded that His people remain holy. He was a loving God but demanded His people to walk in His ways and be satisfied. If not, punishment was lying at their door.

In Genesis chapters six through nine, we read the story of Noah's Flood. The entire population of the known world was drowned because of the horrible evil that was in the world at that time. Only Noah's family of eight people survived. This was a catastrophe that was so overwhelming that God had to promise that He would never do that again.

Sodom and Gomorrah are another one of those catastrophes that is mentioned in the Bible and that is told in different cultures. Each of the epics in these cultures carries a little different twist to the story depending on who is telling it. While many would say that's cause for doubting the story I say that it perfectly corroborates the Bible record. It proves that it is unrehearsed, un-coerced, and shows that many peoples and cultures believed this story. The reason for the difference in reporting the event is that many nations were formed outside of God's perfect plan for them as recorded in the Bible. Many nations were disobedient to His plan. Therefore without the accuracy of God's word through His prophets, the event was remembered because it was major, but the circumstances were reported according to their own culture.

In Luke 13, it mentions two catastrophes. Pilate allowed Roman soldiers to arrive at the Passover sacrifices of the people from Galilee. It was during these sacrifices that the Roman soldiers desecrated these rites and slaughtered innocent people while they were fulfilling their sacred obligations. The historian Josephus writes that as many as 3,000 people were killed during these types of atrocities and another time, 2,000 were killed. In the same chapter it mentions the tower of Siloam falling and crushing 18 people. It was an accident that no one expected, and Jesus made it clear that it's not because one group of people were worse sinners than another group. Instead, Jesus gave a clear message in this chapter for both of these incidents and the message was one of repentance.

Luke 13 verses three and five say, *"Unless you repent of your sins, you too will perish"*.

It isn't a matter of how you die that's important, but repenting of sin and being prepared to meet God when you do die. God's will is for us to make it to heaven. Catastrophes are horrible but how we get there is of less consequence than actually getting there. Jesus used these events to illustrate that just as sure as death will take us from this life, we will need to bring holiness into our lives through repentance while we are still living. Someday we will stand before God and He will want to know if we have turned from our sins. Every time we hear of automobile accidents, an air disaster or some other catastrophe, it is designed to make us think, "what if that happened to me" and "am I ready to meet God?" We need to keep our heart right with the Creator of life.

Much more could be said about how God allowed the killing of innocent children and babies. The most notable loss of children was at the birth of Jesus Christ. Out of jealously, Herod massacred innocent boys that were two years old and younger in an attempt to kill Jesus who he thought would be a threat to his earthly kingdom. Of course, Christ's Kingdom was not a physical kingdom but it was in the hearts of men and women everywhere as described in Luke.

Luke 17:20-21 Jesus said, *"The Kingdom of God isn't ushered in with visible signs. You won't be able to say, `Here it is!' or `It's over there!' For the Kingdom of God is within you."*

In the Bible, we see that God also allowed executions, beatings, violence, and the plundering of cities and people. Even the people of God were subject to suffering and persecution. We are given many examples of this in the Bible but a good recap of their plight is found in the book of Hebrews.

Hebrews 11:33-38 says, *Who through faith subdued kingdoms, wrought righteousness, obtained promises, stopped the mouths of lions, quenched the violence of fire, escaped the edge of the sword, out of weakness were made strong, waxed valiant in fight, turned to flight the armies of the aliens. Women received their dead raised to life again: and others were tortured, not accepting deliverance; that they might obtain a better resurrection. And others had trial of cruel mockings and scourgings, yea, moreover of bonds and imprisonment. They were stoned, they were sawn asunder, were tempted, were slain with the sword: they wandered about in sheepskins and goatskins; being destitute, afflicted, tormented; Of whom the world was not worthy: they wandered in deserts, and in mountains, and in dens and caves of the earth.*

In Luke chapter twelve it mentions that man can sometimes determine what the weather patterns will be, but does not know how to apply any spiritual discernment to what he sees. We need to be aware of the messages that God is trying to send to us.

Luke 12:54-56 says, *"Then He also said to the multitudes, "Whenever you see a cloud rising out of the west, immediately you say, "A shower is coming'; and so it is. And when you see the south wind blow, you say, "There will be hot weather'; and there is. Hypocrites! You can discern the face of the sky and of the earth, but how is it you do not discern this time?"*

THE NEXT BIG HIT

There has been an increase of the frequency of mid-sized earthquakes all around the world. The frequency of huge earthquakes of 9.0-9.9 has had little or no change over the past 15 years. There is usually anywhere from one to three earthquakes of that size in any given year. Some years there are none of that size. It is the small to mid-sized earthquakes that have increased dramatically. The 0.1 size earthquake to the 4.9 earthquake has increased by large percentages in the past 15 years.

* In 1990 there were only 4,493 earthquakes of the 4.0-4.9 size while in 2003 there were 8,466.

* In 1990 there were only 2,457 earthquakes of the 3.0-3.9 size while in 2003 there were 7,626.
* In 1990 there were only 2,364 earthquakes of the 2.0-2.9 size while in 2003 there were 7,726.
* In 1990 there were only 474 earthquakes of the 1.0-1.9 size while in 2003 there were 2,491.
* In 1990 there were no earthquakes of the 0.1-0.9 size while in 2003 there were 134. (5).

Of course, better technology has helped in tracking these earthquakes. However, as you can tell from the statistics there seems to be an increase in earthquakes during the past two decades. It certainly has seismologists keeping their eye on those statistics and watching for the vulnerable spots in the earthquake zones.

There are numerous fault lines in North America, such as the ones under New York City, the Mid-West, and of course California. The West Coast of the United States has seen major earthquake and volcanic activity in the 20th century. A couple of thousand miles or so off the coast of California sits the state of Hawaii that is considered a hot spot danger zone that is possibly primed for involvement of massive volcanic and tidal wave activity. "Volcanic eruptions spew hot, dangerous gases, ash, lava, and rock that are powerfully destructive. People have died from volcanic blasts. The most common cause of death from a volcano is suffocation. Volcanic eruptions can result in additional threats to health, such as floods, mudslides, power outages, drinking water contamination, and wildfires. Health concerns after a volcanic eruption include infectious disease, respiratory illness, burns, injuries from falls, and vehicle accidents related to the slippery, hazy conditions caused by ash."(6).

It's quite possible that in the United States, California will be the next big earthquake catastrophe that will take place. People are banking on the fact that a big earthquake probably won't happen but many scientists are expecting that something major will happen there, it's just a question of time. No one seems to be sure but one thing that is certain, California is on shaky ground. At least the potential for a major earthquake is there and if it does happen, it would have devastating results.

Now I'm not sure if part of California will fall into the Pacific Ocean even though it is sitting on a well-defined fault line. However, there were five earthquakes there in June of 2005, and hundreds of small earthquakes and aftershocks that continued to plague the area after that. With the major fault lines that run through California, a major earthquake or series of earthquakes could potentially cause much death and major damage. Much of California could be totally destroyed and the interruption of the lives of Californians and its services could happen again and again for years to come.

There is the possibility of a massive earthquake and tidal wave that could be a part of what hits the California coast. Because of the type of fault line that it is some geologists are not that concerned about a massive tidal wave. This fault line called the San Andreas Fault Line is part of a continuous line that geologists call a Ring of Fire. The Ring of Fire extends all the way from Southeast Asia, north through Japan and the Aleutian Islands just off the coast of Alaska and continues down the coast of California and on to South America. Because of these fault lines, these areas are the most vulnerable to earthquake and volcanic activity. They are in the greatest danger.

Reminiscent of the hurricane and breached levees of New Orleans in 2005, other coastal cities should be concerned about their safety. Places like San Francisco and Sacramento, California that are protected with levees should be alert. If strong enough earthquakes occurred in that region, it could create great havoc and contamination of the drinking water for millions of Californians and threaten many lives.

Not only should California be thinking about rain, wind, floods, mudslides, earthquakes and tidal waves, it should be concerned about the next terrorist attack. We are not sure where the next attack will be if there is one, but California is one of the most exposed sites to be hit and probably high on the hit list of the terrorists. In 2005, individuals connected with terrorism were arrested in California. If there is a 2nd wave of terrorism after the 1st wave that hit New York City and Washington, DC in 2001, I would think that a place in California or perhaps a place like Chicago would be the next big hit.

Most terrorists groups are not under one single leader. They have splintered into multi-terrorist cells with their own leaders and agendas all around the world. They can create terrorism on multi-levels. They are amassing their own naval fleet of ships and tankers that can strike anywhere in the world. They can bring containers on ships full of nuclear, chemical, or biological weapons and deliver them to any port and time them for destruction. They will look for the soft underbelly or weakness of any nation, particularly the United States. The coastal cities on the Ocean or on the Great Lakes must particularly be on guard.

So much is said about California and the West Coast that not many people talk about the East Coast of the United States and the potential for earthquakes. With the Mid-Atlantic Ridgeline separating the African Plate and the North American Plate, an earthquake and powerful tsunami is possible for the East Coast if an earthquake disturbs the African Plate under the Canary Islands. A tsunami could travel the thousands of miles westward and could hit the East Coast of the United States and cause major devastation and loss of life to the Massachusetts, New York, New Jersey and other East coast areas.

Past earthquakes have created valleys, plains, and shore areas. People tend to gravitate to these areas, and build large cities there. Large cities attract diverse people who bring their sinful activities with them. An amazing thing is that in some cases, sinful people seem to be attracted to the most dangerous places in the world. The symbolism is that the world seems to build on the shaky spiritual ground of sand instead of on the solid ground of the rock of God's Word.

We see the difference of the two types of builders in Matthew chapter seven. Either we hear and obey the words of Jesus Christ and build our lives on the solid rock or we disobey Him and build our lives on the sand.

Matthew 7:24-27 says, *"Therefore whoever hears these sayings of mine, and does them, I will liken him to a wise man who built his house on the rock. And the rain descended, the floods came, and the winds blew and beat on that house; and it did not fall, for it was founded on the rock. But everyone who hears these sayings of mine, and does not do them, will be like a foolish man who built his house on the sand. And the rain descended, the floods came, and the winds blew and beat on that house; and it fell. And great was its fall."*

Masses of people have taken residence in the sinful cities of San Francisco and the movie Industry Empire of Los Angeles in California right over the San Andreas Fault line. It seems like these two areas have built their earthly house on shaky ground. Other major cities of the United States such as New York City are rife with sin and primed for difficult days ahead to say nothing of major cities around the world.

There are fault lines in many parts of the world but there is an important fault line that runs through the nation of Israel that divides the Arabian plate from the Indo-Australian plate. This fault line is important and will figure in quite prominently in the last days. When the Lord returns there will be a mighty earthquake and when He sets His foot on the Mount of Olives it will split the mountain in two. He will then fight the Battle of Armageddon at the end of the Tribulation when the armies of the world are gathered together.

In Zechariah 14:3-4 it says, *"Then the LORD will go forth and fight against those nations, as He fights in the day of battle. And in that day His feet will stand on the Mount of Olives, which faces Jerusalem on the east. And the Mount of Olives shall be split in two, from east to west, making a very large valley; half of the mountain shall move toward the north and half of it toward the south".*

Finally, the earth is not only rotating on its axis it is revolving around the sun. The sun and our solar system is moving through the Milky Way Galaxy, and the Milky Way Galaxy is moving through space just as other galaxies are moving through space as well. With all that movement, is there the possibility of asteroid or meteoroid visitors from outer space that would enter into our solar system and cause devastation like never before? Meteorites are usually too small to create any damage to the earth but such a collision is possible. A large meteorite hit the earth many years ago and created a huge hole 4,000 feet wide and 600 feet deep. It is located in the state of

Arizona and it is known as the Arizona Meteor Crater. It can easily be sensed that if a meteor ever hit one of our large cities, there could be enormous destruction.

Will that be a part of the calamities that are recorded in the book of Revelation? The potential of meteorite collision with earth both now and in that future time is not out of the question. What powerful catastrophes await the earth in an attempt to destroy it as we get closer to the Great Tribulation, the Battle of Armageddon, and the time of the end? Will there be meteorites, earthquakes, hurricanes, nuclear havoc, and destruction of unparalleled proportions that the world would seem to implode in massive waves of utter ruin?

If the dire prediction by the scientific community of global warming is accurate, can you imagine the destruction that is the future of our delicate world? To repeat what was said at the beginning of this chapter, there seems to be a connection between the downward slide of excellent moral living and the upheavals of social ills, geological tremors and other catastrophes around the world.

America has had its warnings from God and in His mercy He has sent Revivals before a catastrophe would strike. The First Great Awakening or spiritual revival came before the Revolutionary War in both England and America. It helped to prepare both those lands for the difficult road ahead in the birth of a new nation. The Second Great Awakening came before the Civil War that prompted a powerful missions and prayer movement. It helped America make a mid-course correction in order to eventually rid the land of the scourge of slavery. Then the Azuza Street Revival occurred in 1906 in Los Angeles, the same month that the 1906 earthquake hit San Francisco. It showed how God was going to shake the flourishing nation of the world both physically and spiritually and prepare them for the great wars that lay ahead. That 1906 revival, which was an outgrowth of the great Welsh revivals in Great Britain in the previous centuries, continued in 1904 and set the stage for a Holy Spirit Renewal. The outgrowth of that started numerous Pentecostal denominations in the United States during the first half of the 20th Century. Many religious historians overlook that revival, but I call it the 3rd Great Awakening in America. It was a rebirth of the Holy Spirit that eventually led to the Charismatic renewal and it infused the Holy Spirit into churches across the nation and around the world. There are now 600 million Pentecostal believers worldwide. That revival eventually made an impact on most of the main line denominations by the second half of the 20th Century. This has changed many styles of worship and now you sometimes cannot tell the difference between the worship of a Pentecostal and believers of other denominations.

What great spiritual awakening does God have in mind to warn the richest, most powerful, and most influential nation of an impending doom in the 21st Century? What doom will first come to awaken this spiritual giant? Will it be the continued acts of terrorism, war, earthquakes, hurricanes, pandemic flu, or some other catastrophe that we least expect? Will Christians in America help turn our nation back to God?

It is up to the people of America to make a choice. God has been sending powerful messages with 9-11, the hurricanes that hit the gulf coast, and other worldwide disasters. Either we side with cultural immorality and "political correctness" or make the choice to stand with God in repentance and righteousness. God has always had a remnant of people who would stand on His side despite the collapse of the moral culture all around them. It is up to us to make the choice to continually live for God. America seems to be living as in the days of the book of Judges found in the Bible. The people of that day vacillated consistently between serving the Lord and not serving the Lord so God sent them punishment when they disobeyed. They ended up doing what their selfish hearts dictated. Then God sent destructive armies and at other times unthinkable catastrophes to their land so that they would repent. It would be a terrible shame if America were unable to learn the valuable lesson that God wants us to learn. He is looking for a people who will seek Him and follow the commandments of His Word!

Judges 2:18-19 says, *"Whenever the Lord raised up a judge for them, he was with the judge and saved them out of the hands of their enemies as long as the judge lived; for the Lord had compassion on them as they groaned under those who oppressed and afflicted them. But when the judge died, the people returned to ways even more corrupt than those of their fathers, following other gods and serving and worshiping them. They refused to give up their evil practices and stubborn ways."*

Judges 21:25 says, *"Everyone did what was right in his own eyes."*

CHAPTER SIX:

The influence of evil over global powers

—⁓—

This is the greatest catastrophe. We are living in a generation that is de-generating right before our eyes and at a faster rate than at any other time in history. The catastrophe of the massive spiritual evil influence in the world today is greater than the physical catastrophes that were discussed in the previous chapter. With a propensity toward evil, we are inundated with a "cultural war" where there are "no absolutes" and where there are plenty of cultural insecurities to go around. We seem to have lost our cognitive powers of awareness and reasoning in relationship with God. If anything will incur the wrath of God and cause a collapse of our societies, it is the blatant promiscuity and willful disobedience to God and His moral laws.

This chapter and chapter seven deal mostly with the cultural evils of the United States but is indicative of what the world is going through as they deal with their own cultural evils. The values of the world are evolving as each generation deals with a gradual diminishing of those values that affect the next generation. The major Superpowers usually set the stage for powerful worldwide evil influence as God usually deals with its culture and morality. The collapse or change of morals in cultures worldwide is due in part to the pervasiveness of the Superpower nations.

When it comes to social issues here in America, whether or not you are liberal or conservative depends on if you are talking about religion or politics, or some other issue. It's easy to be liberal about one subject but be conservative about another. It all depends on the issue. Do we look at issues through a cultural traditional view that keeps our customs intact, or a cultural secular view that seeks to alter our society to fit the calls for changes that lead to immorality? After all, a strong Judeo/Christian philosophy and principle has heavily influenced America since its inception.

Many people struggle with the term's conservative and liberal, but the dictionary makes it clear. A conservative person is someone who is inclined to keep the same customs, would oppose radical changes, and would tend to be cautious. A liberal person is someone who would not tend to be literal or strict. They would be in favor of progress and reforms with the idea of changing society no matter if those changes were good or evil. The Liberal will say it's the freedom of expression that is important.

Some people feel that being liberal in policies and conservative in social mores is hypocritical, but in actuality, the Bible is both liberal and conservative. It is very liberal when it comes to helping the poor and when dispensing God's love, mercy, and forgiveness. While some religious teachers use part of the following verses in Luke to encourage financial gain, the verses actually refer to the liberality of being kind to others and how that blessing will come back to us.

Luke 6:36-38 says, *"Be merciful, just as your Father also is merciful…Forgive, and you will be forgiven. Give, and it will be given to you: good measure, pressed down, shaken together, and running over will be put into your bosom. For with the same measure that you use, it will be measured back to you."*

The Bible is conservative however when it comes to personal behavior patterns and when a line is crossed that will lead individuals or a nation to sin against God's Commandments. God's call is for individuals and nations to conservatively adhere to the morality

218

of God's Word in personal behavior. Then they will discover the liberality of God's love and forgiveness. For many years now, the conservatives have overlooked the practical aspect of being generous in helping others. On the other hand, the liberals have overlooked the spiritual relevancy of morality in applying it to society.

There are many cultural issues that anyone can raise for debate and how they should be applied. Discussions about nuclear weapons, the environment, energy, disability rights, privacy rights, matters of conscience, the death penalty, civil rights, workers rights, poverty, and social and economic justice are all important. The question however always comes down to the interpretation of some of those issues and how they should be applied. Both liberals and conservatives want to keep the "Bill of Rights intact that protects citizens. All of these concerns fall within the political realm, but are spiritual issues as well.

The liberals have led the way in keeping many of these issues in the forefront. In the past, the conservatives have lagged behind and have had to compromise and agree that the liberals had been right with many of them. We have fallen short at times in meeting the needs of the helpless and the poor, as was the case with hurricane Katrina in New Orleans in 2005. All of us have had to do our best to meet these needs. Liberal thinking goes a long way in helping the poor and the needy.

While great strides have been made in many areas as an improvement to the quality of life, it's the moral and personal behavior issues that can lead to decadence. They are the most controversial and disruptive. I believe that among all of the cultural issues in America, the issues of abortion and homosexuality along with homosexual marriage, are the most challenging and powerful "pieces" of the puzzle in the cultural war that we are facing today. The reason is that these issues together, involve the "giving of life" and the "living of life." They have become its symbols.

These two issues are the biggest political hot buttons in America today, and they too are crossover issues into the spiritual realm. One of the reasons they are so hot is that there doesn't seem to be any compromise on the part of the liberals as the conservatives have done with the other social issues that were mentioned. The liberals want to deal with them only as private matters and don't want to face them as moral, cultural issues. They won't agree that they are morally destructive and that we must do our best to teach America different lifestyle patterns. Liberal thinking says that these two issues are innocuous but just the opposite is true. They are harmful and provoke strong emotion. Twenty or thirty years from now they may not be such hot topics as they are now, but the damage will already have been done to the spiritual and moral life of America. These issues along with other moral issues will contribute greatly to America's moral decline in the world.

Dealing with all this is a dilemma and a source of difficulty for the liberal thinkers because they are for the downtrodden, those who are out of the main stream, and those that have their rights misused. The problem for the liberal is that they have to allow the throwing of moral behavior out the window at any cost, even if it means grave consequences to the moral fabric of America. For them to be "politically correct," they have bound themselves to the freedom and "rights of individuals" due to the First Amendment. They display intolerance toward any intrusion into private behavior even if that intrusion is for the good of society as a whole. As far as individual rights is concerned, they don't allow much room for a consciousness of guilt. They feel no need to follow any particular spiritual rule or thought of behavior. This makes it difficult for them or the followers they endorse to come to any decision about repentance and a changed life. It's easy to live their kind of lifestyle that is devoted to self-satisfaction.

I was raised in the 1940's and 1950's by parents who taught me many of the values that have been in our country for decades. It was an age of innocence and higher morals. They taught me that black was black and white was white. There were no gray areas. I knew the value of God and country. They taught me not to commit any crimes or I would go to jail. They said that if I got in trouble at school that I would also get in trouble at home. They would never threaten anyone with a lawsuit just because they were inconvenienced in some way. As a child I was not in control of my parents, my parents were in control of me. Adultery was not called an "affair" and homosexuality was not called "gay." Sin was sin! Those and other immoral issues were not in control of our country but a wholesome morality was, and that is what everyone expected and accepted.

America may not be a Christian nation officially, but it is the most powerful remaining Christian culture in the world today and allowed by God to be established that way. We either influence or clash with other cultures of the world. But we are being ripped to shreds internally by an obvious lapse in morals and character. We are at war with the "Cultural Elite" of our society that tries to give the impression that they are a cut above the rest as a social class. They feel they are "enlightened" because they are casting off all "Christian" moral restraints. According to their own liberal standard, they view conservatism as a form of bigotry when in actuality, it is the liberals that have obstinacy, cruelty, and unreasonableness attached to their viewpoint. They are bitterly intolerant to conservatives who believe it is possible to separate belief in morality from the lifestyle and viewpoint of those who hold to the "new tolerance" in our society. They want us to be "politically correct" and accept everything they are espousing without allowing us to offer any disagreement. There is no tolerance for the conservative point of view.

Tolerance is the name of the game. Unless you act in the name of tolerance you cannot be a part of the 'real' world of those who are advocating this brand of tolerance. They want us to endorse every conceivable variant and deviant act that they wish to perform. We need to break through all of their depravity. Dr. Charles Crabtree said "Tolerance is the new holiness for the world. The world wants us to bow at their shrine of tolerance. Without the supernatural, we can do nothing to help this culture and this generation. Helping them cannot be done with our genius or our methods."(1). In other words, our culture needs the help of God.

We are on a slow, steady but gradual slide into a deception by Satan, as most everyone seems to be immune to the grip that it has taken on our society. One thing leads to another as our world continues to reel back and forth through the vicissitudes of life. We laugh at the days of prohibition but we are repelled at the acute alcoholism in our society and scorn the drunk drivers who today are responsible for nearly half of our highway deaths. We protect the rights of pornographers but grimace when a child is molested or murdered and pornography is found in the perpetrators home or on his computer. We applaud the homosexual and his freedom but denounce the "dirty old men" and some respected leaders, ministers, or priests that have helped to foist this plague upon us. We openly accept the scenes of adultery on our television programs but lament the sky rocketing sexually transmitted diseases, and look the other way when it comes to a comprehensive program to eliminate the AIDS epidemic in our world. We have set aside the spanking of children but cannot see and won't admit that the behavior of children has hit a new low since the introduction of psychological behavior modification programs to replace spanking our children. All of these things are the consequences of an increasingly depraved society.

We say the evolutionists have their rights in schools and the creationists have none. Therefore, an anti-creationist theme has fostered an anti-god idealism in the minds of our children. With no allegiance or accountability to a higher power in our schools, the children have run rampant with violence, disobedience, mayhem, and drugs. We have kept quiet as millions of our children, given the choice, have left the public school system sponsored by our government. Many are now in parochial, charter, private, and Christian schools or they are being home schooled. What does that say about the reasons behind this mass exodus from our public schools over the past four decades?

The kind of thinking that has turned us from God has lowered any moral standards that we have had here in America. It has influenced a change in the moral fiber of our country, which in turn has affected its financial stability and its political direction. There is a major connection between politics and morality that has come from our various religious teachings of the past that has produced an economically stable country.

All of us are capable of committing evil acts and we all have a propensity to do wrong. That is where God must be brought into every action of our nation for without a moral compass, acts of violence and sin only intensify. In reality, evil like that has prevailed throughout the world and has influenced all of the nations, including the United States.

Morality and politics may be strange bedfellows but they are absolutely necessary partners. Politics has ridden on the back of religious morality even before the inception of our country. Now with the cries of separation of Church and State here in America, politics is now saying that it would rather walk than ride. The problem is that you cannot live in the arena of legitimate religion or legitimate politics without morality because of their equal demands for a moral code of ethics. Both of them have had their immoral setbacks, shameful exposure of sin, and extremism, but now politics is crying that they want their own morality without religion. The politicians and liberal thinkers have forgotten that politics received their morality from religion in the first place. They are casting off the one thing that can keep our society intact and their political job secure. They want their own brand of morality without religion and its influence.

The end result is that there is a powerful hedonism that is prevalent in America. Our capitalistic system has gone amuck without a moral base. We call ourselves Christians here in America but we are more like buffet style "Cafeteria Christians." We choose what part of morality we want that God is serving, and we leave out what part of morality we don't like.

Years ago I heard a well-known liberal talk show host debating these kinds of issues with his guests. In trying to appeal to his secular audience, he would ask, "If we are going to teach morality, whose morality are we going to use"? His reason behind his question I'm sure was that he was opposed to bringing morality to the forefront. As a Catholic his faith had long languished and he wouldn't have had a clue as to what to do. He would rather keep morality a private thing so he wouldn't have to answer to anyone for his own morality or lack thereof. I may sound somewhat sarcastic but my answer is, "Please, use someone's basic morality without its extremism, be it the Pentecostals, the Mormons, the Baptists, the Muslims, or the Catholics. Any morality is better than no morality!" For being a good Catholic boy he really hit bottom when he asked that question. He soon lost his ratings and he was off the air.

Of course, there has always been immorality throughout history, but the Internet, television, movies, and the theater have given it a major fast-forward boost. Today we are in a state of moral decay and collapse accompanied by a sense of moral relativism here in America. Hollywood, the press, and humanistic influence are telling us, that anything goes in regard to standards of decency.

The problems that we face in America center on the satisfying of a person's ego and the difficulty when anyone doesn't understand them. For many people, life has to focus around their hurt, selfishness, and why things aren't going their way. Everything must bring attention to their life, income, happiness, and what pleases them, instead of focusing on God. The Bible talks about this kind of people.

II Timothy 3:1-5 says, *"But know this, that in the last days perilous times will come. For men will be lovers of themselves, lovers of money, boasters, proud, blasphemers, disobedient to parents, unthankful, unholy, unloving, unforgiving, slanderers, without self-control, brutal, despisers of good, traitors, headstrong, haughty, lovers of pleasure rather than lovers of God, having a form of godliness but denying its power."*

This kind of immorality was propelled during the days of drugs and free love in the 1960's as it gave us the attitude of freedom without restraint. There has been an increase of outrageous behavior just in my lifetime alone. *We have become the people that our parents warned us about.*

A GENTLEMAN'S AGREEMENT

All this freedom of expression centers on the 1st Amendment. The biggest thing that is stuck in the throat of the U.S. Constitution is the current idea of separation of church and state. There has always been the separation of church and state. It used to be a gentleman's agreement similar to the respect of a man's word that comes with a handshake. The church respected the state and the state respected the church. The lines were drawn but if someone crossed those lines there wasn't the outcry as there is today. That type of understanding of the separation of church and state continued for over 175 years throughout the history of our country and it was acceptable by nearly everyone. It was never interpreted as it is today.

There was a religious freedom that dated back to the earliest days of life in America. If there was an intolerant view of others it was usually one religious group against another, not the government trying to suppress religious expression. The fact that there was intolerance to other religions unfortunately is proof that the Separation of Church and State was not viewed then as it is today because the government did not suppress them. Religious fervor flourished. An example was the Quakers, who did not see eye to eye with the Puritans. If anyone wanted to dissent, many times they had to start another religious group elsewhere, as was the case with Roger Williams when he moved from Massachusetts to Rhode Island. The city of Providence was started because he wanted a haven for religious dissention and toleration. It was so named Providence because they expected and desired the guardianship of Divine protection. William Penn, another very religious individual, was a progenitor of the people and state of Pennsylvania. These religious men and others like them were very involved in community life. There was more of a tolerance back then with religious laymen and clergymen expressing themselves in politics.

Today we are being told that we must respect other people's religion by not mentioning the name of God or the name of Jesus lest we offend someone else's idea about God. That's a smokescreen just in order to get religion off the front page of society and into the back rooms where it will "hurt no one". But how do you respect someone else's religion or how do you create a dialogue that would bring that respect, if you cannot mention God's name. How do you learn respect if you do not participate publicly? They say that by mentioning the name of God we are imposing our view on them. I'm definitely in favor of respecting other religions but how absurd is it that we are accused of imposing our views on them! Religion is a free choice. Even if one converts to another religion, it's still their free choice. Protestants have converted to Catholicism and vice versa. Jews have converted to Protestantism and vice versa. No one forces them. My parents converted from Catholicism to Protestantism before I was born. I have cousins who converted to Catholicism. Forcing individuals to change religions was part of the archaic religious relics and rites of the past, and a part of the religions of terror and tyranny today.

The thought of offending someone else was never implied during George Washington's day as it is being presented today. Thomas Jefferson fully supported the rights of all in religion, including those who practiced the faith of Mohammed. He saw no interference with anyone else's faith if all were allowed to practice their faith freely. It was never thought of during more recent Presidencies such as Franklin Roosevelt or Dwight Eisenhower, or for that matter during any of our early Presidents from James Monroe to Abraham Lincoln. Religion was allowed to work out their differences themselves unless it involved criminal activity. Religion was part of what shaped our country.

Taking that into consideration, does that mean that I should be offended when I hear views from the political, scientific, or the historical arenas? Should I feel that they are imposing their views on me and that they should keep silent lest they offend me? Again, how absurd! I may disagree with the evolutionist, the abortionist, and the liberal, but we all influence each other in one way or another, religiously, politically, and socially. This imposition idea is all being presented as something bad through the pretext of the atheistic viewpoint of the separation of church and state as atheists and humanists interpret it today.

An example is the right arm of atheism such as the American Civil Liberties Union (ACLU) and the People for the American Way, who have stood in favor of the theory of evolution being taught in our schools. Those views are being expressed to our Christian children. They are not alarmed about the imposition of that view upon our children. Out of fear they have helped to effectively keep Creationists from teaching their view in our schools despite the fact that it was taught there even before America was birthed as a nation. We are forced to live with their imposition.

The question isn't about whether we can respect someone else's religion. That isn't the question at all. The question is about atheism, secularism, humanism, and neo-socialism. It's about those who purport this view that don't want to hear about religion, God, Jesus, faith, or the Bible in the public arena, particularly the political and social arenas. It comes down to the warfare between the idea of God, and man wanting to be god himself by not having to answer to a higher power other than self. Those who believe in these social orders don't want to hear clergymen and politicians mention any thing about God in an open forum of any type. Yet they all give themselves a "free pass" to say whatever they want to say against the expression of religious freedom and thought in the public arena. They don't want to hear anyone mention the name of Jesus as the Savior of the world because they consider that too narrow of a view. In their eyes, it's OK if Muslims say that their religion is the correct way, but Christians cannot say that.

Atheism, secularism, and humanism are giants like Goliath who taunted the armies of Israel as they cowered in the fields in front of him. The young man David defeated him and killed him in battle as he came against Goliath in the name of the Lord. In the same manner, these all-powerful philosophies will have to give obeisance to God in the time of eternal judgment when every thought will have to be brought in subject to Him. Secularism and humanism are self-destructive, yet set themselves up as gods and cannot support the longevity of societal relationships because of their self-centered ideology. These social expressions play into the hands of personal moral liberalism and pit themselves against every moral teaching of the Bible.

With the ACLU on the haunt, Christians are on the "endangered species list" when it comes to laws governing religious expression! The ACLU continues to support and impose other drastic measures upon the United States all under First Amendment rights and as a direct affront to Christianity. They seek to legalize homosexual marriage, promote the acceptance of homosexuals as Boy Scout leaders, and protect the Man/Boy Love association so that men can have sexual relations with boys. They want to remove the words "In God we trust" from our currency and "under God" from the Pledge of Allegiance. They are also supportive of the removal of any and all Christmas and Christmas displays and associations in the public arena.

The psychological imprint of most religions is that there is only one way and usually they tell everyone that they know what that way is. The fact that there is only one God is an open door by which all of us are received of Him. The problem is that man's religious and denominational idealism gets in the way but his basic "follow me to God" approach is a reality to him. The difficulty is in finding the right way. In the gospel of Mark chapter nine we see the story of one of the disciples telling Jesus that he saw someone doing God's work in the name of Jesus but not following them. The message Jesus gave was quite clear.

Jesus answered him in Mark 9:39 saying, *"Don't stop him! No one who performs miracles in my name will soon be able to speak evil of me."*

Jesus was only interested in people's needs being met. So we don't want to get into the idea of "my way is the only way", but we do want to point them to Jesus. It is through Christ Jesus that we can be saved. That's what Jesus Himself said in the following verses.

In speaking about Himself in John 3:18, Jesus said, *"He who believes in Him is not condemned; but he who does not believe is condemned already, because he has not believed in the name of the only begotten Son of God."*

He said in John 14:6, *"I am the way, the truth, and the life. No one can come to the Father except through me."*

So we have the right to say in America that Jesus is the right way just as the Muslims have a right in their own country to say that Islam is the right way. There are not many ways to God, but one way!

JEFFERSONIAN JARGON

I've seen changes in regard to the separation of church and state since the time I became a minister in 1963. The wall of separation of church and state as it is being interpreted today is not based on the First Amendment as the courts and the politicians are currently telling us. Rather, it is based on a letter that Thomas Jefferson wrote to the Danbury Baptist Association in Connecticut on January 1, 1802.

He penned a statement in that letter, which in part influenced the First Amendment. He said, "I contemplate with sovereign reverence that act of the whole American people which declared that their legislature should 'make no law respecting an establishment of religion, or prohibiting the free exercise thereof,' thus building a wall of separation between Church and State."(2). Notice that the words "a wall of separation between Church and State" was not written into the First Amendment.

So, I ask emphatically, when has congress ever passed a law respecting an "establishment of religion" that would have caused the courts to rule against its "free exercise"? When? It has never happened and what's more it never will! If it has never happened, why has there been all the uproar in the past 50 years about the separation of church and state? Even the insertion of the words "under God" in the pledge of allegiance during the 1950's does not endorse or respect a particular religion. God is used interchangeable for many religions including Christians, Jews, and Islam, that uses the name Allah.

Because Jefferson mentioned the phrase "building a wall of separation between church and state" liberals say it means that the church should not interfere with the state. In other words, stay out of the governments business by not mentioning the name of God. In actuality Thomas Jefferson meant just the opposite. Jefferson was guaranteeing to the Baptist Association that the state would never interfere with the church. The First Amendment was not meant to hinder religion but to keep the government from intruding into it. Now mind you, there was well over 150 years between that letter and the first big outcry that people thought that there was a problem with the lack of separation of church and state powers here in America. My, how did the government get along all those years under such church restraint?

In the same letter Jefferson said, "Believing with you that religion is a matter which lies solely between man and his God, that he owes account to none other for his faith or his worship. Adhering

229

to this expression of the supreme will of the nation in behalf of the rights of conscience, I shall see with sincere satisfaction the progress of those sentiments which tend to restore to man all his natural rights, convinced he has no natural right in opposition to his social duties."(**3**).

The liberal "Elite" has used the simplicity of Jefferson's letter to turn the 1st Amendment "gentleman's agreement" into what has now become a series of convoluted phrasings and speech. They try to raise the level of conversation about it to be so specialized and technical, that we cannot go back and operate under it as America had in its early years. Not everyone is happy with that arrangement. The Courts have ripped the 1st Amendment in half by separating the "establishment clause" from the "free exercise clause" which has made talking about it something that is now nonsensical, incoherent, and meaningless. In other words, jargon! If it weren't so heart breaking, it would be laughable.

Using Thomas Jefferson's phrase of "building a wall of separation between church and state," atheists and humanists have managed to drive a paper wedge of separation between the church and state institutions. A paper wedge! It's all about a piece of paper, a letter, and not original Constitutional law. To be sure Jefferson had plenty to say about the freedom of religion in his writings and that it must be left alone to be ruled by church leaders.

In his Second Inaugural Address Jefferson said, "In matters of religion, I have considered that its free exercise is placed by the constitution independent of the powers of the general government." He said that he has "left them, as the constitution found them, under the direction and discipline of state or church authorities acknowledged by the several religious societies."(**4**). According to Jefferson, religion was endorsed by the Constitution to be practiced freely and not hindered by Federal, State, or Court rulings.

Jefferson also declared, "all men shall be free to profess, and by argument to maintain, their opinions in matters of religion, and that the same shall in no wise diminish, enlarge, or affect their civil capacities." In other words, you could be religious and it would not harm whatever civic duties you wish to perform, be it President, Governor, or Senator. In that same draft concerning religion he said, "we are free to declare, and do declare, that the rights hereby asserted are of the natural rights of mankind. And that if any act shall be here-after passed to repeal the present or to narrow its operation, such act will be an infringement of natural right."(**5**). Did you hear that? Any law that would be passed after the statement you just read written by Thomas Jefferson would come against our natural right to freely practice our religion. I say that the courts of the United States of America have over and over again passed such laws to narrow the operation and infringe the natural rights of its citizens to practice their faith freely in the public square!

Of course, Jefferson was greatly involved with the Declaration of Independence, and he signed it. He was also involved with estab-lishing the laws of the Constitution of Virginia. He served in both the Virginia legislature and the United States Congress during his lifetime. In writing in his autobiographical notes about his term in Virginia, Jefferson wrote that all faiths were protected under the law. They made sure of this protection because belief in God was so strong in the early days. The intention of some was to ensure a Christian nation but they stopped short of being exclusive by becoming inclu-sive. The early fathers of the State of Virginia felt that the "protection of opinion was meant to be universal. An amendment was proposed by inserting the word 'Jesus Christ'" during the writing of their Constitution. Jefferson wrote that "the insertion was rejected by a great majority, in proof that they meant to comprehend, within the mantle of it's protection, the Jew and the Gentile, the Christian and Mohammedan, the Hindu, and infidel of every denomination."(**6**). During the early days of our country, the name of Jesus Christ being written in State legal documents was one thing, and they rejected that. However, allowing the freedom of religious expression was encouraged, even publicly, as so declared by Thomas Jefferson while the Virginia Constitution was being written. In other words, the faith of everyone was to be protected, not pummeled.

Even though every state Constitution makes some reference to God, the founding Fathers were opposed to a national Church. However, they were not in favor of the isolation of God from the State. There already were established state churches in some states such as Massachusetts and Virginia. They continued for some time after the United States Constitution was written. While these state churches weren't ideal, nevertheless, they existed for a time. Thankfully, no national Church was established.

The threatened concept from liberal thinking in America is that if we become like the Evangelical "religious right" movement, we may become a theocracy, which is a government ruled by or subject to religious authorities. America becoming a theocracy is ludicrous. If it didn't happen during the early days of our country under the Puritans and other religious extreme movements it is not going to happen in the future. Besides, God will not be interested in a theocracy until the time of the Millennium when He sets it up after Jesus Christ returns to the earth. As stated previously, democracy is too weak, it is unable to form such a religious system.

What the courts have done in the 20th Century is chain the thoughts of spirituality and the words of religious thinkers of our day to their pulpits and away from the public square. The separation of church and state as it is has been decided by the courts today is a modern day anomaly that has been fraudulently enacted as a maxim of the First Amendment. The same "separate but equal" nonsense that we have rejected as a living arrangement in the United States between blacks and whites is being accepted among politicians as a good living relationship between the church and state. Ironic, isn't it?

FIRST AMENDMENT

The same individuals who want religion limited will say nothing about the First Amendment and how it has been taken out of context. When you compare it with the rest of the Constitution you will see that the Constitution enforces good behavior in regard to the three branches of government. There are safeguards that protect us when anyone of our political leaders abuse their power through treason, felony, breach of peace, bribery, or other high crimes and misdemeanors. That goes for members of Congress, The Supreme Court, and The President of the United States. All three branches of Government are held to a prescribed set of checks and balances if they abuse their freedoms through their own personal bad behavior in connection with the office that they hold.

The First Amendment that guarantees free speech, a free press, and the right of the people to peaceably petition the government is being upheld without any regard to any limits placed on it. There is no fear of the consequences of any abuse or misuse by any individual or group. The First Amendment is taken out of context from the entire Constitution, all in the name of freedom. We have made the First Amendment a non-restrictive piece of our Constitution that no longer allows us to confront anyone about his or her behavior, whether good or bad. We hold our political leaders to a strict code of the abuse of public life but not the actions of any of our everyday citizens that are considered to be under the 1st Amendment, no matter how immoral they may be. We have made a mockery of the 1st Amendment. You can say anything you want (except religiously), print what you want, and protest all you want even to the point of treason, with no restraint and no punishment. Other than religious speech, about the only other unacceptable word that liberals quote that you can't erroneously say is "Fire" in a crowded theater. How petty!

On the other hand, religion that is addressed in the same amendment and listed first and given a free pass when emphatically stating that you cannot "prohibit the free exercise thereof", has been restricted by the courts and local authorities to the fullest degree possible. Only the fear of a major uproar by the people, who are by and large still religious, is preventing a total crack down on religion and their institutions today. The real feeling of the anti-religious expression crowd, and that includes the American Civil Liberties Union and the People for the American Way, is to keep religion in its proper place and away from the public square. I'm sure that if those two groups had their way, they would be the first to rise to support a major crackdown on religious expression. Certainly, the American Civil Liberties Union and the People for the American Way aren't the kind of organizations we want defending the Constitution and the First Amendment in the first place.

Not abridging the freedom of religion is directly inferred first and foremost as a guarantee of freedom before any of the other freedoms we have such as the freedom of speech, the press, or the right of the people to assemble. Yet it is religion that everyone is clamoring to prohibit. The same phrase of the First Amendment that guarantees that Congress shall not restrict religion under the "establishment clause" and the "free exercise clause" is the same phrase that is being used by everyone to restrict religious rights and freedoms. Do you see a misrepresentation, a double standard? Have the decisions of the courts run amuck? The courts have singled out religion as being separate from the state. Under that same amendment, what if the courts ruled on separation of free speech from the state, or the separation of the press from the state, to limit their activities in public areas? There would be a massive outcry from practically everyone.

The courts have attempted over the past 50 years to restrict public religious participation that has created a dearth of religious expression. After being in our schools for over 175 years, the Bible and prayer was shunned and cast out. This has opened the door for the evil of secularism to become more prevalent and run rampant throughout our society, which in turn impacts the world. The atheist and secularist in America knows that the best chance to remove every vestige of Christianity from public venues is through the liberal court system.

The Supreme Court did a grave injustice to the separation of church and state. Why did the Supreme Court interfere with religion in the first place and attempt to rule on the "establishment clause" and say nothing about the "free exercise clause?" The First Amendment goes out of it's way to mention religion specifically, that "Congress shall make no law respecting an establishment of religion, or prohibiting the free exercise thereof". That statement underscores the right of religion not to be interfered with by Congress and yet the Courts and local officials have done just that. The First Amendment guarantees that religion can be practiced anywhere. The Courts have perpetrated a grave injustice. They have helped ingrain it in the psyche of liberal thought and even in some conservative thought as well, that religion should not always be expressed in a public forum because of separation of church and state. A recent example was when a Nevada high school class valedictorian in June of 2006 had her microphone cut off because she expressed her faith in God while speaking. If you're talking about "rights" in America, what's wrong with a Christian talking about Jesus, a Jew saying they don't believe in Jesus, or a Muslim expressing his faith in Allah?

The faith of everyone was meant in the First Amendment to be protected by the law and not stymied or obliterated. The congress was never to interfere with religion. The courts were never to interfere and "prohibit the free exercise thereof" as they have time and time again. It is common that "The court today divides the religious clauses of the First Amendment into what it calls 'The Establishment Clause' and 'The Free Exercise Clause.' The current application of the 'separation of church and state' metaphor actually represents a relatively recent concept rather than the enforcement of a long-standing constitutional principle. Subsequent over-zealous applications by State and local officials...frequently lead to even greater religious restrictions than those handed down by the courts"(7). This standard became policy in the 1947 *Everson v. Board* of Education case.

The mind-boggling thing is that because of the First Amendment, many clergymen support the humanist's view of separation of church and state as it is interpreted today! They have been brainwashed by the cultural and intellectual elite that they sat under in the 1960's and 1970's, and that includes what they learned from the liberal seminary professors who taught them. They have fallen prey to the smoke-screen that hides the bigger picture of what God is attempting to do with this world. They have been duped into believing the lie that God must be kept separate from national and international affairs. Nothing could be further from the truth, and nothing will take us down the road to disaster and dissatisfaction with America's ideals faster than these evil cultural influences. I believe in separation of church and state in practice, but in principle the state must rely on God just as they did in the days of the Bible. First Amendment rights have become an anomaly for destructive behavior patterns. Our Constitution is in a state of behavior "meltdown."

BURN, BABY, BURN

The First Amendment has been cited for the right to burn the flag, which by the way, became a big issue in the 1960's. The liberal thinkers say that the American right to freedom includes the right to burn the very flag that represents that freedom. They say the flag is just a symbol and a man has a right to burn that symbol. The conservatives are painted by the liberals as sitting around as "good old boys" reminiscing about the "good old days" and that we don't want anyone to touch our sacred symbols.

Of course, it's only a symbol, but so are our national monuments and we wouldn't want them destroyed! Burning the flag is like burning your marriage license or marriage certificate in front of your spouse. What if you held it up in front of your spouse and said "Honey, it's only a symbol, only a piece of paper," and then burn it. For most couples, it would cut to the heart of their spouse because of what it stands for. You see, it's what it represents that matters. It represents fidelity and everything sacred in the marriage, so you hang on to that precious document, you frame it, hang it on a wall, or put it among your precious documents. Some would say, "well, it's only a piece of paper." Theoretically, it's always been about a "piece of paper!" The piece of paper meant having someone's blessing. In the days of the Bible it was the blessing of the Father. It evolved into the blessing of the family and then the local officials of the nation. It became the business of the state to then issue the "piece of paper." So you see it's always been about a "piece of paper, meaning someone would authorize and bless the marriage union." The "piece of paper" means something that is very important!

It's the same thing with the flag of the United States. Men have fought to see it wave. To them, respecting that piece of 3 by 5 cloth is like defending San Juan Hill, Midway, Iwo Jima, the Battle of the Bulge, Normandy, or revenging Bataan.

What flag burning amounts to be is an expression of an arrogant, angry, and hateful spirit by the perpetrators. They are expressing an "in your face" attitude that "no one is going to tell me that I can't burn the flag." Not that there is any practical or legal Constitutional purpose behind burning the flag, it's just that it becomes a challenge and they want the notoriety it gives them. Burning the flag becomes "their right" but represents that person as one who is egocentric.

I laugh when someone says during war, "you're fighting for my right to protest the war and burn the flag." In other words, "you're fighting for my freedom so I can protest the fact that I am not in agreement with you fighting for my freedom." Or they may mean, "I'm burning this flag because I don't agree with you fighting for

236

my freedom to burn this flag." Does that make any sense? It's an oxymoron, and according to the dictionary that means, "a rhetorical figure in which two incongruous or contradictory terms are combined." Adhering to that "right" to burn a flag is rank and file stupidity. The principle of fighting for freedom is constructive and has a purpose, even though death is involved. Burning the flag is destructive and has no purpose. I dare say that if it was left to the "flag burners", there would never be another "Remember the Alamo", "the Maine", "Pearl Harbor," nor would there be "Remember the World Trade Center."

What if an Arab who was a suspected terrorist but had done nothing that we knew of in the form of terrorism, and he burned an America Flag on American soil and an American decided to stand with him? Is that his right? And what would we do if we found out that flag-burner was connected with terrorism? What would we do to the American? Would we say that it is the American's right or the Arab's right to burn the flag anyway? What happens if even the display of the American flag is not allowed and becomes lost in a flurry of flag waving by immigrants from other countries that want to wave their native flag? Will the waving of our flag come under ill repute because of this brand of "political correctness"?

What would be next with those who stand behind the rights of those who burn flags? Shall we allow the burning of the Constitution of the United States in the public square as well? Why not! Let's burn the Constitution! How many of us would be appalled at that fiery display? Indeed it's a precious historical document but it's only a symbol and worthless unless we adhere to the laws it represents.

Just one other little note, while burning is the proper way to dispose of a flag, we have no record in American history of "attention hungry" flag burners in the latter half of the 18th Century when our country was founded. Flag burning was not an issue in the 19th Century in the expansion of our country, or the first half of the 20th Century when we fought in two world wars. Hmm, interesting! I say, cherish the flag!

GOD IS NOT IN THE CONSTITUTION?

Then you have those individuals who have wanted to remove the words "under God" from the pledge of allegiance and the printing of God's name on our currency. They have also fought to have prayer removed from the Presidential Inauguration of 2004. In television interviews, when they are told that the Declaration of Independence mentions the "Creator", they mimic what every other liberal says that "the Declaration may mention God but the Constitution does not". I say "the Constitution does mention God!" It says in Article VII of the Constitution of the United States, that it was finished "the seventeenth day of September in the year of our Lord, 1787". Did you hear that, "In the year of our Lord." Who else is the "Lord", but "God"? Isn't the Lord, the God of the Universe? The mention of God in that manner was more than a mere formality, or "pro forma." As small and as insignificant that it may be, the framers of the Constitution gave recognition to God. Their writing of the Constitution gave recognition to the legally understood AD Christian era that was based on the birth of Jesus Christ. They could have just said "September 17th, 1787, but they said "in the year of our Lord". Amen to that!

The Declaration of Independence and The Constitution are not two separate documents from two separate governments. They are two separate documents from the same government. It wasn't that they forgot to mention God, it was just that any further mention of Him other than acknowledging the date in connection with God in the Constitution was unnecessary. Their proclamation of God was found in the Declaration of Independence that preceded the Constitution. The Constitution has a Preamble, but the Declaration of Independence was the precedent and America's formal statement, and is the Constitution's introduction and mainstay of faith. "The Declaration of Independence...is structured upon a Judeo-Christian base in two fundamental ways. First, it professes faith in a 'Creator' who works in and governs the affairs of men in establishing absolute standards to which men are held accountable. Second, and even more fundamentally...there is the idea that man is a fallen creature and, hence, cannot be his own lawgiver and judge."(8). The Constitution was therefore an outgrowth of the Declaration of Independence to provide law to a fallen people, and the declaration they wrote was put forth in part, as the Constitution's statement of faith. Man may have penned the Constitution but God authored it.

During the writing of the Constitution, Jefferson was very upset that certain declarations were left out such as ensuring the freedom of religion. In letters to James Madison and George Washington, he expressed his objections. He advocated and pushed for amendments to the Constitution, which included the freedom of religion. I heard someone refer to Jefferson's statement that when it comes to one God or 20, "It neither picks my pocket nor breaks my leg." In other words, it is left up to the individual, and the gods of others did not affect him. That statement is in one of his queries that he wrote about religion. Some would have you believe that because he said that, religion wasn't important to Jefferson. In the same query however, he vigorously defended religious expression and very eloquently stood for its freedom. He wanted the separation of church and state to ensure that religion would not be stymied in any way, shape, or form.

It has been said that during the writing of the Constitution, Benjamin Franklin's proposal to open the meetings with prayer was rejected by a majority of the delegates. One thing for sure, there was much prayer during the founding of our country. The absence of mentioning God in the Constitution was an endorsement for freedom to worship as one pleased and to be sure that the government was not going to stand in its way. They didn't forget to include God because in just the previous decade of Revolutionary War, Jefferson writes that there was appointed a day of general fasting and prayer. His writings show that he supported the 1st day of June for "a day of fasting, humiliation and prayer, to implore heaven to avert from them the evils of civil war, to inspire us with firmness in support of our rights."(**9**)

Because of his thoughts about the Constitution, some people present Jefferson as a Deist. A Deist believes that God created the universe but assumes no control over life. The presentation of Jefferson as a Deist may be true, but his statement about prayer shows that he wasn't the hard-core Deist that many make him to be. It must be that his earlier Christian upbringing influenced him somewhat. The conclusion some make about his belief in Deism is unreasonable and absurd because some of his writings show that God could intervene in the affairs of men. Apparently, Deism which Jefferson and some of our founding fathers believed, lost influence in America to other religions. Those same founders were in favor of the right of those other religious expressions, even though they may have disagreed with them.

Deism lost its effectiveness in America due to their self-fulfilling prophecy that God assumes no control over life. Deism doesn't offer much when it comes to God influencing man, so no control is believed in or sought after. On the other hand, traditional Christianity, Judaism, Islam, and all other major religions believe that God does get involved in church, family, and yes, the nation. The past 200 years of religious influence in America has proved the very thing that Jefferson's Deist religion would support. Jefferson thought that reason should rule over religion. His reasoning supported the right of other religions and their influence in the daily life of man, even though he may not have believed in those religions. Deism says that God is a matter of reason, not experience. Traditional Christianity says that God is a matter of reason, and experience with God. The Deist that emphasizes the mind over the heart misses the full experience of God by 18 inches.

Today, America seems to be split in its thinking because we are in the downswing of a religious pendulum as a tremendous social shift in our nation's morale is taking place. America needs prayer! The evil of the other cultures of the world has come down upon the United States and we are being influenced by that evil.

CONSTITUTIONAL CRISIS

We have a Constitutional crisis on our hands. It is looming larger with each national election and with each Supreme Court appointment. It can be seen in the voting results of the 2000 and the 2004 election. Former President Jimmy Carter whose comment that George Bush was elected in the year 2000 by 5 judges in the 5-4 Supreme Court decision in Bush's favor, was an insult to the election process in which 100 million people voted that year for both candidates. His irresponsible remark shows the country's polarization.

The reason America is in a crisis is because the Constitution is based on religious moral laws. There have been a countless number of rejections of morality by the courts, and a refusal to adhere to a 10 Commandments basis of jurisprudence that was connected to the Constitution by its draftees. Therefore, the Constitution has lost its cohesiveness in maintaining governmental separation of powers. The separate powers have begun a process of political degeneration within the framework of the Constitution itself. At times, each of them have been against the opposing separate power, because the cries for morality still echo from the Constitution's pages and from America's constituents as these powers try to separate religious morality from its politics. The majority of the people have begun to realize the moral basis of the Constitution and its spiritual ties to moral absolutes.

The courts have stood in favor of abortion, homosexuality, transvestites, the transgender, the criminal, and against the police, death penalty, and the 10 Commandments. Because they have done that over and over again during the past 40 years, a crisis has begun to happen. Morality has been lost in the oblivion of poor choices and in a landslide of human failure.

What is happening to the Constitution of America would be like any corporation that may change its philosophical direction. Sometimes when the founders of a corporation are no longer in charge, new corporate officers change the philosophy of the original corporate ideals. Company policy may be re-interpreted and make the old and long established ideas of no effect. The standards of the company are lessened and the quality of their product is cheapened. The company loses its purpose and direction. The workers or investors try to enforce its basic principles but the philosophy has changed and there is deep division within the corporation.

In the same way, there is a power struggle that is going on between the Executive Branch, the Congressional Branch and the Courts, as the debate between life and death is being played out in the public's eye. There has been a lack of morality in our country and an acquiescence of our leaders to its lack. Their endorsement in favor of decisions of death instead of life through poor cultural choices, are tearing our Constitution apart because our Constitution

241

was framed with the morality of life in mind. Not that this is the first time that our political system has been polarized and that the balance of power has been in question. It is coming however, at a critical time when a lapse of civility is center stage at this juncture of our nation's 200 plus years of history.

These severe disagreements also lead to power struggles over other programs and policies as well. We have concocted a series of multifaceted laws in order to appease the "politically correct" syndrome in America. These laws are a conundrum and sometimes conflict and work against each other to the extent that they seem to cancel each other out and destroy the truth. It has become confusing and there doesn't seem to be a way out of the nightmare we are in.

Our modern technology has extended life but it has brought us into the arena where we have to make decisions like God as to who will live and who will die. Once you start being God, you have to start making decisions like God. It's at that point when cultures begin to fall apart because they have usually already begun to reject God's morality as America is doing so now. We try to act righteously, but without acknowledging God and His help, we are doomed to failure.

Isaiah 64:6 says, *"But we are all as an unclean thing, and all our righteousnesses are as filthy rags; and we all do fade as a leaf; and our iniquities, like the wind, have taken us away."*

CRAZY COURTS

In the recent past, the liberals in the Senate have filibustered and consistently blocked the nominations of conservative judges who would help to keep our country on a consistent conservative moral path. They claim that they have approved most of the nominees for judges, but the reality is they have blocked some of the most important and strategic ones. This is indicative of the cultural war that has been waged over the past 50 years. The conservatives threatened to use the "Nuclear Option" which is to shut down filibustering in order to get the nominees approved. It is an ominous sign of the future difficulties of judicial appointments. Consider how many liberal judges that Presidents have appointed in the past 50 years. Conservatives have had to live with those appointments, yet the liberals will do anything they can to prevent conservative judges from coming up for appointment.

Were the laws protecting our conservative heritage wrong for the first 175 years of our nation? President Dwight Eisenhower regretted his appointment of Earl Warren as Chief Justice because of his liberal view on issues. He thought that Warren would have been more conservative in his leadership and rulings but he proved to be just the opposite. Was Eisenhower wrong for feeling that way by wishing that Warren would have been more conservative? Eisenhower was fooled and of course other Presidents have been fooled also.

President George W. Bush has had the opportunity to appoint some conservative judges and to make a powerful impact on the direction of the Supreme Court. He can make some of the most critical changes in the direction of the court over the past 50 years due in part to the great return to conservatism in America. It won't happen however, without President Bush's appointees having to tip toe through a "mine field" of political haggling in front of a disheveled Senate judiciary committee.

The radical social agenda and the changes in our culture have not only been brought about by the elected officials of our nation but by the non-elected members of the Courts of our land. They have been forcing these changes on the American people for decades. The Courts have shown poor judicial self-restraint and have left their Constitutional mandate of interpreting the law, and have taken upon themselves the power to make the laws.

For the first 175 years of America, the Courts of our land, including the Supreme Court were conservative in their decisions when it came to personal morality. In the past 40-50 years the Supreme Court had become a more liberal court but has now swung back to a "middle of the road" centrist court. The liberal politicians don't want it to shift back to a conservative court. The liberals continue to call for Supreme Court justices without any litmus tests, and they don't want to have too many justices with one particular persuasion, neither conservative nor liberal. That's because they don't want the Supreme Court to swing back to the conservative way of thinking as it was in the beginning of America. They want to keep it as liberal as possible. Trying to keep the Supreme Court as a centrist court is the 2nd best option for the liberals. A liberal court is out of the question for now, because liberalism is not the mainstream of thought in America. Therefore they are fighting to keep it a centrist court.

The conservative country that we have been came from the religious framers of our Constitution who implored God for His help. If succeeding generations cast God off and do not acknowledge and maintain His help, then all hope is lost. We will continue on our path to physical, mental, emotional, and spiritual death. Even if our courts become more conservative, we are in a life and death struggle for the future of America.

In 1892 in the "Church of the Holy Trinity v. United States" decision, the Supreme Court ruled that many of our laws and our institutions reflect the teachings of Jesus Christ. They referred to the people of America as a historically religious people and that it is affirmed in many ways. Their conclusion was that these matters, and many other things "add a volume of unofficial declarations to the mass of organic utterances that this is a Christian nation." Can you imagine the Supreme Court today acknowledging the fact that America is a Christian nation? I think not!

We desperately need changes in our court system in the way of "tort" reform because liberal judges have freely protected the rights of criminals. They have sought to change the law over the years, protecting the rights of those criminals over the wrongs committed to their victims. They have thrown case after case out of court because of technicalities brought up by expert trial lawyers. In the past, so many have gotten off through the Miranda ruling in 1966 by the Supreme Court that says, "You have the right to remain silent and have an attorney present". While I agree with a degree of criminal rights, I have disagreed with how the judges in the past have set criminals free when police officers failed to arrest the criminals properly.

The police have been unable to perform their duties because the courts have tied their hands. Of course we have had rogue cops who have used excessive force, but many good cops have been frustrated in the performance of their duties. They have demonstrated that frustration by over zealousness in dealing with criminals during arrests. The criminal knows it so he pushes as many of the cop's emotional buttons as possible in order to get off the hook and get the cop in trouble. Some cops have been so fearful of wrongfully being accused of over zealousness that they have backed off during some times of crisis. Of course the cops are blamed for that response too for not carrying out their duty. The bottom line in troubled cities is that there is a dynamic of mutual distrust between the population and the police. There simply are not enough police officers with the support and respect they need for the responsibilities they have. Police have a tough job to perform.

> Romans 13:1-7 endorses their responsibility. It tells us that *"the powers that be are ordained of God"*.

> It tells us not to resist these powers because if you do you are resisting *"the ordinance of God. For rulers are not a terror to good works, but to the evil"*.

> Supporting their rule over us it says, *"He is the minister of God. But if you do that which is evil, be afraid for he bears not the sword in vain"*.

Consistently, judges prejudice most cases by not allowing the jurors to consider all the evidence that could be presented in a trial. They have been too free in throwing out confessions or other admissible evidence because of technicalities. They cite the idea that if the jury had all the evidence they may become prejudiced. Aren't the judges prejudicing the cases by withholding certain pieces of evidence from the jury and not allowing them to see or hear all the evidence? We are to be judged by a jury of our peers and not by the judge. All the evidence should be allowed in court except perhaps in cases that are nulled. With the proper instruction from the judge, we should trust the jurors to be mature enough to know what evidence to accept and what evidence to reject. They can be instructed on how not to be influenced or prejudiced in each case. Some people have been wrongly convicted because not all the evidence has been allowed in court. Sometimes it was found out later that with proper DNA findings, some who were supposed to be guilty, had to be set free. How sad for those innocent individuals!

The jurors are to prove a person's innocence based on the "letter of the law" and "beyond a reasonable doubt." Many times the letter of the law doesn't make sense because there is certain evidence that the jury is not allowed to consider. A juror may know if a person is guilty or innocent based on information that they are not allowed to consider. Yet they have to stick to the letter of the law and ignore that information. Jurors sometimes "cave in" or they are "intimidated" so they side with the majority. Too often after a trial is over jurors will step forward, realize their mistake, and change their mind, but it's too late. Either they didn't have all of the evidence or they were pressured into a rushed decision. Something is wrong with the judicial system!

The courts have turned our system of justice completely upside down. Sometimes were not sure if a person is guilty or innocent but they are forced to plea bargain and say they're guilty to a lesser charge, and serve less of a jail sentence. The way the courts are set up it is better if a person lies about what criminal act they may have committed. Some individuals have their lawyer lie with them and jump through all the judicial hoops in order to get them off with a lighter sentence. Then if the courts can prove a conspiracy, they try and get some of the individuals to plea bargain the case for a lighter sentence and pin the rap on someone else. This makes the prosecution of the case look good. They corner someone and dangle the carrot of an easy sentence in front of them to testify against someone else. Isn't that backwards? That's not how God deals with you. With God, you admit your error or you sin, ask for forgiveness and He gives it to you even though you may pay the consequences for your sin. There's no plea bargaining with God. You're either guilty or innocent.

Another big problem is criminals who commit crimes themselves and then turn states evidence, point their finger at someone else and then get off with a slap on the wrist. While that may work when dealing with career criminals testifying against each other, it's a shame when criminals get off easy when testifying against a first time offender. Still another problem is that the courts have been too technical in allowing the idea that a disturbed crime scene has no value in court.

We are paying a price for all of that as criminals now know they can easily get off with technicalities of all kinds. We have gone too far to protect the criminal. We are making it easier for the criminal to live and work in America, both those who already live here or have immigrated here. We are too prone to make sure their rights are protected.

LIFE AND DEATH

The struggle for who lives and who dies in our court system is seen in a recent example of the case of the man in Atlanta, GA. who shot a judge, a court recorder and two police officers in 2005. How did he get a gun? Of course by protecting his rights, he was brought into court without handcuffs so that the jury would be kept from prejudice by seeing him in those handcuffs and thinking he was guilty. He and many others like him are allowed to come into the courtroom unshackled. The consequences were paid when he grabbed an officer's gun and promptly killed the four. He also held a woman hostage in her home before he was finally captured. By the way, it was when the hostage reasoned with him about God, which was a religious act that centered itself on a judicial situation that convinced the criminal to surrender. Do we really want God out of the courtroom?

In Florida, also in 2005, a 5-year-old girl made a frantic call to 911 and said that her parents had been shot in bed. It was a reprisal killing because the mother and father had been a witness against a known criminal. The parents requested a restraining order to keep the person away from them but the judge refused to grant a court injunction because according to law there needed to be two past incidents reported against this individual. Technicality, technicality, technicality! Well, the parents paid with their lives and the five-year girl lost her parents all because a judge wanted to abide by the law and refused to show any mercy or understanding to the parents. The judge should lose his job.

There was also the case when a Minnesota judge released a man after he came before him for molesting little boys. Instead of keeping him locked up he allowed him to be released on low bail. He skipped bail and went to Idaho where he killed a mother, father, their 9-year-old son, and kidnapped and sexually abused their daughter for weeks. What a shame!

Then, in 2006 we had a couple of "out of this world" decisions by two judges. In Vermont, a man was sentenced to 60 days in jail for raping a girl for four years who was under the age of 10 years old. The judge felt that his sentence should be in rehabilitation and not in jail. After a public outcry, he then gave the man a paltry 3-10 years. In Nebraska, a man received probation after sexually assaulting a 12 year-old girl. The judge thought he would face to much violence in jail because he was short in height. That is how far our court system has fallen. It's outrageous! Similar slaps on the wrist have occurred for child molesters in a number of other states as well.

Whether or not to keep seriously ill people connected to feeding tubes is a big development of life and death issues that sometimes involves our court system and seems to capture the news headlines. The courts have ordered feeding tubes removed from a number of people in the past as doctors have determined that the ill individual was believed to be brain dead. However, "for many Christians, the withdrawal of nutrition and hydration is never appropriate under any circumstances, since it is a natural means of preserving life, not a medical act."(**10**). Many times the situation involving parents, spouses, and the seriously ill person's life itself are only pawns in something that is far deeper than that person's right to live or die.

The Terri Schiavo case in Florida involved the Governor who wanted to hold on to any hope of life and would have pitted him against the legality of the Court system who ordered her feeding tube removed. Those wanting the feeding tube removed told the others who wanted to keep it in, not to politicize the case, but the problem is that politics and the morality of life and death are insepa-rably linked together. These types of struggles are part of the battle over the cultural issues that are tearing at the heart of America.

Years ago a doctor from Detroit whose cases involved assisted suicide was indicative of the mindset that is trying to lead our society in the direction of death. Why is it that liberal thinking stood for that doctor and stands for death and immorality and conservative thinking stands for life and morality? Why? It certainly doesn't necessarily mean that liberals are more immoral than conservatives are or that they are not religious. It's just that liberal thinkers in principle will stand for the First Amendment rights of those who are immoral even if it means allowing their freedoms to go unchecked. It's a bad concept and one that will not bode well for America.

There are the preponderance of decisions that fall on the side of evil and wrong and against life and the understanding of common sense. The moral decisions that the courts have made for over 150 years were based on ideals that came from Christianity. If the courts have discarded Christianity, then they had better find and use some other religious morality because secular morality won't work. The courts have stood on the side of the criminal again and again all in the name of freedom as we have seen an overall rise in hostage situations, school shootings, murder, rape, robbery, and gangs.

We have gone to any extreme to protect criminal rights. We have tied ourselves up with so many technical laws such as pleas for insanity that we can no longer practice common sense in the courtroom. If we wait too long to bring criminals to justice because of technicalities, we risk the fact that crime will get worse and will create havoc in our society, with little deterrence of crime. Read this Bible passage that mentions that the more we put off the swift punishment of the criminal the more evil will be prevalent in our society.

Ecclesiastes 8:11 says, *"Because the sentence against an evil work is not executed speedily, therefore the heart of the sons of men is fully set in them to do evil."*

Connected with all of that is the problem of all the frivolous lawsuits involving insignificant infractions that the court system is allowing and using up the time needed to pursue serious crimes. That's why we have to have so many plea bargains, because of all the time wasted on unnecessary lawsuits that courts should never allow to even be considered. Trials and investigations that put a

250

premium on various mitigating circumstances have left our court system inept. To be sure, there are legitimate times for a lawsuit but unfortunately, we have become a litigious society.

The trauma of "Eminent Domain" is yet to rear it's ugly head. With a recent Supreme Court ruling, the government, whether it is state or federal, can decide if your property does or does not fit in with their plans. They can rule to take your property from you and award it to someone that will fit in with their community plan or increase their tax base. Those organizations that are particularly at risk are those with tax exempt status. Churches are ones that may run the highest risk. This may be more of the erosion of America and the onslaught of evil against anything that is Christian by nature. Can you picture the American Civil Liberties Union jumping on this one as it develops over the years?

With the way the Supreme Court judges have become activists for liberalism and "politically correct" thought, and have now made laws instead of interpreting laws, we shudder because they are all serving their court terms for life. The legislature should decide the law and the courts should simply uphold the law. Instead of possessing a good sense of judicial acumen, they have plagued the Supreme Court with 50 years of judicial activism that has politicized the entire court system. They have reversed many decisions that the Congress, President, and the people have voted on. We have given the caretaker assignment of the Constitution to an activist Supreme Court. The scary thing is that they are the final interpreters of the law. "It's like letting the fox guard the hen house". Thankfully, conservatism in the courts can and will return.

The question may be asked, "Where would the civil rights movement be without the activist judges that served a few decades ago?" Activist judges propelled the civil rights movement, and rightly so! However, they were activist judges for life and the living rights of African-Americans and they reversed terrible laws of the past in regards to race. There have been activist judges for women's rights, the right to vote, the worker, and the poor, which are all living issues and well justified. Judges today are activists for death, abortion, the criminal, the pornographer, and have let drunk drivers free to kill others. They won't rule against immoral sexual activity and perversion that help lead any nation to disaster. Issues have become so complicated that the courts have been unable to separate the living rights for Americans from the rights that involve death and immorality. Judges are also activists for the rights of liberal women who themselves have become the greatest advocates for the death of the unborn.

Judges have ignored hundreds of years of customs of early American morality. They side with European Jurisprudence and their custom and laws. Under the Latin definition of "Stare Decisis" the judges cite, adhere to, and are bound by United States case precedence, and can ignore United States Constitutional law. That also means that they have bound themselves to the liberal precedence of the past 40-50 years. We are forced to agree with all of that liberal precedence and if we don't, we are labeled as "not supporting the Constitution." When the laws changed from a conservative base 50 years ago, wasn't that "not supporting the Constitution?" Of course precedence must take effect in some cases because the Constitution doesn't cover every aspect of detailed law but in recent years the liberal courts have made sure that liberalism survives.

The courts are in favor of absolute reform for America with the idea of changing society no matter if those changes are good or evil. I hate to be a prophet of doom but an unraveling of our great democracy will echo out of the failures of the European powers of the past as America's judges seek to connect our court system to the bleakness of Europe's slide into a jurisprudence of oblivion. As Europe reawakens and rises in prestige and power that prepares for the advent of the Antichrist, America will begin to follow the pattern of Europe's past decline to become a second class power. Just as there has been the rise and fall of world powers in Europe and around the world, the same fate awaits America as her failure leads to a collapse of morality into an abyss of depravity.

Judges and other political officials who say that religion does not play a part in their decisions are either not being honest with themselves, don't understand their inner morality and how it relates to God, are misguided, or are simply not telling the truth. They say they can keep their liberal or conservative faith and morality separate from their decisions. They say it hasn't or doesn't influence them. Good luck! Who are they trying to kid?

One final thought about our courts. Cameras in the courtroom make the courts a vehicle of entertainment. There is something unsound about being entertained with other people's problems, struggles, and difficulties. The prejudice in the minds of those television observers can be seen as they watch courtroom scenes on television. The viewer is not there so it is difficult to grasp all the pertinent facts and to sense the drama of the trial in person. Cameras are fine in other areas such as security, protection, and honesty in business, but in the courtroom it creates a bias and undue influence on the judge and the attorneys. In my mind this is a big factor in determining that the courtroom is no place for television.

LIBERAL MEDIA

Although they continue to deny their liberalism, that's exactly what the media is, liberal! Thankfully, conservatism in the media has been on the rise in recent years as more conservative points of view are being expressed! With the introduction of conservatism in the media, it has forced the liberal left to move more to the center. As we have seen in the past, the liberal media has been for the rights and freedoms of individuals and opposed to the stringent guidelines needed to keep extreme immoral individualism at bay.

The reason that conservative thinking fares better than liberal thought is because it makes more sense to stand for the morals that were key to the birth of America and that we all remember from the time when we were young. These are the morals that are based on the history of our country rather than on the morals that the liberals are espousing. Most people want to aspire to live morally right. Basically people don't like abortions but they have been convinced by pro-choice rhetoric. They may be disgusted with homosexual relationships but recoil from saying anything because of those who play the "intolerant," homophobic blame game. Many people feel that although liberals may live a good moral life, many times they stand for life-styles that are offensive and morally degrading, all in the name of freedom. It is time for the liberal thinkers of our society to realize that "trying to defend liberal thinking that flies in the face of God is indefensible."

Liberals blame the religious right for all that they feel is wrong in America. Wrong! They had better realize and realize it soon that America is trying to swing back to its conservative roots, and the conservative press is having a lot to do with it. There is a conservative press that is now out there once again. They are not going to let liberal Senators get away with their kind of verbiage anymore as they speak out on many of the liberal topics and issues. They are not going to let other liberal Senators get away with words that stand for the rights of the immorally depraved. The criticism against that liberal thinking and other liberal thought is not only coming from the religious right but from the ranks of the conservative press. It is piercing the liberal heart of America. No matter if Democrats or Republicans win upcoming elections or who may be in control of the government. The need to swing back to a conservative point of view in personal behavior is essential to the life of America if we are to survive as a nation.

As mentioned in a previous chapter, the philosophy of liberalism is not to sacrifice freedom for security even for those who are fighting against the United States. A case in point would be the Iraqi prisoners at Guantanamo Bay in Cuba in which the liberal press has constantly tried to remind the public of any abuses. The Geneva Convention rules will eventually be applied, as something will have to be done with that situation.

One Senator had compared the treatment of the detainees at Guantanamo Bay to the torture done by Nazis, the Soviet gulags, or by the Cambodian Pol Pot who was a mass murderer. With blame going to the President and with some calling the Bush Administration an Imperial Presidency, there is no way that Hitler and Stalin can be compared to the leadership of any American President. There is no way that the Constitution can be suspended, as some are purporting that the President can do, without an outcry from the heart and soul of our republic. The moment that would happen, we would see a similar justice as in Watergate, or America would first split apart along cultural and religious lines. These comparisons are political scare tactics that have no value.

Then there is the prison abuse scandal at Abu Ghraib that rocked the military when prisoners were mocked by being paraded nude in front of the guards. Those who committed these crimes were punished and well they should have been. Some of the press wanted to show as many disturbing photos as possible in order to try and influence the war's outcome and blame the war on our leadership, just as they did during the Vietnam War.

Given the fact that there are so many extreme terrorist groups, all that abuse and the excessive reporting of it did nothing but inflame the terrorists. America has used interrogation in the past but is not supportive of physical and inhumane torture period. America has had to endure the insinuated and exaggerated accusation in the press that it has a torture policy.

Other examples of innocent Iraqi civilians being murdered by American soldiers have been uncovered and may lead to murder charges. As bad as these were, they were being touted and compared as evil by the media in an attempt to show how despicable our soldiers and leaders are in this Iraqi war because they disagreed with it. In my opinion, the capture, torture, treacheries, mutilations, and eventual decapitations committed on Coalition forces, and individuals prisoners is just as evil, if not worse. Civilians who are maimed and killed by suicide or homicidal bombers, all in the name of Allah by Al Qaeda and other terrorist groups is religious tyranny. What does the liberal media say about that?

The liberal media and the media in general need to double-check their own standards. We have seen the inept and irresponsible reporting of Dan Rather when in a news broadcast he told of some false information about President George W. Bush's military record. Mr. Rather apologized and resigned, but he stood by his story in what has been called "memo-gate."

Then in May of 2005, Newsweek falsely reported that some of our military flushed the Koran down a commode, which infuriated the Islamic World. This faulty reporting on the part of Newsweek led to riots that broke out across many of the Muslim nations, causing numerous deaths. Newsweek apologized because they could not substantiate the report, they then stood by their story and later retracted it. Their outsource was anonymous tips that failed good and honest journalistic guidelines. Sometimes Americans don't understand how Muslims feel when their religion is defaced. The American media is quick to protect Islamic sentiments with an apology and rightly so, but they should do the same with Christianity.

Some Americans, the liberal bias, and the media won't give the same courtesy to the conservative right when their beliefs are trampled on! Do the liberal media view the reporting of abuses to the holiness and sacredness of faith in the Bible the same way they report the abuses of the Koran? In the past we haven't even been able to take our Holy Book, the Bible into many of the Federal and State institutions in America, such as our schools, without being scorned for it by the Courts and by over-zealous state and local officials. The Courts have sub-consciously influenced the state and local officials over the past 40 years with their rulings.

The Bible is falling into disrespect and ill repute among Americans because it's authority has been targeted for dismantling and challenged by our Judges for decades. I see hypocrisy and a double standard in the media with the honored stand they take for the Koran and the poor stand they take for the Bible. This liberal influence and thinking has convinced some hotels and motels to remove the Gideon Bibles from their premises. It's possible that someone complained and now they may be afraid of being taken to court. Today thankfully, some States are allowing schools to use the Bible with their curriculum as a historical book to be studied. Continue to pray for the reversal of decades of illegal law imposed on Christianity.

Though Thomas Jefferson freely endorsed the freedom of the Press, in his Second Inaugural Address he voiced strong disdain over its abuses. He said, "During this course of administration, and in order to disturb it, the artillery of the press has been leveled against us, charged with whatsoever its licentiousness could devise or dare. These abuses of an institution so important to freedom and science are deeply to be regretted, inasmuch as they tend to lessen its usefulness, and to sap its safety. They might, indeed, have been corrected by the wholesome punishments reserved and provided by the laws of the several States against falsehood and defamation; but public duties more urgent press on the time of public servants. The offenders have therefore been left to find their punishment in the public indignation."(**11**)

Thomas Jefferson was upset with the abuses of the press leveled at his administration, referring to it as "artillery." According to him, those defamatory publications would have boundaries under state law but he wasn't sure that public officials would have the time to reform such abuses.

CENSORSHIP IS NOT A BAD WORD

Jefferson was leaving it all up to the court of public opinion, and today the court of public opinion has registered its disgust and disdain. The court of public opinion has a question to ask the press. "When will the media withhold certain information that is morally detrimental to the public and admit their ignorance, bias, and confusion on many of their facts?" When will they work to censor themselves? When will they face the fact that their rush to be the first to report a story when they do not verify whether it is right or wrong, can cause much harm, grief, and embarrassment?

The runaway reporting done by the press was seen in the unfortunate mine disaster in West Virginia in January of 2006 in which 12 miners were killed. The information that came from the mine officials was wrong when they first reported that all 12 miners were alive when in reality only one had survived. The press registered disgust with the mine officials and repeated calls came from them for an explanation and an apology. The press never held themselves up to the same kind of examination for their part in the rumor mill that left the families devastated.

There is much general information given that is consumed for the public good but with the freedom of the press should come responsibility on their part to censor themselves. It is better to show restraint when reporting a story, to make sure it is accurate and, and to make sure their reporting of moral issues does not create undue influence of society on their part. It is better for some things to be left unreported.

When will they censor themselves if a story is harmful to the public's moral standing? The moral stability they overlook, the problems they face, and their unwillingness to make any lasting corrections all show their utter mismanagement of their media empires. We no longer live in a democracy but we live in a media-ocracy, where media is king!

I know that today, censorship is a hush-hush word. No one wants to talk about it. But what ever happened to the restrictions that the press and public figures placed on themselves and continued to prac-tice up until just a few decades ago? What ever happened to the check on morality freely done by the press? Self-censorship shows restraint, discipline, dignity, fairness, and concern for the human beings involved with, or affected by the reporting. Self-censorship was a badge of honor. Everyone practiced it. It sets moral bound-aries. They withheld stories, pictures, or certain words that were unsuitable for public consumption. An example of the lack of self-censorship is the unflattering portrayal of the Prophet Mohammed in the Danish press in 2006. They did not care about the sensitivity of portraying the sacredness of religion disgracefully. With no apology from the Danish press, it led to much unrest in the world.

After the hurricane that devastated the city of New Orleans in 2005, I was watching a news program on one of the television stations in Boston while I was on Cape Cod, Massachusetts. It defended it's right to show dead bodies floating or laying around in that city. It was stated that in order to properly portray the disaster they needed to show those dead bodies. Why? Did other viewers or I need to be convinced of the devastation in that city? Are they a station that is gripped by a gruesome and gory desire to show dead bodies? Did they have a political agenda in mind that wanted to expose respon-sibility of the aftermath of the hurricane? I wonder! If the media disagrees with a particular point of view on the part of our political leaders, self-censorship is not in their vocabulary.

The producers of television shows today say just turn the dial. They accept no responsibility. Their rating system has gone nowhere and is simply a "laugh." They have conveniently forgotten that we live in a society with "latch key" kids, single parent homes, and some irresponsible parents. It is very difficult to watch your children 24 hours a day and restrain them from viewing certain programs when the parents are at work. It is also difficult when they may be in someone else's home. With the additional problem of Hollywood movies, Broadway theaters, and the Internet, the problems only escalate. One only has to see the easy prey our children are to predators on the Internet to conclude that it is time for the producers to rise up and accept some responsibility. Censorship is not a weakness in society, but strength. It shows respect, courtesy, and a vision of wholesome influence.

Another example is when the press withheld pictures of a disabled President Franklin Roosevelt because he wanted to present a picture of strength to the American people and not weakness. Today it isn't necessary to avoid showing a person's physically impaired condition, but that was censorship back then, right? Were the leaders of a free America in the first 200 years of our country wrong about censorship because they voluntary practiced it?

Today we are inundated with the rights of any movie producer and director to show anything on television or on the big screen, no matter how violent, immoral, and sexually degrading that it is. After all, the courts say it's their First Amendment right. A strong stance against censorship is exactly what is leading our country down that slippery slope into the morass of oblivion.

I'm sure the press would love to see a Federal Shield law enacted to protect the media from being forced to reveal it's sources of information. When it comes to the security of our nation, some in the liberal media make political distinctions among themselves and will reveal security secrets particularly if they disagree with any presiding administration. The press thinks nothing of disclosing vital, secret and sensitive information even if the government requests that they withhold such information for national security purposes. The government in June of 2006 requested the New York Times and other newspapers to withhold such information but they printed the story anyway. These news outlets that demand First Amendment rights to hide their secret sources won't afford the same right to the government to withhold their secrets. They openly inform the public under the guise of "their duty and responsibility." They will not censor themselves like the demands of censorship they make on religion either. They would want to have similar protection that some states allow priests, ministers, and attorneys. If that happens, it could only get worse.

When the media is onto a story, they have an incredibly insatiable appetite to find answers or report a story with little or no restraint. Like a hungry pack of wolves, hyenas, or a pride of lions and circling vultures, they are never satisfied until they get the answers they want. Their aggressiveness for sensationalism reflects a runaway fever-paced press that constantly pushes for snapshot images and a rush to be the first with a big scoop. We are in the age of information, but the media is just like Adam and Eve who ate of the tree of knowledge of good and evil, too much information cost them their rights and freedoms. The media is playing that game without a moral base. They are abusing their rights and it will cost them, but they don't see it that way. Pity!

HOLLYWOOD HYPE

Our children are targeted and influenced by Hollywood, liberal lifestyle changes, pornographers, pedophiles, and prostitution. The fight has ensued on the turf of school, television, radio, newspaper, and magazines. We have seen an onslaught of mayhem, murder, licentiousness, violence, and sexual escapades from Hollywood. The violence that they produce on screen has led to an aggression on the streets and is irreversible in today's culture. We have watched with disdain at the overwhelming outpouring of graphic displays of sex, pornography, sexually suggestive commercials, advertisements, homosexuality, alarming music videos, gangster rap, violent video games, situational ethics, and sexual gutter-like sitcoms on television, in the movies, on videos, and now on the Internet. Ouch! A total overall immoral behavior is the seedbed that helps germinate a hunger for child pornography and a passion for a sex-trade industry for children.

It has gotten so bad that the some of the very ones who have perpetrated this lifestyle on America have openly admitted that they wouldn't let their own children see or hear some of the very things that they themselves have produced. How shameful! Many movie stars are treating their children conservatively and won't allow them to watch bad programming on television or see morally question-able movies. They view much of what is in entertainment as trash and poison.

It must be their background and the influence of Christianity in America that has come into play in their decisions. Good for them and they have to be admired for that. However, they decide this while marketing multiple millions of dollars worth of their own immoral and violent works of art. They do it all in the name of freedom of expression. It's too bad that they won't exercise the same courtesy to the millions of other children and youth as they have toward their own, by not exploiting them with their trashy work. What gives them the right to draw the line where they say it should be drawn, when they have been upset with others for drawing a line and saying that their work is too raunchy. That's the inconsistency of artistry in which the artist says it is innocent enough to be displayed for the public to consume, but too evil for their own children to see. It's an ugly world, a sheer catastrophe!

Hollywood has bombarded us with programs that used to be censored. They take pleasure in glorifying the promotion of trans-vestites, transsexuals, cheating wives, or homosexual lifestyles. The film industry is the biggest promoters of homosexuality and other related deviant lifestyles. We are being served a continual delivery of Hollywood trashy terrorism that is fast turning us into a culture of terrorists. We don't have to turn to the Middle East to be overwhelmed by terrorism because it is taking place right in the living rooms and bedrooms of our homes through television and the Internet. We wonder why we have child kidnappings, pedophiles, murderers, violence, and rebellion when practically every kind of perversion is easily displayed and reached for by anyone. The Bible gives us a warning as to what we should look at.

Psalm 101:3 says, *"I will set nothing wicked before my eyes."*

Not looking at something evil is pretty difficult to do in our society so we can't be prevented totally from seeing things that are not wholesome to look at. What the above scripture means is that I will not "lay hold of or set my mind" to any evil with my eyes. In other words I will not become fixated with any evil or wicked thing that I see and let it become a part of my life and involved in my life-style. It's there, and I've seen it but I can make a conscious decision to remove it from my viewing habits. Our eye-gate and our other senses are the vehicle to our mind where like a computer, things are recorded and stored. Some day we all must answer to God for what we may think, act, and do, including those who promote such life-styles, when the books are opened at the Day of Judgment.

Hollywood and the public media of television and radio who refuse to place any restrictions on themselves and cry out when the Federal Communications Commission and conservative America want to restrict them say that they are only portraying what society is already doing. They say it is "art imitating life." Of course they refuse to accept any responsibility that "life can imitate art". They say that they have nothing to do with influencing society. As long as they can sell their wares and earn their profits, they just don't care. Yet we know that commercials, sit-coms, news programs, politicians, theologians, teachers, and others, influence people through the media and in just about every other way as well. We have teaching videos that we use in school and at home in order to influence our children. We bring in educators to our classrooms and assemblies to create influence in the public school. Shouldn't we accept responsibility for what we show them?

How does Hollywood think that they are not creating any influence when they show something that is violent and sensual, and accept no responsibility for it. Yet they will accept praise for their influence they have on the public when they show something that is wholesome? How can they then accept awards such as the Oscars when they feel they are not creating any kind of influence? They do create influence, both good and bad. However, just like Pontius Pilate in the Bible, the media rushes to wash their hands of any guilt found in their productions. But America knows and God knows that Hollywood and the media will be held responsible. Hollywood is out of touch with mainstream America. It's like they are a culture all their own as they help bring evil down upon America.

There is no stigma for many of the lifestyles that used to be considered wrong, such as adultery and divorce. Many times a couple is being portrayed as divorced but yet living near each other and still talking for the sake of the children. There is nothing wrong with getting along no matter what the situation is for the sake of children. Divorce however, is treated as such a common thing to be accepted, and to not say anything bad about, and not to ruffle any feathers. Very few in Hollywood try to teach or say that it is better not to commit adultery and it is better not to be divorced. Many Hollywood couples marry with the idea that if the marriage doesn't work out divorce for the usual "irreconcilable differences" is an option. They do this rather than trying to keep the marriage intact.

We have lost the home life in many of our families, as both parents are interested in their careers and the money they need to earn. Many of those same families end up being fractured by divorce. Then we want to pass laws to elevate and legitimize homosexual relationships to the status of marriage. Marriage is no longer sacred and its standards are lowered because of couples who are simply "living together. It's a no win situation in the battle over the decay in our culture. America will pay a price and much of Hollywood is leading the way in promoting these lifestyles.

There is a depravity that is coming from Hollywood, and with their depravity is coming a sense of spirituality, but their spirituality is not the proven, traditional sense of religion. They are being led down the path of false religions similar to the idolatry revealed as "ungodly" in the Bible. Madonna has relied on Kaballah, Buddhism influences Richard Gere, and Tom Cruise has turned to Scientology. They are leading the way into strange religious ideas through their notoriety and those who follow them will spin out of control with them spiritually. They are involved with the mysticism of healing, the occult, reincarnation, spiritualism, divination, and channeling with spirit guides. Hollywood is constantly trying to re-invent itself, never satisfied, and never quite acknowledging the true Creator God.

Anyone involved with such spirituality assumes a power that God did not give. They offer things that are beyond the natural and peer into the future that God did not allow, and they delve into the spirit world that God has not authorized. Their entrance into the spirit world by talking with spirits is what God wants to reserve for the end of their life when their spirit meets God. By their intrusion, they are looking into the spirit world that they normally would not understand and then get it confused by misrepresenting God's Spirit and God's intent. King Saul did a similar thing when he visited the witch of Endor in order to speak to the deceased Prophet Samuel in First Samuel chapter 28.

We all know the popularity of those who attempt to make contact with those who have already passed into the spirit world through death. As far as contact with the dead is concerned, God simply asks two questions. Those questions are found in the book of Isaiah.

Isaiah 8:19 says, *"When men tell you to consult mediums and spiritists, who whisper and mutter, should not a people inquire of their God? Why consult the dead on behalf of the living?"*

America is a country that has really lost the concept of "one nation under God." Instead we are one nation under many "gods." We have seen an abundance of religions infused into our society that are Eastern and foreign by nature. Those religions combined with the rebellious attitudes of atheism of the 1960's have caused a confusion of purpose and direction in a country that was once founded on a good moral understanding and teaching of a righteous God.

The reason that much of Hollywood is liberal and on the "left" is partly a reaction to the conservative era of "McCarthyism" during the 1950's when much of Hollywood was under suspicion of communism. "Black lists" were created and many actors vocations were in jeopardy. Hollywood's response was to become a very intolerant and exclusive group. They had their own political, social, and religious agenda. As evil as "McCarthyism" is portrayed, it was the "dark side" of the cold war and a minor blip as part of a major force that eventually shook Communism to the core. It became a two-edged sword by which McCarthyism was deemed deplorable, and Communism was vilified in the psyche of America. It was the sting of McCarthyism that forced movie actor Ronald Reagan to walk through its path and form his own resolve that eventually confronted Communism during his Presidency and help in its dismantling. Once again, the ugliness of man played into the hands of the program and plan of God. The bedrock of atheistic Communism will be tossed onto the ash heap of history at the Battle of Armageddon.

After McCarthyism it was not fashionable to be Republican or conservative, with a few exceptions of course like Ronald Reagan who changed from being a Democrat to a Republican. The pendulum then took a drastic swing during the 1960's. During that time, the rights of every individual were guaranteed regardless of how corrupt their right may be. America's leaders handed our country over to anyone who wanted to teach anything contrary to our history, or to be involved with showing and displaying any despicable act of pornography on television, in the theater or Hollywood. That older generation of actors from that time who became a part of the 60's and 70's was an anomaly that promoted permissiveness, tearing our nation apart.

Thankfully there is a conservative move in Hollywood today. Writers, actors, producers, and directors that are conservative Christians are making their mark. Conservatives like Mel Gibson are bringing a note of hope to the Hollywood industry, particularly after 9-11. Many of the up and coming young of Hollywood who are under 35 years of age are Christians and very conservative. They stand for God in society and are against abortion and homosexual marriage.

Many of them have left the old "Hollywood lifestyle" that stood for the drug addicted, womanizing, self-centered, counter-cultured, and easy living, egocentric individual. Young conservatives have abandoned the Hollywood leftist type actors who wanted to be the mainstream for socialism in America's future who were anti-life, anti-war, and "politically correct." Has liberal Hollywood missed the relevancy of Godliness in the past and is there hope with this new conservative movement?

MUSIC MEGALOMANIA

The music industry has pumped racy videos and music into the minds of an "out of control" generation of today. They are using every means possible through radio, television, and the Internet. The upbeat music of rock, hip-hop, rap, and gangster rap, and the portrayal of explicit video sexual escapades, control and influence the fertile emotions of our nation's teenagers.

Their songs have created a negative, devastating out of balance cultural view that is not in line with the morals of previous generations. An example is the seemingly innocent 1960's Beatles song "Imagine," that helps us to imagine what this world would be like with no heaven, no hell, no religion, and living for today. There may be good lines within that song but John Lennon who wrote it, was trying to create an imaginary world of the 'here and now'. It shows us what that generation and succeeding generations of music moguls have been thinking about and how they have influenced the minds of our youth. It is a view of a world without God.

Out of a decent time at the conclusion of World War II came the improbable; a group of culturally appointed musical gurus that created the rise of a generation of musical sensationalism. They have glorified the use of drugs that has altered the minds and behavior of our youth and young adults. With the haven of drug running now through the border with Mexico, these drugs are grown on farms and injected in the arms of the youth of our society. Their minds have already been jaded by the music they have heard most of their adolescent years. Many adults who are still haunted by drugs and alcohol that they have been addicted to since they were teenagers have affected the genetics and behavior that they pass to their children.

We are beginning to see more than just the tip of the iceberg when it comes to how far their music has taken our culture. We are seeing the effects of how our young people are being led astray be heavy metal and hard core rap music and a demonized hip-hop music which is centered around the Zulu culture of Africa. With the promise of immortality, some of our youth have become fascinated with cults, vampirism, and ritualistic murder. Some of those who have sung Rap music have died and it's their music that has contributed to their death. They have glorified sex, drugs, violence, and guns all in the name of "art" or "role-playing." Some of them have been arrested for brandishing guns during various confrontations. Their songs have been about killing innocent people. Some have died at the abuse of the very things they sing about. If they haven't died of some sexually transmitted disease, they have died of a drug overdose or at the hands of someone else with a gun.

White Corporate Executives who run that type of music industry glorify the use of drugs and show women being demeaned. With each succeeding generation comes the tearing of the fabric of our society. Our sins are being revealed through our young people who have been influenced by a "culture of corruption."

HOMOSEXUALITY IS NOT GAY

Some feminists who where burning their bras are now having second thoughts about where the feminists movement is going psychologically. With women in the military, and as CEO's, they are finding that there is a definite distinction between men and women. No longer can they accept what Gloria Steinem has stood for, in which she has inferred that there isn't any difference between the sexes. I assume she meant psychologically and emotionally. Gender distinction is becoming more important than ever before but many times our lifestyles easily influence transgender confusion.

One unfortunate thing about gender distinction or the perceived lack thereof, is that the word "gay" is used for the homosexual lifestyle and defines homosexuality. It is unfortunate that the homosexual community has robbed the English language of a beautiful word that means "cheerfulness, lighthearted excitement, merry, bright and lively especially in color, and given over to social pleasures." They have used it to promote their lifestyle in order to be more accepted. Homosexuality is anything but gay!

Many who are caught up in that life style end up wanting to be free from it. Some of them give testimony to the delivering power of Christ to set them free, just as others testify about being delivered from adultery and pornography. There have been some studies that have discovered a nearly 80% success rate of homosexuals changing their sexual orientation to heterosexuality.

With the nation of Canada becoming the third country to pass a bill granting same sex marriage, we will begin to see many more countries doing the same as a further breakdown of morals in the western world occurs. Canada joins the Netherlands and Belgium in now making it federal law. You will notice that it will be many of the States in America and the Western world countries that will follow suit and not any of the Asian countries. There may be some exceptions perhaps due to the fact that they have been infected by our western culture. All of this will have a grave impact on the world as morals begin to worsen and decline.

During the primaries of the 2004 election, Congressman Richard Gephardt spoke on the campaign trail at a gathering that was very much pro-homosexual. He was running for President. While he was speaking, he mentioned that his daughter had left her marriage relationship with her husband for a lesbian relationship. He went on to say that he admired his daughter's courage for taking that step. He said nothing about the relationship she had with her husband and nothing about how wrong it was for her to have broken her covenant vows with him. He was just keeping in fashion with being "politically correct" as long as he could appease the homosexual community and get the votes needed for his election. That was the biggest thing that mattered to him. How two-faced!

I've heard various clergy say that homosexuality is not mentioned in the Bible or that it means something else. They've also said that the punishment of Sodom and Gomorrah was not about homosexuality, but about the violence of the homosexual men that was done to the men who were with Lot. As you read the text in Genesis 19 you discover that the violence that these clergy were concerned about was never carried out because the homosexual men were smitten with blindness before any violence could occur. So what violence was there? Did God destroy a whole city because of intended violence or did He destroy it because their sin of homosexuality had messed up the community and that it was an abomination before God? If violence was the sin, why did Lot offer his two daughters to the men for sex, who were virgins? Wasn't he concerned about the violence that would be done to them? If the concern was violence, his daughters could have been killed. He would rather, give his daughters up for adultery, and that of course was horrible itself. To me it was clear that Lot wasn't concerned as much that any physical harm was going to be done to any of them. He just would not allow these men who were more than likely angels appearing as men, to be abused in the unacceptable and despicable act of homosexuality. A similar incident happened in Judges 19:22.

Another thing, when you carefully read the text, you will see that no homosexual act had been committed either. So why did God destroy the city? Was it for intended violence or intended homo- sexuality? You have to go back to the 4,000-year historical under- standing of the term sodomy and not change it to appease the sins of our modern society, its sexual preferences, and "political correct- ness." Sodomy meant, and has always meant abnormal and unnat- ural sexual behavior and it has never meant violence.

I agree that violence is wrong within any sexual behavior but the men of Sodom had one sin and one sin only that God was going to judge that city for, and that was the homosexual perversion that the men were already practicing. The historical understanding of the text clearly means that the homosexual men wanted to have sex with Lot's friends. They knew that Lot's friends had come to judge them not realizing that they were angels sent from God. They were mad and wanted to inflict their brand of sexual influential harm on them and on Lot as well. That of course is the violence the clergy may be talking about, but you cannot whitewash the homosexuality.

More importantly, it could not have been violence that God was punishing them for. God had already noticed the sin of Sodom and Gomorrah before He had it destroyed, and before the men had arrived at the city, and before any violence was even thought of by those homosexuals. The destruction of Sodom and Gomorrah occurred in Genesis chapter nineteen and its sin had already caught the eye of God in chapters thirteen and eighteen. Even Abraham knew of their sin ahead of time. God called their sin "very grave," meaning to be weighty, or heavy. God took their sin very seriously. They had already been practicing homosexuality. If it were not a city full of sin, God would have known it and He would have spared it.

Genesis 13:13 says, *"But the men of Sodom were exceed- ingly wicked and sinful against the LORD."*

Genesis 18:20-21 says, *"And the LORD said, Because the outcry against Sodom and Gomorrah is great, and because their sin is very grave. I will go down now and see whether they have done altogether according to the outcry against it that has come to me; and if not, I will know."*

Some clergymen give an improper exegesis of the passage of Sodom and Gomorrah. It's true that God would have known the future of that sin of violence if it would have occurred. However, long before any act of violence could have occurred, it is clear that God had something other than violence on His "plate of destruction" and that was the sin of homosexuality.

Where do they think the term sodomy came from over the past 4,000 years? Did it come from the intended violence that was going to be carried out that day? Do they think that's the reason Sodom and Gomorrah were destroyed? The mission of the angels to Sodom and Gomorrah can be detected in the written tone of their voice. Its destruction was about something more sinister and corrupt than intended violence that those men were going to carry out.

These angels speak in Genesis 19:13 and say, *"For we will destroy this place, because the outcry against them has grown great before the face of the LORD, and the LORD has sent us to destroy it."*

In a related scriptural passage of Matthew chapter 10, Jesus was instructing His disciples about preaching the Kingdom of Heaven in the cities of Israel. Jesus described those who would not believe their words. His words of judgment are quite revealing!

Jesus said in Matthew 10:15, *"It shall be more tolerable for the land of Sodom and Gomorra in the Day of Judgment than for that city."*

Did Jesus pronounce that kind of judgment for not accepting His words because of the intended violence of those men at that time? Some have compared Sodom and Gomorrah to America. "Isn't God going to have to apologize to Sodom and Gomorrah if

He allows the evil of homosexuality to continue in America without punishment?"

My clergy colleagues are caught up in the fact that violence done to anyone is an unacceptable ill in our society. But that's the only thing they see. They choose to tickle the ears of their listeners about the sin of violence, but ignore the sin of homosexuality. They pick and choose the sins they wish to talk about. Shame on them! They have joined the chorus of those who are trying to get us to accept the homosexual lifestyle such as homosexual clergy, lay elders, and deacons in their various church denominations. Their stance is reprehensible!

It is unfortunate that the homosexuals compare their own cause as equal with the civil rights cause of African Americans. I've heard them say that just as African Americans struggled to be accepted in the military under President Harry Truman, so they are fighting to have their lifestyle accepted here in America. Well, their cause can never be compared to the plight that African Americans struggled with during slavery and segregation in America. How can you compare the rights and mistreatment of a race of people with those who are trying to assert themselves through a lifestyle of homosexuality that has been looked at as an immorality for over 4,000 years? Some African Americans are offended with that comparison and frankly, if it were compared with my national background of Italian some how, I would be offended also.

Homosexuals and other liberals refer to conservatives as homophobic. Wrong! Homophobia means that someone has a fear of homosexuals. They are only using the term homophobic as a smokescreen to get everyone's minds and thoughts away from the morally degrading act that it is. There is no fear of homosexuals nor is there a fear that the homosexual lifestyle will be the dominant lifestyle throughout the world. It's much different than that. To paraphrase a remark made by a recent President, "It's a morality issue, stupid"! We are obligated to raise the moral bar against this lifestyle that was condemned in the Bible, equal to those who use the discrimination factor and push for their acceptance in the community. Homosexual marriages only add further confusion that is already in the world when it comes to raising children in a family without both a viable mother and father. Their absence can do much damage to the raising of children. The Public School system doesn't help matters either with their agenda of endorsing the lifestyle of "two mommies" or "two daddies."

The practice of homosexuality relates back to the Greek word "Pornos". In the Bible, "Pornos" is indicative of fornication in the English language, both heterosexual and homosexual. A fornicator is someone who practices his or her sexual vice over and over again. They either cannot or do not want to be set free from it. Jesus used this word and it is associated with adultery, prostitution, homosexuality, incest, and bestiality. Also, the word fornication is related to our English word pornography and that's definitely a vice that requires deliverance. There is a connection between these two vices of homosexuality and pornography that can maintain a grip on someone until being set free by the Holy Spirit. There is enough scripture that speaks about homosexuality.

Leviticus 18:22 in talking about men says, *"You shall not lie with a male as with a woman. It is an abomination"*.

That scripture is sandwiched right between a prior verse talking about the sin of adultery and the following verse talking about the sin of having sex with animals. Now how much clearer can the sin of homosexuality be as an abomination in the eyes of God when it is mentioned in the same context of those two other sins?

Leviticus 20:13 says, *"You shall not lie with a male as with a woman. It is an abomination. They shall surely be put to death. Their blood shall be upon them."*

Homosexuality has been with us since the beginning of time. Jesus did not have to address it as opposition to it was already in Jewish religion and culture. It was a settled issue. Thankfully, even though the government still exercised the death penalty, the religious leaders were no longer to put to death those who committed those types of sexual sins. Christ came and changed that, like when He asked for mercy for the woman caught in adultery. No religious leader could cast a stone at her because they were all guilty too. God is the only one who decides our position to be either in heaven or hell. But did that mean that Jesus condoned her sin? On the contrary, He opposed the sin of the adulterous woman and told her to be free from it.

Jesus said to that adulterous woman in John 8:11, *"go and sin no more"*.

And that is what the religious leaders say and should be saying to the homosexual. "We are not here to judge you or condemn you to hell, but God does want to deliver you so you can be set free from that gripping sin!" Our mission is not to speak against the person but to speak against the lifestyle. God can and does forgive the sin of homosexuality! To be sure, we are not to hate the homosexual but love them through Christ and we must definitely oppose any violence done toward the homosexual community. Violence such as the man in Texas who was dragged and beaten to death a number of years ago by those opposed to homosexuality was clearly wrong.

The Apostle Paul spoke about homosexuality and other sins in Romans chapter one and the judgment that God will bring upon them. In chapter two he calls for us to be careful how we judge others if we do not come to repentance ourselves. In other words we have to look at our own sin first. Jesus also told us of the seriousness of judging others.

Matthew 7:1 gives us the command from Jesus that says, *"Judge not lest you be judged"*.

The Greek in the above verse carries the inference that none of us can make the final judgment that would condemn that person or any other person to hell. We are not allowed to judge any person in finality and totality. That's God's responsibility. That doesn't mean that we are not allowed to speak against any sin or moral failure because we are told to make sure that we know who the true followers of God and His word are.

I John 4:1 says *"Believe not every spirit, but try the spirits whether they are of God"*.

Matthew 7:20 says, *"Every tree that does not bear good fruit is cut down and thrown into the fire. Therefore by their fruits you will know them."*

There are other scriptures that talk about homosexuality and it is important that we recognize their viability. The homosexual mind is described in Romans as being depraved, meaning in its original thought that it is unapproved and rejected and Corinthians lists homosexuality with other sins. Then the book of Timothy describes the conscience of the homosexual.

Romans 1:26-28 in talking about disobedient mankind says, *"Because of this, God gave them over to shameful lusts. Even their women exchanged natural relations for unnatural ones. In the same way the men also abandoned natural relations with women and were inflamed with lust for one another. Men committed indecent acts with other men, and received in themselves the due penalty for their perversion. Furthermore, since they did not think it worthwhile to retain the knowledge of God, he gave them over to a depraved mind, to do what ought not to be done."*

I Corinthians 6:9-10 says, *"Do you not know that the wicked will not inherit the kingdom of God? Do not be deceived: Neither the sexually immoral nor idolaters nor adulterers nor male prostitutes nor homosexual offenders nor thieves nor the greedy nor drunkards nor slanderers nor swindlers will inherit the kingdom of God."*

I Timothy 4:1-2 says, *"The Spirit clearly says that in later times some will abandon the faith and follow deceiving spirits and things taught by demons. Such teachings come through hypocritical liars, whose consciences have been seared as with a hot iron."*

The book of Timothy goes on to say that God's law is for the sinners to understand and to be helped by it. The following scripture is so simple to understand. It can change the life of the homosexual.

I Timothy 1:8-10 says, *"But we know that the Law is good, if one uses it lawfully, realizing the fact that law is not made for a righteous person, but for those who are lawless and rebellious, for the ungodly and sinners, for the unholy and profane, for those who kill their fathers or mothers, for murderers and immoral men and homosexuals and kidnappers and liars and perjurers, and whatever else is contrary to sound teaching".*

The question is always raised as to whether or not a homosexual person is born as a homosexual or influenced by the environment of the homosexual lifestyle. Is it nature or nurture? The homosexual community would like us to believe that they are born as homosexuals. In major studies on the difference between heterosexual and homosexual men, focus is usually on specimens of the brain structure. There is no conclusive evidence in these studies that any difference causes one man to be heterosexual and another to be homosexual. That means that it cannot be proved that homosexuals are born homosexuals.

I'm sure that they want to compare the homosexual with the heterosexual in saying that they are both born the way they were born. They want us to believe that there was a mix-up in their genetic code. Some have said that they have felt this way all their life and they knew since a child that they were homosexual and that there was an attraction they had toward someone of the same sex. With the genetics of both sexes in our gene pool, a choice has to be made. Many may be born with a genetic propensity toward homosexuality but the same thing can be said about the adulterer, the thief, the liar, and murderer. We call it original sin and it must be confessed to God and dealt with.

The problem is that the homosexual community doesn't want to admit that generally speaking, homosexuals can and do influence others into the homosexual lifestyle. We do know that it is a definite factor. Ask any child after they reach maturity about their experience when an adult sexually influenced and prematurely heightened their sexuality either in a homosexual or heterosexual manner. This has hurt many of them and they will tell you so. The homosexual community wants us to forget the fact that for generations, no, millenniums, homosexuality was considered wrong. Some in the homosexual community along with some in the heterosexual community even want us to believe that sex with children is OK. How disgusting!

Homosexuals want to become an acceptable part of the community of life. They don't want us to talk about the fact that just as someone can influence another to commit adultery, look at pornography, or become interested in sex with children, so a person can be taught the way of homosexuality. If a child or a teen looks at pornography and becomes interested in it, does that make it naturally right for them or do we try and steer them away from it? If a child is molested, aren't we concerned for them and then have them properly counseled so that they don't become predators themselves when they are older? Don't we deal with the child molester and alert the community when one lives in the neighborhood?

I am a heterosexual born from the line of Adam and Eve who were also heterosexual. I am a sexual being born within the heterosexual concept of God and I came from a loving heterosexual relationship between my parents, one male and one female. I learned heterosexuality, not in the bedroom, but by observing the lifestyle of my parents and their parental relationship with my siblings and me. That's why we tell parents to talk to their kids about sex, to teach the proper ideas about heterosexual relationships, and not about homosexuality. That's the way it's been since the time of creation.

In Genesis God gave Adam and Eve the physical ability to have children. The reason homosexuality was so unacceptable by God for society was because the natural process of pro-creation would have been interrupted. In the 6,000 years of history of this world, I don't know of one child that was physically and naturally born out of a homosexual relationship. None, nada, zilch! Maybe science will change that someday in the future, but that's exactly what it will be, science!

One final thing about homosexuality: my wife and I have had homosexual acquaintances over the years. We did not ignore them nor did we always present an "in your face" challenge to them. But they knew where we stood on the issue and what we believed.

ABORT ABORTION

In other words, end abortion! Abortion is a blight that is striking at the core of human understanding and at the heart of Western civilization. None of the aborted babies are given their rights to "life, liberty and the pursuit of happiness."

Genocide in America is creating a culture of death as we are being asked to compromise our position on abortion. The truth is we have already compromised our position that has been engrained in society for thousands of years, as over 45 million babies have been aborted in the United States since 1973. In 2013, less than ten years from now we will be coming to the 40th anniversary of Roe vs. Wade. In the Bible, 40 years was usually marked as a time of testing for God's people and for the nation. With these laws of abortion so embedded in our culture, what is in store for our nation on, before, or after that 40th anniversary as we continue to make poor and immoral choices?

To be sure, abortion has been with us throughout ancient history. For hundreds of years in America and long before Roe vs. Wade, abortion was considered wrong because it was an attack on human life. By the 19th Century, every existing state had passed measures outlawing abortions. Those who wish to reverse the current abortion law of Roe vs. Wade that was foisted upon us by the courts of our land are now considered as going against the law. Didn't the courts go against the law of the states and of human decency in the first place when they passed Roe vs. Wade in 1973? We are considered the outsiders or on the fringe when really we are the mainstream. We are not the right wing but we are the hearts of decency.

Then there is the question as to when life begins. It is now proven that these precious little ones are more than the medical term "fetus" that is ascribed to them. After conception and while they are in the womb, these little "babies" have DNA. It should make everyone shudder when thinking about abortions, especially when the "partial birth abortion" law was in effect and partially born babies were murdered before they were completely birthed. These babies are living beings, and when it comes to abortion we must air on the side of caution and life. The debate and uncertainty as to whether life begins at conception or at birth is all the more reason to protect the unborn.

How is it that we won't prosecute those who commit the crime of abortion and yet we will prosecute those who kill a pregnant woman and her unborn baby? We then charge them with double murder of both the mother and her baby as it was in the case of Scott Peterson in California. If it's because at some point his wife's baby was discharged from her in the water where she was found, aren't they just making that a technicality? Of course, "pro-choice" critics would argue that she had no choice in the matter and that her husband chose to abort or murder the baby. They conveniently draw a distinction between someone else killing the baby and the mother killing the baby. Is there a double standard there? Why will judges allow abortion, or murder by the mother and her doctor because it is only a fetus and then condemn someone who kills a mother and her unborn baby?

Of course I am opposed to violence done at abortion clinics and violence done to abortion doctors. In 1993 a doctor in Florida was the first of a number of abortion doctors to be murdered. A few years ago an abortion doctor from Buffalo, New York was killed in his home in front of his family by a sniper that shot at him through his kitchen window. The man who shot and killed that doctor never gave him the opportunity to change his opinion about abortions. He just condemned that doctor in his mind, was convinced that he deserved hell, and shot and killed him. That killer did the very thing that I mentioned a few paragraphs earlier that you shouldn't do.

Matthew 7:1 tells us, *"Judge not lest ye be judged"*.

That means that God does not allow us to make the final judgment on anyone that would condemn them to hell. We must give them ample opportunity to come to Christ! God forgives those who have had abortions and those who have been involved with abortions.

It has been said that abortion has little mention in the Bible. Well, there are many verses that describe a baby in a mother's womb. These verses can be taken both literally and figuratively.

For instance in Job 10:8,11-12, he talked as if God took great care in creating him. It says, *"You formed me with your hands; you made me. You clothed me with skin and flesh, and you knit my bones and sinews together. You gave me life and showed me your unfailing love. My life was preserved by your care."*

Psalms 139:13-16 gives David's description of God's tender care of him in his mother's womb. *"You made all the delicate, inner parts of my body and knit me together in my mother's womb. Thank you for making me so wonderfully complex! Your workmanship is marvelous—and how well I know it. You watched me as I was being formed in utter seclusion, as I was woven together in the dark of the womb. You saw me before I was born. Every day of my life was recorded in your book. Every moment was laid out before a single day had passed."*

Isaiah 44:1-2 gives an analogy of God, who knew the nation of Israel before it was even formed, *"But now listen, O Jacob, my servant, Israel, whom I have chosen. This is what the LORD says. He who made you, who formed you in the womb, and who will help you: Do not be afraid, O Jacob, my servant, Jeshurun, (poetic name for Israel) whom I have chosen."*

In Jeremiah 1:4-5 we read how God not only knew Jeremiah before he was born but called him and selected as His spokesman, *"The LORD gave me a message. He said, I knew you before I formed you in your mother's womb. Before you were born I set you apart and appointed you as my spokesman to the world."*

Finally, in Exodus chapter 21, there are laws and ordinances regarding murder, kidnapping, fighting, and other issues. Included in that same chapter are laws that talk about premature birth and accidental abortion.

It's found in Exodus 21:22-23 and says, *"Now suppose two people are fighting, and in the process, they hurt a pregnant woman so her child is born prematurely. If no further harm results, then the person responsible must pay damages in the amount the woman's husband demands and the judges approve. But if any harm results, then the offender must be punished according to the injury. If the result is death, the offender must be executed."*

The harm that would have resulted would have been the death of the woman, or her child, or both. God placed a great premium on the unborn! And again thankfully because of Christ's forgiveness, the religious leaders were not to execute these types of offenders anymore even though the government continued to enforce the death penalty. But abortion – not much mentioned in the Bible? How about the term murder! That's mentioned in the Bible plenty of times. But the liberals and the abortionists don't want to call it that.

And what about stem cell research, the forbidden science? Stem cell research is another subject that is medically and technically very complicated. My nephew, Mike Siriano has multiple myeloma, which is cancer of the bone marrow, a type of blood cancer. He needed a stem cell transplant from a sibling but his two brothers who were not a genetic match couldn't help him so the decision was made to harvest his own stem cells. During one of his medical procedures, the doctors extracted the stem cells from his blood. The stem cells of course being the building blocks of life were treated, and after he received a high dose of chemotherapy, they were placed back in his blood. My nephew told me that sometimes it works and sometimes it doesn't and that he had only a 30 percent chance that it would put him in remission. He quoted my grandfather Ulisse Cecchini who also had cancer and that the pain from the cancer was like "holding fire in his hand." My nephew said that in his case the bone pain was like the pain of a hot knife.

He doesn't agree with embryonic stem cell research because he said the use of discarded embryos with all the possibilities of the needed mutations can become a "sick science." Various cancers have responded to stem cells from donors and has shown some promise for cures. Side stepping abortions, umbilical cord blood can show promise as well.

My nephew said that America and the world are obsessed with "a pursuit of immortality." I thought, what a testimony coming from a man who could if he wanted to, leave this life with bitterness because he was dealt a "bad hand." Instead he has taken a mature approach to his own mortality and eternal life.

Sometimes we don't want to let go of this life when in reality we should be ready to meet God anytime. The devil wants us to believe the lie that we can live forever. He offers us life but it carries with it spiritual death! Ever since the Garden of Eden when he tempted Adam and Eve to eat from the tree that was forbidden by God, the Devil has been the exponent of life according to his terms. His idea of life included death so Jesus called him "a murderer from the beginning"...and "a liar." That includes his instigating the lie that abortion is not murder. On the other hand Jesus is "the way, the truth, and the life." Jesus told us not to fear the death of the body as much as fearing the second death that is spiritual.

Matthew 10:28 says, *"And fear not them which kill the body, but are not able to kill the soul: but rather fear him which is able to destroy both soul and body in hell."*

If stem cell research involves the giving up of one life for the life of another, that's a shame, and we are playing right into the Devil's lie. In Korea and in other nations, stem cell research and experimentation has opened up a Pandora's Box when it comes to the creation of life and the cloning of individuals. Ethical lapses occurred in Korea and the credibility of stem cell research suffered because of that as it came under great scrutiny from all parts of the world. Scientists are saying that stem cell research will be done with tight security and nothing will go amiss and that the technology will not be abused. According to them there will be no attempts at the Creation of life, or cloning. How can they guarantee that? They say that more good will come of it than potential harm but how can they be sure? That guarantee cannot be guaranteed! It won't work!

281

Like I said earlier in this chapter, once you start being God, you have to start making decisions like God. That's where cultures begin to fall apart because at that point they have usually already begun to reject God's morality. Sadly, that's where America is right now! After we are dead and gone what will the next generation find more acceptable? Will it be the encouragement of euthanasia to rid society of the elderly, the total acceptance of suicide, and the movement toward the creation of life and cloning?

There are some that are personally opposed to abortions but believe it's a woman's right to choose or if it involved their daughter such as in a rape situation, they back off and say, it's her decision. They don't want to sound hypocritical by saying that they would let their daughter have an abortion. In other words they don't even have the tenacity to say that they would help her to make an informed decision about keeping the baby. Many mothers have kept their baby in a rape situation or kept it even though it was an unwanted pregnancy, and that child grew to become a productive member of the community.

Many political leaders apply similar conditions of hypocrisy to their own belief system because liberal thinking is in the clutches of the abortionist and are heavily influenced by them. There are many that oppose abortion but say we live in a pluralistic society so it's the woman's choice. That just won't cut it anymore and won't do as an answer when our society comes unraveled at the seams. There has to be alternatives to abortion and we must convince the abortionists who are earning a living performing abortions to pursue those alternatives. There are exceptions to abortion to be sure, but that's what they should be, exceptions!

LET'S MAKE A DEAL

Some say that it's OK to be homosexual, or commit adultery, or have an abortion, but it's not OK to be a child molester. Why can they have their say as to what is right and wrong and draw the line where they want to but not give the evangelicals or the conservatives the right to draw the line where they want to?

The liberals want the conservatives to compromise on the death penalty. They say it is hypocritical in standing against abortion and in favor of the death penalty, because conservatives want to save life on one hand and take a life on the other. Incidentally, the Bible, world culture, and American culture have had the death penalty for centuries.

Usually liberals are just the opposite as they are in favor of abortion and against the death penalty. Doesn't that make them hypocritical too? Ironically, it's usually the very ones that have protested against wars that God uses as I mentioned in a previous chapter, that support the abortion platform and have innocent blood on their hands.

Those opposed to the death penalty or who are not sure of it, cite the Bible passage that says, "you shall not kill," meaning there should be no death penalty. However, the same God who gave that 6th Commandment to Moses also told him to "put to death" those who commit egregious crimes against society. In the New Testament, mercy was extended in a number of situations as redemption became the keystone of Christianity, but the death penalty was not eliminated. The death penalty, which should be beyond a shadow of a doubt, comes under the authority of the government and is no longer carried out by the church.

There is a difference between abortion and the death penalty. America kills between one to one and a half million babies a year through abortion, but usually less than 100 people a year are put to death under the death penalty law. That's quite a profound difference in choices. Anyway, how do you compare the capital punishment of serial killers, cop killers, rapists, child molesters and murderers who should be put to death, with the murder of a million and a half innocents without damaging the fabric of our society? An unborn child is the essence of innocence in society and those serving on death row for heinous crimes are the extremes of society. How do you compare the two and how can you compromise the lives of the babies? But that's the difference in how a conservative thinks and how a liberal thinks.

I know that abortionist's do not equate the death penalty with the death of a baby in the womb. They don't call abortion murder. So let's make a deal! I have always been in favor of the death penalty but would be more than happy to change my position and I would say many other evangelical Christians would as well, under one condition. If the United States House, the Senate, and the Supreme Court would go back to their chambers and vote to change their position on abortion then we would be glad to change our position on the death penalty. If all of the churches would stand for life, the Evangelicals would be ecstatic to exchange the 80 to 100 individuals that are put to death each year for the one to one and a half million babies that are murdered each year. We would be thrilled to change how we feel about the rapist, child molester, murderer, and cop killer, and get them off death row if they would let the innocent babies live! The liberal won't stand for life when it comes to innocent babies, but they will stand for life when it comes to those kinds of individuals. Again, that's OK, let's make a deal! Let's change our positions and let both sides stand for life. If they'll work to free the fetal fatalities, then we'll work to let the losers live and remain in jail! It's true, mistakes can be made when it comes to the death penalty as some individuals were jailed or put to death for crimes they did not commit. If the liberals will work to change the laws on abortion then the evangelicals will stand behind the laws of ridding this society of the death penalty and make the maximum penalty to be life in prison. Let's all stand for life.

Television personalities Jim and Lori Bakker talk about post-abortion trauma. Lori had 5 abortions before she became a Christian and she describes what women can go through who have had an abortion. She describes the trauma of eating disorders, alcohol and drug dependencies, depression, and other life changing experiences. Jim says men can go through the process of abortion and that their "pain comes from the fact that men are not the final decision-makers in the abortion process. The scars from that decision are burned deeply on their souls."(**12**).

Essentially men are told that their choice has nothing to do with it even though it's their sperm that has impregnated the woman. A woman contributes half of what makes the baby and the man contributes the other half, but the woman has been duped to view it as her choice and most of the time won't even consult the man because it's her body. How selfish is that? Of course abortion is never viewed as murder!

Pro-choice displays the saddened problem of a people that has lost its faith in a Creative God. When a woman insists that it's her choice and won't consult her partner, that choice shows the crippling sin that has gripped our culture and stands in the way of the scripture that endorses the partnership of a man and woman. God created man and woman to be as one.

> Genesis 2:23-24 says, *"And Adam said: "This is now bone of my bones And flesh of my flesh; She shall be called Woman, Because she was taken out of Man." Therefore a man shall leave his father and mother and be joined to his wife, and they shall become one flesh."*

Again, much is said about the woman's right to choose. The doctors and the courts make it the woman's choice and no one else's. I compare the woman's right to choose because the baby is only a "fetus" with the Supreme Court's decision in the Dred Scott case in 1857 that stated the blacks were not citizens. By a woman's choice she is declaring that her baby is not or will not be a citizen.

A 14-year-old girl can have an abortion after being told by doctors that she doesn't have to tell her parents or consult with them. Yet if she wanted to get an aspirin in school the school authorities would have to call her parents. That's simply an upside down principle!

To be sure, there are cases when the man is so immature or his situation perhaps because of his abusiveness is so bad, that his decision shouldn't even be taken into account. There are times however when the woman is immature as well. Pro-choice won't even look into whether or not the man is a decent man. They emphatically say, it's the woman's choice, period, because it's her body. Well, she'll have to answer to aborting that baby when she stands before God. The right of privacy is important but should never take precedence over the will to murder.

IS THERE AN ANSWER?

While some will say that diversity is not threatening, it is all of these cultural influences that are having a profound effect on America and its position as a global power. It is the cultural changes of America that will affect our Super Power status. Our moral structure as a society will be weakened because other societies and religions will be challenging our changing cultural beliefs. We are not necessarily in a physical state of war but in a war against certain unwholesome behavior patterns that have not been culturally accepted in our world for millenniums. Now they are being accepted in America.

If you follow the definitions of Conservatism and Liberalism that I presented earlier in this chapter, the scariest, craziest, and most bazaar of all thoughts in my mind is that within the next 30-50 years or so, the application of those terms could reverse. If the liberal thought becomes the mainstream of society, then they would become the conservatives who want to hang on to the same customs they are used to and would oppose any radical changes. The conservatives on the other hand would then become the liberals who would be in favor of progress and reforms, in which they would then want to change society. Amazing!

The fact of the matter is that many of the liberal laws over the past 40-50 years have changed the course of conservatism, and have already been ingrained in American society. A reversal of liberal and conservative thought is what has happened with the abortion controversy. It has happened since the pendulum swung from an anti-abortion society to an abortion society by the law created by Roe vs. Wade in 1973. That is also what is happening with the endorsement of same sex marriage laws of today.

One of the biggest challengers in the future will be the nation of Islam as it tries to influence America with its fundamental principles of right and wrong. The Muslim's who don't believe in separation of Church and State could become a powerful force in America in the future just as they are becoming in Europe. With the liberals effectively moving the restraint of Christianity out of the way, will Islam be a payback to America for the corruption that liberal thought has brought to America? The principles of Islam will be a radical change for America. Instead of that happening, will we seek to change our culture to fit the biblical pattern of instruction to make the necessary changes ourselves? I hope so!

In the 16th Century, Martin Luther nailed his 95 theses or statements to the door of the Wittenberg University Cathedral in

Germany in which he exposed certain abuses made by the authorities of the Church. I have read his theses and would dare say that his issues with the Church pales in comparison to the cultural issues that divides Catholicism and Protestantism today. If He could see how his ideas of reformation has led mainline Protestantism on such a divergent path so vastly different than the Catholic Church of today in regards to homosexuality and abortion, he would be appalled. He would regret the day he ever formulated his theses to help divide the Church!

The cultural disasters in this chapter are worse than the earthquakes and other catastrophes that may take place in our world. This affects our stand with God as a nation as we head for the end time. Our wickedness in the sight of God has been unconscionable. Our societal changes offer a confusing set of moral choices that worsens with each passing decade. Just as God gave the Jewish people the choice between good and evil in Deuteronomy, so God gives that same choice to any nation in the world today, including America.

Deuteronomy 30:16 and 19 says, *"...I command you today to love the LORD your God, to walk in His ways, and to keep His commandments, His statutes, and His judgments, that you may live and multiply. And the LORD your God will bless you in the land which you go to possess...I have set before you life and death, blessing and cursing; therefore choose life, that both you and your descendants may live."*

With no moral absolutes of black versus white, unbelievable stress is added to our society. The moral impasse that is developing between God and us will seriously affect our stand in the community of nations. Our excessive compulsion with our "rights" and the cultural changes that are taking place in America internally will bring our nation to its knees.

America falling to its knees can be taken two ways. As a warring nation, we can be physically embattled and overcome as a superpower nation and we can no longer have the effectiveness that we are enjoying now. On the other hand, we can willingly fall on our knees and implore God for His help and guidance. God will always honor a people and a nation that turns from their sin. Over and over again in scripture we see the hand of God move in favor of his created people when someone stands to make amends for all the evil that is in their land. Let us pray that happens before our world falls apart all around us.

We have all contributed to the cultural collapse of our world because of our sin, but God has always said that He would forgive the penitent. It matters not how much or how deep anyone has sinned, if one confesses their sin to God, it is forgiven. Any sin is between that sinner and God, and God will reach out in love to them. He has always had a remnant of people who served Him no matter how much evil prevailed. The presence of Christ is standing over our cities and over our nation. Let us pray that there will be a revival in America to bring us back to God.

Let us pray and ask God to change many of the cultural abuses mentioned in this chapter and believe God for a revival of our standards of decency and morality on which this great nation was founded. God's master plan is far above the political foray, the protests, and rhetoric that engulfs man's world. As God has forgiven my sin, God can change you personally and use us even though we are not perfect. Then and only then can we expect to have a positive influence in the world before Jesus Christ returns!

II Chronicles 7:14 says, *"If My people who are called by My name will humble themselves, and pray and seek My face, and turn from their wicked ways, then I will hear from heaven, and will forgive their sin and heal their land."*

Isaiah 55:6-7 says, *"Seek the LORD while He may be found, call upon Him while He is near. Let the wicked forsake his way, and the unrighteous man his thoughts; let him return to the LORD, and He will have mercy on him; and to our God, for He will abundantly pardon."*

CHAPTER SEVEN:

When history and the Bible conflict!

—◁◅◣◢▷—

We are writing history and becoming history with every tick of the clock, but what happens when the history that is happening all around us, conflicts or is at war with the Bible and it's history? History has been on the side of God because He proves His power over and over again to us through that history. It is when we ignore history and what God is trying to do through history that we get into problems. We don't want to learn the lessons that are important for us to learn today. It's usually when we try to interpret history to suit our particular persuasion and do not compare it with the Bible that we get into trouble.

I became a minister in November of 1963, the very month President John Kennedy was assassinated. I lived through the 1960's and 1970's and viewed with horror the increased development of atheism, secularism and humanism. I was appalled as University and College students, priests and ministers became involved as Vietnam War protestors. They felt that they were acting like Christ by being peacemakers. It's true, Christ was a peacemaker but He would never have been involved in any controversial, political protesting process. Never, never, never! One of His own disciples was Simon the Zealot who was in favor of the overthrow of Roman rule, but Christ Himself never endorsed such behavior nor would he even become involved in the political process. The motto of Christ in regard to the government is found in the Gospel of Mark.

Mark 12:17 says *"Render to Caesar the things that are Caesar's, and to God the things that are God's"*.

Of course that statement was in regard to the paying of a tax to the government. Christ clearly came down in the middle of the confrontation by the Herodians who tried to catch Him in His words as to which He would give allegiance to, God or the government. It meant more than the payment of taxes. Jesus' attitude was to give to Caesar what is due to Caesar and give to God what is due to God. In essence He was saying, let God be God and let Caesar be Caesar! Jesus could have taken the opportunity to protest against taxation, government rule and policy, or about Roman war policies. But He did none of those things. I take it further to mean that we are not to interfere by protesting against government policy but to cooperate with the powers that be! Jesus was not making a political endorsement and neither was He making a political protest.

Some argue that a patriotism that questions authority is far better than blind patriotism. I'm not advocating blind patriotism, but the patriotism that not only asks questions, but then is an affront to authority is not the kind of patriotism that Jesus endorsed. There are some questions that all of us are concerned with. "How involved should the church be in our culture, particularly as it relates to the state?" "Do we oppose the state at any opportunity, endorse it, don't become involved with it or seek to transform it?"

Cooperating with existing governments that we disagree with is not unusual today. Our missionaries cooperate with foreign governments in order to get their job done as missionaries so they will not be viewed as one who proselytizes. They are careful about how they preach in the name of Christ, or they resist only when they are not allowed to preach in the name of Christ so as not to be killed or expelled from the country. Often they work in other job capacities and minister for Christ as God opens the door for them. Indeed they are careful.

You may ask, "what about the atrocities of vicious and horrible governments under the dictatorship of men such as Hitler and Stalin?" There are justifiable reasons that speaking, protesting and rising against a government that is particularly evil is important.

That kind of government needs to be overthrown. However, just because you politically disagree with your government's policy is no reason to try and overthrow it. Uprising and protesting is not the answer. I didn't see the policy of the government of the 1960's and 1970's as a legitimate reason as some did to violently protest against the Vietnam War. Think about it, the governments of Caesar, Herod, and Pilate in the days of Jesus were just as vicious and atrocious as the governments of Hitler and Stalin in our era. God eventually allowed the overthrow of all of those governments because of their sin and God will punish America for its sins. God is in control of the nations. Remember, the First Amendment mentions, "the right of the people peaceably to assemble, and to petition the government for a redress of grievances." That is how we should behave when we disagree with our government.

The birth of the United States was one of those exceptions of independence that was led by a people who synchronized a serious and important revolt. War became inevitable as the British issued a crackdown on the colonists when they sought a redress of grievances from the King of England and bolted against taxation without representation. God has definitely used revolution in governments in the Bible, particularly in the Books of Kings. He has used revolt in nations for a plan that is far beyond what one can see, and God used revolution in the United States for His future plans. Remember that God has the authority and power to set up and remove nations and their leaders.

Others have paid a tremendous price for freedom, and then brought about the changes needed in government peaceably. One such notable example is Nelson Mandela. He was a man that had been jailed but brought change through a peaceful signing of an accord to end factional violence. Mikhail Gorbachev is another example that promoted glasnost (openness) and perestroika (restructuring) in the old Soviet Union. This eventually led to the end of the existence of the Soviet Union as of December 31, 1991. Mr. Gorbachev made some difficult decisions, but it insured a peaceful change in his government. Still another example is Gandhi who won India and the world through his philosophy of non-violent protest.

I believe that Christian leaders should cooperate with our political leaders, and that war and its implementation must be left to those outside the body of Christ and we are not to endorse wars or come against them either. Instead we must support our leaders in all that they do which may include war, and we must let God's overall plan of His usage of the nations and the world's war machine to bring His will to fruition. After all, if He cannot break through the barrier of man's stubborn, cold, and insensitive heart with the message of His kingdom, then He will use war. As a counter to that thought, of course we must speak and fight against the likes of a Joseph Stalin, Adolf Hitler, and Saddam Hussein. We must rise against the terrible rule of a Slobodan Milosevic, who endorsed the evil ethnic cleansing of Bosnia-Herzegovina. Many brutal kings and dictators of recent time and of centuries past had to be deposed and for good reason, but it was in God's timing.

MY FAMILY

My grandparents and my father came to America in the late 19th Century and the early part of the 20th Century. My father-in-law came in the early part of the 20th Century as well. All of them became a part of America not illegally, but with proper registration and citizenship. When my ancestors came through Ellis Island, they did not want to retain a strong identity with their former country and they made plenty of sacrifices to be here. They wanted to identify with America because they felt they were now becoming Americans! They felt so strongly about it that they did not bother to teach us the language from their homeland because they wanted us children to speak English! My parents wanted us to be Americans.

The message on the base of the Statue of Liberty that says, "Give me your tired, your poor, your huddled masses…send these, the homeless…" is still true! The problem today is that many do not want to make the sacrifice and learn to be legal Americans. If we turn a blind eye to those coming across our borders illegally and allow them to work and acquire driver's licenses improperly, it is a slap in the face of my parents and grandparents. They came here through the proper channels and did not sneak in. And that's not even saying anything about the threat to America because of terrorists who may sneak into America illegally and pose a threat to our security.

Today, everyone wants to retain their family's own historical identity, similar to the heritage of my Italian family who were proud of that. Many immigrants are bringing their culture or their religious faith with them and worshipping in the native tongue in their own religious services. There is nothing wrong with that as they blend their culture with America. However, if immigrants come and there is no blending and legal attachment to America, then America that was once called "the melting pot", will lack loyalty and cohesiveness. It will end up being "beef stew" instead, where the components cannot be blended but would remain separate!

The emphasis today is on a multi-cultural society instead of on the pride of nationalism in America. Liberal thinking tells us not to emphasis the character of our history and how this great nation came into being. There seems to be a de-emphasis on who discovered America and how it was founded as a nation. At one time it was thought that the challenges of discovery and the strength of the explorers led them to establish a powerful nation of entrepreneurs. It has now filtered down to appear as a historical malfunction and embarrassment that a certain race of people had forced their culture on another race of people. The eventual liberality of the United States government has become a great blessing to the peoples they previously had suppressed. What opportunity there has been for the uplifting of all races of people, who were already here, who came to America or were brought here unlawfully by others.

From the early 1600's when people from Europe first started coming to America, until 1787 when the Constitution of the United States was written, the dominant power in North America was not the United States but the French and the English. Wars were fought even with the aid of the people who were already in America. The United States wasn't formed until people from Europe had already inhabited this land for over 150 years. People did not come to America to see who they could dominate, they were looking for new land and new freedoms!

Its not that the United States has done everything right in it's past, because it hasn't. However, many do not understand nor would they accept the historical fact of the shifting of global powers as we discovered in chapter two. Time and time again this has happened in the history of our world when one group of people dominates another group of people in their land. If we think America owes someone because of how it was founded then we would have to trace back in time to unscramble all of the political influences of one nation over another throughout time. We would have to reverse the domination of those people and make all of the necessary and rightful reparations. It would be utterly impossible.

The emphasis now is being placed on the idea that three great peoples of the world came together to start America: the Native Americans, the Africans, and the Europeans. That may be OK but not at the expense of the historical values and understanding that are already in place. That is how some historians want to change what we emphasize in our history. All of that will play into the scheme of things as America as a nation becomes weaker and weaker as a mighty force in the world today. As addressed in a previous chapter, America will be divided as we witness a rise of the various power cultures in America that will maintain their individualism. This includes the most recent cultures of people that have come through Mexico, many who have entered America illegally. Confronting those various culture problems will backfire and worsen an already delicate problem. We as a nation will give in to the will of the people and cease to be the great nation that was strengthened by the strong leadership that we have seen in our past history.

OUR PREDECESSORS

When our forefathers came to America and landed in Jamestown and Plymouth Rock, they were hard working, committed to their social community, very religious, and had a strict moral and righteous code based on the Bible. This belief system came with them when they sailed from Europe. The history and legacy that they left for us was peppered with a godliness that cannot be denied.

For over 350 years their religious practices had been embedded not only in those early settlements but also in the founding of our country until the mid 20th Century. America continued on a conservative path and avoided any liberal interpretation of what they had been practicing all those years. Most of the first 100 colleges and universities founded in America were founded on Christian ideals and for Christian principles. It is very difficult to understand why today, conservative thought is shut out of debate in many of our liberal institutions of higher learning.

Conservatism in early America meant that there was not the separation of Church and State as it is being interpreted today, and there was a freedom to believe in God and to practice it openly and freely. Abortion was not accepted in society, and neither was homosexuality. There was no acceptance of same-sex marriage, cross dressing, or sex changes. They did not believe in Euthanasia or assisted suicide. They were tough on crime, believed in the death penalty and were supportive of police authority. Adultery was looked down upon as was child molestation.

Our forefathers were not in favor of liberalizing the laws that their religious beliefs had dictated. The American Civil Liberties Union and other liberal thinkers are sincere in their belief that freedoms such as abortion, homosexuality, and pornography will actually free our society for the good. That's actually taking our freedom too far. Instead, those freedoms will chain us as a society to new behavior patterns that we won't be able to free ourselves from, and will make that kind of freedom a two-edged sword. In actuality, sin and wickedness will destroy a nation and take their freedoms from them.

The following verses are in chapters that tell us to surrender to both the authorities in the natural world and the spiritual world. We are not to abuse either one of them with our extreme bad behavior.

The Bible warns us in I Peter 2:16 not to use our *"liberty for a cloak of maliciousness (wickedness or evil)"*.

Galatians 5:13 says that we *"have been called unto liberty; only use not liberty for an occasion to the flesh (sensuousness)."*

To repeat again what was said in the previous chapter, when it comes to social issues here in America, many people struggle with the term's conservative and liberal. A conservative person is someone who is inclined to keep the same customs, would oppose radical changes, and would tend to be cautious. A liberal person is someone who would not tend to be literal or strict and would be in favor of progress and reforms with the idea of changing society no matter if those changes were good or evil. The liberals say it's the freedom of expression that is important. They say that's what counts.

America was so conservative in its religious and social ideals that they even had local "blue laws" that kept businesses closed on Sundays out of a deep respect for religious practices. By the time Franklin Roosevelt became President he wanted to increase the Supreme Court justices from nine men who served on the court to fifteen in order to push his social agenda through and affect its conservative base. He wanted to get his social programs moving so badly that he was willing to "stack the deck" of the Supreme Court. Thankfully he didn't get his way but of course most of his programs were passed in the "New Deal". Roosevelt established institutional programs that helped the unemployed and the poor. His social programs were great for that time. He helped America get out of the Great Depression. But what worked then and contributed to America's power, greatness, and rise from depression will be the very thing that will bring America to its demise.

There are problems facing America that stem from the Roosevelt "New Deal" days, and "The Great Society" that was introduced in the days of President Lyndon Johnson. Government entitlement programs cannot answer the needs of every human being in its society. As much as we would like to see that happen, it would be impossible. The consequences are that America will face financial chaos in the future that will eventually impact the world. Americans can no longer afford to, nor pretend that they live in the "Great Society" that was once promoted by Johnson. In fact if you really think about it, America has never lived in the "Great Society" because there has not been the long term effect that was needed to sustain the "Great Society." The time clock on the success of the welfare programs of Roosevelt and Johnson has run out a long time ago. The entitlement programs are killing us and are part of the very thing that will bankrupt America. It is no longer about being a Democrat or a Republican, we just simply cannot return to the New Deal, Fair Deal, New Frontier, or the Great Society. The old social programs as they were, won't work in our economically depressed society. We are trillions of dollars in debt.

All those social entitlement programs from that time were put in place in the name of liberalism. Today, social liberalism is in its death throes but if it does gain momentum again, it is what will drive the nail in the cultural coffin of America. It will lead us to financial chaos. There is the utter impossibility of meeting all of the financial demands that is expected by everyone, including Social Security recipients. In fact, Social Security is at the top of the list, as individuals will struggle with their own retirements. "There is no pool of investment assets set aside in 'trust' to pay benefits of retirees. The phantom 'Social Security Trust Fund' contains nothing more than IOU's from the United States Treasury. One hundred percent of the surplus paid into the Social Security system has been spent to fund other government programs."(1). That's part of what leads the world into its financial woes that we see in the end-time just before Armageddon.

President Bush is facing mounting debt with the continued war in Iraq and with his programs of helping the survivors of recent natural disasters. He has just as much entitlement programs as Roosevelt did, if not more. Our politicians will never admit to wanting to return to pre-Roosevelt days. However, we may be forced to do so because of economic and political failure.

The liberalization of our laws that have always demanded decent moral behavior is relatively new in America. The conservatives are painted as lurking at ever corner, trying to force their ideals of moral behavior on others as if they were the outsiders looking in. In actually the conservative thought had been the mainstay on American soil for nearly 400 years when it comes to decent moral behavior, and liberal thought is more the newcomer. Even today, America is more conservative, but many have been duped to believe that they must allow some of their thinking to be liberal for the sake of "political correctness."

50 years ago, it didn't matter if you were Democrat or Republican. America was a conservative nation. Conservative morality supported liberal thinking. The Republicans continued to be conservative as

the Democrats took on the policies of Roosevelt and Johnson and eventually the policies of liberal demagogues, who are trying to change conservative America.

CHRISTIANITY CRUSH

There are those who want to push Christianity out of the picture, yet want their freedoms. They fail to recognize that Christianity has everything to do with their freedom. Christianity created our modern day freedoms and gave it to the Western World and those freedoms created our prosperity. Much of the rest of the world does not have the freedoms that we have and almost none of the prosperity. There are those who want to make us feel guilty because we have the least amount of output but use up the greatest amount of resources. Using all of those resources has helped us share all those resources with the rest of the world and is what has made us the great nation that we are today. All those resources come with prosperity and Christianity gave us the freedom to pursue those resources. The bottom line of all that prosperity and its ensuing tragedy is that our unchecked and unrestrained prosperity is what leads to our greed and only Christ can reverse that trend. Sadly, America will face the dilemma that greed poses as explained in the book of I Timothy.

I Timothy 6:9-10 says, *"But those who desire to be rich fall into temptation and a snare, and into many foolish and harmful lusts which drown men in destruction and perdition. For the love of money is a root of all kinds of evil, for which some have strayed from the faith in their greediness, and pierced themselves through with many sorrows."*

Those who want to push Christianity out of the way simply don't understand. The irony is that the more they push Christianity out of the way, the more they pull the rug of freedom out from under themselves. In the place of morality, righteousness, and religious freedom will be the freedoms of immorality, decadence, and disobedience, which will tear any nation apart at the seams. It will place chains around them, restrict their choices, and bind them to the freedom of Aids, murder, drugs, divorce, broken families, multi-family relationships, child molesters, rebellion, delinquency, and greed. It will allow criminals to prey on the weakness of our society and sell illegal drugs and weapons. All of this will be damaging to our society as a whole. Compared to the 1950's, we seem to be losing the cultural war. The following scriptures are a picture of the Last Days behavior pattern and a revelation of any society that is out of control.

II Timothy 3:1-5 says, *"In the last days perilous times will come. For men will be lovers of themselves, lovers of money, boasters, proud, blasphemers, disobedient to parents, unthankful, unholy, unloving, unforgiving, slanderers, without self-control, brutal, despisers of good, traitors, headstrong, haughty, lovers of pleasure rather than lovers of God, having a form of godliness but denying its power. And from such people turn away!"*

Matthew 15:19-20 says, *"Out of the heart proceed evil thoughts, murders, adulteries, fornication's, thefts, false witness, blasphemies: These are the things which defile a man."*

What an impending indictment against the United States! My view may be fatalistic, but those scriptures describe the present evil that has a distinct influence on our culture today. America desperately needs our prayer!

Some people want to make the United States a secular, humanistic or atheist country without a trace of religion anywhere in government. They don't want politicians talking about God and they don't want the clergy anywhere near government. They want to de-Christianize our culture striking at the heart of America with anti-Christian, anti-Protestant and anti-Catholic influences. They want to bring meaning to life without spirituality, which will fail. That is part of the evil that is exerting its power over the United States in what seems to be one of the last great Superpowers before the end time. As I have already said, the separation of Church and State should be like it used to be in its simplest form, a gentleman's agreement.

There is no such thing as a totally atheist culture. Religion played a part even in the suppressed Soviet Union under Josef Stalin. The Soviet Union lasted 74 years under atheistic Communism, from 1917 until 1991. Given that track record, Communist China that began in 1949 should last just a few more decades before atheism as its foremost principle becomes a relic of the past and they are caught up in Armageddon. Thankfully, China has a powerful underground church that is growing each year.

When an attempt is made to become an atheist government, it usually runs its course, tears apart, or is eventually overturned in succeeding generations. Pity the United States if they take such a course of action. How long do you suppose America would last in that condition before its government collapsed? Would it last as long as the Communist Soviet Union lasted? Remember atheism becomes the suppression not only of religion, but also of every other essential freedom that a nation enjoys.

Remember also that the freedoms of pornography, abortion, and homosexuality are not freedoms, they are restrictive and cruel by the implications of their deeds alone. Predators are a part of the evil of any society that tries to go it alone without God. When they are a little older and a little wiser, many that are involved with pornography are usually glad when they get out of that business and many times go back and try to help others who are still in the business. Many of those who have had abortions are tied to psychological depression, are ensnared in post-abortion trauma, are in need of counseling, and usually encourage others to avoid having an abortion.

We are trying to ignore history and the lessons that our forefathers believed in and practiced. None of them would have stood for the type of shameful behavior that is allowed to exist in America. History will not be kind to us as our ill-fated history will come back to haunt us, expose us as to how we really live, and be in conflict with the Bible.

RIGHT WING, LEFT WING, SOUND OFF

The idea that anything coming out of a religious viewpoint is wrong and would not be acceptable in the public debate is totally ludicrous. Left-wing liberals are telling conservative evangelicals that the intensity of their faith closes them off from the rest of society's discussion about ideals. They make it sound as if they are ineligible to speak about causes in our culture and that they should be exempt from speaking about them because their thoughts come from their religious code of ethics. Liberals accuse conservatives of having no conscience, and they believe that the very religious should have no part in the political process if they are too outspoken about their faith and convictions. Just the opposite is true. Our religious code of ethics is what makes us eligible to speak about those issues. We all speak from a religious code of ethics, both the liberals and the conservatives. Liberals want religion kept at the level of a private matter, behind church doors and in the quietness of the home. The problem is that without religion you have no ethics. Without the discussion and encouragement of public participation in religion, there is no public, decent, authoritative, or good moral cultural behavior, period!

The liberals want to shut religion out of the debate. The only thing they will debate about religion is that it should be kept private. They say that there should be no public prayers and no public religious displays on federal and state property. In so many words they say, the 1st Amendment says "nada," it's separation time! Gulp! How demeaning to God! How disastrous for both liberals and conservatives! Secularism is on the rise in America and threatens us all.

The Evangelical Christians are painted as right-winged religious fanatics. The idea that they will be successful at imposing all of their Christian ideals on the entire society is totally out of the question. The reason that Evangelicals express their belief so strongly is because of society's moral misbehavior. Society has become immune to good behavior and has accepted immoral behavior. Evangelicals also realize we have liberal courts that have gone mad. The court's agenda has endorsed those evil trends and has shut out Christian ideals for decades. Much of the Evangelical strong public stance is reactionary to the morally depraved trend in America. Faith in God or the lack thereof for both Evangelicals and the liberals has a powerful impact on our nation. Faith wields a great amount of influence and can keep any culture on course.

Besides, what are the liberals going to do when radical fundamentalist Islam makes an impact on America as is happening in Europe? It is looming larger and larger and it will come to America. We had better hope that we have a huge head start in espousing our faith or we will see a remarkable change in America, beginning with "The Separation of Church and State" which Islam doesn't believe in. Wouldn't it be better to choose Christianity now and allow it to ferment in society?

The rights of freedom have replaced the resolve in America of winning at any cost. We are led to believe by the liberals in our society that security cannot replace or come ahead of rights and freedoms. That is why the liberals are so opposed to the Patriot Act that they say is too intrusive into our privacy. They don't want the stringent rules to guard against illegal acts against our country if it means giving up some of their rights. Freedom thinkers give the impression that the more freedom there is, morality will take care of itself and will fall into place. In actuality, morality will disintegrate.

Of course, they would be against profiling of any kind. Unfortunately, profiling is done whether we like it or not, and it's done in many situations. An example of Gender profiling would be, if a woman murdered someone in a fight, the police wouldn't be looking for a man, they would be looking for a woman. Racial profiling would be if an Asian held up a bank, they wouldn't be looking for an African American, they would be looking for someone that looked Asian. When Islamic Fundamentalists hijacked our airlines and flew them into our buildings in New York City, the police weren't suspecting that Catholics did it, they were looking for Islamic terrorists. They weren't looking for a little old grandmother either. We've got a problem, because all of that is profiling! Of course, good intelligence is the first step in our fight for security. However, the American Civil Liberties Union is against asking personal questions of airline passengers at airports to help weed out terrorists because it disrupts civil liberties. All I know is that I want to be protected when I step onto an airplane or go anywhere else in America. I don't care how personal they get with questions or searches if it keeps us safe from Terrorists. Let's admit it that all races of people discriminate and we must seek God's forgiveness.

The conservatives are hanging on for dear life in what they believe the United States has historically been. The liberals are hanging on to what they think the United States should become. It matters not if democrats win in upcoming elections and control any or all branches of government. The liberal thought in history as far as personal morality is concerned is far outweighed by the conservative thought so the liberals need to make a shift closer to what the conservatives are hanging on to.

STIFLE POLITICIANS AND CLERGY?

The evil in America has tried to prevent the politicians and the clergy from speaking out about God. That idea puts the Bible in direct conflict with the history of America that is forming right now. What is wrong with politicians freely bringing God into their personal lives and then speaking about it in a public forum? When Senator Joe Lieberman of Connecticut was chosen as the Democratic Vice Presidential candidate during the 2000 political campaign, he freely spoke about the fact that he felt that God had chosen him as a Jewish individual and that he was put in that position by God. He felt favored by God. I applauded him for his remarks. He had a right to speak his mind. I'm sure at first he received no criticism because no one wanted to be chided for speaking out against him because he was Jewish. The criticism slowly rose and he had to temper his speech concerning how he felt that God had selected him. What a shame it was for such a God fearing man to be stifled in his faith by the oft-misinterpreted establishment clause of the First Amendment!

On the other hand, at the funeral of Coretta Scott King in February 2006, some politicians were able to freely speak of their faith and read from the Bible. That's the way it should be. Others sadly, used the occasion for political rhetoric. Politicians and Clergy should be able to speak of their faith at public forums on religious property and on government property without the fear that government is endorsing a particular religion. In America, the religious playing field is level for all to participate.

Of course, the Bible supports the fact that there must be a clear distinction between the religious and political leadership. A politician should not perform religious duties such as the case when King Uzziah tried to do so in Second Chronicles chapter twenty-six and was smitten with leprosy. On the other hand Prophets and other religious leaders had access to the political leaders of their day in order for God's message to be clearly heard for all the people to obey. Such was the case when the Prophet Nathan confronted King David in Second Samuel twelve about his adultery and the murder he committed. The political process and religion both need each other to make any culture work. Therefore, belief in God is not a religion, for that implies that we should all adhere to a particular denomination with a particular set of rules. Belief in God is a philosophy or way of life and is germane for the welfare of the people of America and the World.

My own personal ministry has included numerous occasions involving the blending of politics and religion. Years ago, there was not the Separation of Church and State as it is being touted today. On more than one occasion I've had the local mayor of a major city in New York who was a Christian, come to our Sunday morning service and address our congregation. He always gave his personal testimony about his relationship to Christ and what it meant for him to be a Christian. He didn't agree with our religious principles in all areas, but it was a beautiful blending of religion and politics with no coercion.

In 1964 I was asked to read scripture, and in 1966 I was asked to pray the benediction, both times at the High School Baccalaureate services in Bristol, Vermont. Fellow ministerial colleagues of different denominations were also there who offered prayer and spoke in the same service. I wasn't offended and they weren't offended. We shared the same podium in the same service. The idea that we may have been imposing our religious ideals on each other didn't even enter our minds. The fact that there may have been an atheist in the service didn't even cause any uproar. There was no call for separation of church and state in those days as there is today. There was a mutual guarded respect for the school and they had the same for us as clergy. When we read scripture and prayed, we weren't interfering with their business of the daily operation of running the school and they weren't interfering with our running of the church.

In 1968 I was also asked to pray in the state of Maine House of Representatives. My name appeared as "Reverend" on the House Advance Journal and Calendar. I represented Christianity in my prayer and no one said anything derogatory to me. I wasn't criticized. Instead I was respected. I crossed over into the political arena with prayer and it was accepted. Legislative members were there that I'm sure did not accept my particular world or religious view and again there was no outcry. That's because prayers have been said in our legislative bodies since the founding of our country. All of our States' Constitutions mention the name of God.

In 1971 I was asked to pray the Invocation, not at a Baccalaureate Service but at the Graduation Exercises for the South Burlington, Vermont High School. I was accepted by the community and by the school. Again, I did not interfere with their operations and they did not interfere with mine.

By the early 1970's things began to change. The U.S. Supreme Court stopped school sponsored graduation prayers in 1992. Thanks in part to the efforts of Madalyn Murray O'Hair who worked effectively through our court system to help remove prayer from our schools. This gave the atheists the foothold they needed when it comes to anything connected to the state and federal governments. Atheism had reached a peak that influenced many people. History and the Bible began to conflict in an even greater way.

It's not that we necessarily want prayer to be re-instituted back into the school systems, although that would be fine. It's just that the courts and local officials for the past 40 years have "in your face," told us, you can't pray in school! Our freedom of religion in many public places has been taken away from us. I have no problem with hearing a public Jewish or Islamic prayer, as other religions can be honored or respected in that manner also. The problem is that we have been lied to when the courts have said that it is no longer our right to pray or speak about God in State or Federal public areas. America has done it for years when it was organized properly.

Also during the early 1970's I had a Native American speaker in our church for a series of children's ministry services. We had the opportunity to have him dress in his native garb and speak in two assemblies for the local primary school. In one of the assemblies at the school he mentioned the "Great Spirit" and in the other assembly he mentioned the name "God", all as part of his Native American culture. Nothing else religious was mentioned and there was no mention of conversion, or what church to attend, or even whether or not a person should believe in God. It was a simple expression of what Native Americanism is all about and he included many other aspects of his culture in his presentation that day.

One of the children mentioned this to his atheist mother who then complained to the Superintendent of Schools. The Superintendent called me to say that the law said that it was not permissible to mention God. It was not permissible to mention God? My, how times had changed since the time in our early American history when the Bible was part of the curriculum and was one of the major textbooks in our schools! Prayer was in vogue and recited daily. Now I'm not suggesting that we return to all of that. I am suggesting that we've gotten our freedoms because of Christianity and we are going to lose them because we are shunning Christianity by not letting it flourish where it may! It's just more of the history that we as the people of America are writing and the conflict that it is creating with the Bible.

COMMANDMENTS – CURSE OR CURE

Then there's the problem of the 10 Commandments. Some problem! The 10 Commandments are a composite of what comprises the behavior pattern of most cultures. The reason is that the 10 Commandments are one of the oldest recorded instructions for human behavior ever recorded. Over the millennia they have impacted every society on the face of the earth. While the world already had some of these ideals because of God's early impact on society, the 10 Commandments as a whole did not come from Buddhism, Hinduism, Islam, or the writings of Confucius. They came from Judaism, one of the earliest of cultures and have been copied by other religions and cultures. Judaism impacted all the cultures of the world with those Commandments. What culture doesn't punish murderous acts, stealing, or the giving of false testimony? What culture doesn't honor and respect their parents, and their god? What culture doesn't recognize the stigma of adultery and doesn't encourage respect for your neighbor and their possessions? What culture doesn't set a day such as a Sabbath, or use a partial time set apart for religious purposes? What culture doesn't use the basis of the 10 Commandments in their society? All decent cultures use the 10 Commandments even though they don't call them that, and are more than likely unaware as to where those basic rules of respect came from. The Bible makes reference to some of those basic ideals from the very beginning.

Even if a culture has never heard the name of the Creator God or His Son Jesus Christ, they can still come before Him with confidence because of the created world that they observe. No one can stand before God and say, "I've never heard about you" or "I didn't know who you were." All of God's creative powers can be recognized and believed in through the observation of His creation. It is then that a person can know who God is and God of course would know them.

Romans 1:19-20 says, *"Since what may be known about God is plain to them, because God has made it plain to them. For since the creation of the world God's invisible qualities – his eternal power and divine nature – have been clearly seen, being understood from what has been made, so that men are without excuse"*.

It further states in Romans 2:14-15, *"When Gentiles, who do not have the law, do by nature things required by the law, they are a law for themselves, even though they do not have the law. Since they show that the requirements of the law are written on their hearts, their consciences also bearing witness."*

There may be some cultures and people that do not know about Jesus or the Bible, but if they are fulfilling the commandments of God even without knowing it, their conscience should tell them that there is a God. That's the benefit of the Word of God and the 10 Commandments even though some cultures don't even know that they are obeying them.

Of course Christianity also picked up on the Commandments and brought them to the western world and to America. But oh, the intelligence of the Courts has struck down the display of the 10 Commandments over and over again. Shame, shame, because with few exceptions, you cannot display them on state or federal property. After all, we don't want to influence anyone about God and about moral living now do we? There shouldn't be any undue spiritual or religious influence on anyone now should there? The bottom lines is, we better get over our resentment of the influence of the 10 Commandments, because it is not so much of a religious issue anymore as it is a societal issue.

It's not that we want all state and federal properties to start displaying the 10 commandments. Again, it's just that the courts have taken the "in your face" position that this is the improper place for them to be displayed even though similar symbols such as these have been on Federal and State properties for years. Liberals want public displays of religion to be removed. It's a lapse in freedom for Christians.

The courts have dismissed the 10 commandments, stood on the side of the right to die, and with the criminal, and have allowed one frivolous lawsuit after another where people sue someone for the most insignificant thing. Then they have forced us to live in a society where the courts have ruled against parental authority, and have protected pornography, homosexuality, abortion, and easy divorce. We have substituted intellectualism for our basic common sense. Today, anything goes, with no moral restrictions, regardless of the downward spiral that America is headed for. Unfortunately, there are no "moral absolutes" anymore!

We have ignored the history that Presidents, Congressmen, Judges, Lawyers, Doctors, Schoolteachers, and College Presidents have practiced and taught us for centuries. We are writing our own history and it seriously conflicts with God's Word. It even conflicts with the Islamic Koran and it's five pillars of their faith, and it conflicts with common sense and decency.

Liberal courts have also ruled against displaying a crèche or other religious items on public, state, or federal property as well. There have also been objections to crosses along federal highways. Liberal thinkers believe that the showing of symbols mean an endorsement or support of a particular religious view. That is so far from the truth. Tell that kind of liberal thinking to the founding Fathers that had religious symbols carved in statues and monuments throughout our federal buildings and landmarks. Some of our founding Fathers were Deists and not necessarily church goers, but they felt symbols didn't mean support of religion, it meant religious freedom.

Besides the liberal thinkers who want the 10 Commandments removed from public view, you have the "politically correct" organizations and institutions that in 2005 wanted to change "Christmas tree" to a "Holiday Tree." and say "Happy Holiday" instead of "Merry Christmas." How ludicrous! Of course we know that the word "holiday" has it roots in the words "holy day," Christmas trees and manger scenes were not in the Bible, and we're not even sure what day Christ was born on. All of that however is not the point! What is happening is more sinister than that. It is but a small part of the work of a spirit of atheism and secularism that is alive and well and growing stronger each year that wants to remove Christ out of every vestige of society as possible. What with the recent fictitious writing of the book and release of the movie, "The DaVinci Code," the warfare and confusion has just begun.

Scholars can point to the fact that trying to rid Christ from society has been happening for centuries. That's exactly the point! It is the affect that it has on successive generations in any nation and if we want to survive as a nation we need to allow faith and religious expression to flourish. That's what caused the downfall of those other nations in past generations. The children and grandchildren of those who are touting anti-Christian ideology in America today will rue the day their ancestors ever did. Many Americans have been convinced that a secular society best fits in with the separation of church and state. Nonsense! Do they think we're fools! There would have been no holiday without Christ.

What we're dealing with is the liberal thinking in our society that promotes atheism and secularism and that wants exclusion instead of inclusion. It's an assault on Christianity in which they would rather exclude any thought of Christianity under the guise of pluralism and separation of church and state, than be inclusive and allow all religions and symbols to flourish. In the name of diversity they suppress diversity. It's a smokescreen for atheism and secularism. The conservative view is not to rub out Christianity but to let it thrive and to allow the inclusion of other religions as well. If Christmas were a Native American holiday or African American holiday such as Martin Luther King Day, the liberals wouldn't touch it with a ten-foot pole.

Jesus explained this kind of attitude when He mentioned the parable of the Sower. The seed in this parable represents the Word of God. Many do not hear and understand God's Word because they are so busy with the world that the seed that falls in their hearts is as if it would fall along a pathway, among the rocks, or in the thorn bushes. It does little or no good. But those who faithfully read and accept the Word of God and the seed of it falls in their hearts, it is like seed that falls on good soil so that it can grow.

Matthew 13:8, 23 says, *"But some seeds fell on fertile soil and produced a crop that was thirty, sixty, and even a hundred times as much as had been planted. The good soil represents the hearts of those who truly accept God's message and produce a huge harvest—thirty, sixty, or even a hundred times as much as had been planted."*

When the disciples knew that the people might not understand the parables, they asked Jesus why He spoke in parables. Jesus then gave them his reply in which He explained that with their eyes many people would not be able to see and with their ears many would not hear.

In Matthew 13:13-16 Jesus said, *"This is why I speak to them in parables: "Though seeing, they do not see; though hearing, they do not hear or understand. In them is fulfilled the prophecy of Isaiah:" 'You will be ever hearing but never understanding; you will be ever seeing but never perceiving.*

For this people's heart has become callused. They hardly hear with their ears, and they have closed their eyes. Otherwise they might see with their eyes, hear with their ears, understand with their hearts and turn, and I would heal them.' But blessed are your eyes because they see, and your ears because they hear."

Doesn't that sound like America? Are we not as a nation seeing things we want to see but yet not able to discern what may be good for us? Are we not seeing what will harm us as a nation? Isn't America hearing many voices and not understanding the message from God that we need to hear? Have not our hearts grown hard and callused? God will bless those who take the time to open their eyes and ears to the truth of His message.

CHRISTIANITY CORRECTS ITSELF

Because of the basis of the freedoms brought by Christianity, America and other western nations as well, have dealt effectively with not all, but many of its demons. Some of the issues that were important to change in America were Slavery, Segregation, and Women's rights. As far as Women's right's are concerned, as bad as this sounds, it took our country less than 100 years to begin the changes needed for Women's rights when the first Women's Rights Convention was held in Seneca Falls, New York in 1848. Of course, much needed to be changed for women since that time including their right to vote! That's far different than women's rights buried in thousands of years of abuse and denial in many countries around the world that do not have Christian freedoms. When it comes to women's rights, we were and are light years ahead of most other countries. In fact, we are light years ahead of other countries in many of the social issues, and Christianity has been one of the biggest reasons why that happened. However, a woman's legal right to choose abortion under federal law was not a part of the early woman's movement. Most of the women of that era were against abortion and would not side with the National Organization for Women today and their radical feminist agenda that tears at the throat of Godly marriage and relationships.

There were plenty of other changes that needed to be made in America. The Salem Witch trials are another example that was brought about by narrow-minded religionists. It was seen for its evil and was dealt with by a nation of common sense Christians who knew that it was wrong.

Concerning slavery, Abraham Lincoln said God was dealing with America through the Civil War because of it. "The Almighty has His own purposes. Woe unto the world because of offenses; for it must needs be that offenses come, but woe to that man by whom the offense comes. If we shall suppose that American slavery is one of those offenses which, in the providence of God, must needs come, but which, having continued through His appointed time, He now wills to remove. And that He gives to both North and South this terrible war as the woe due to those by whom the offense came, shall we discern therein any departure from those divine attributes which the believers in a living God always ascribe to Him? Fondly do we hope, fervently do we pray, that this mighty scourge of war may speedily pass away."(2) Lincoln wasn't so much concerned whether or not God was on the north's side as much as he was concerned that the north would be on God's side.

America dealt with slavery but many were guilty as the Dutch, English, Africans, and others bought and sold slaves. Not only were whites involved but people from African nations were involved too. Jack Gaines and John Hatch recently wrote about "a reconciliation conference in Benin, West Africa that saw the President of the nation issue a national apology for the role Africans played in the slave trade. By revealing that the root issue of slavery is not skin color but sin since Africans sold Africans to the European traders."(3). Truly God is able to forgive.

Mr. Gaines went on to say, "Coming of age during the Civil Rights era, I know well the indignities of racism. During my stint as a professional baseball player, there were times when I couldn't eat with the rest of the team because of my color. A lot has changed since then. But there was a time in my life when I was bitter because of my experiences. After accepting Christ, I learned what real reconciliation is. Today I realize that racism isn't really about color; it's a sin issue."(**4**)

What about the early Fathers of our nation that owned slaves? George Washington and other great leaders of our young nation owned slaves but wanted them freed or eventually freed upon their death. Slavery was of second nature with many landowners because America grew up with slaves since the 1600's. In many instances, that's all they knew. Of course, that didn't make it right but the importation of slaves started over 100 years before their time!

Many of those early leaders grappled with the horror and indecency dealt to the slaves but they were trapped by an ideological dilemma that was greater than their own personal slave ownership. It sounds like they lived in hypocrisy and selfishness until you discover the overriding reason behind their decision not to deal with the slavery issue at the founding of America.

Thomas Jefferson said that the issue of slavery had to be put aside in order to win the Revolutionary War. Jefferson mentioned about slavery and "the business of the war pressing constantly on the legislature. I brought in a bill to prevent their further importation. This passed without opposition, and stopped the increase of the evil by importation, leaving to future efforts its final eradication."(**5**). In other words, the birth of a new nation had to take precedence over his desire to see the slaves set free. He also talked about the freedom of slaves born after a certain day, "But it was found that the public mind would not yet bear the proposition, nor will it bear it even as this day. Yet the day is not distant when it must bear and adopt it, or worse will follow…It is still in our power to direct the process of emancipation."(**6**). Ten years later in 1786 he would write, "But we must await with patience the workings of an overruling providence, and hope that that is preparing the deliverance of these, our suffering brethren. When the measure of their tears shall be full, when their groans shall have involved heaven itself in darkness, doubtless a god of justice will awaken to their distress, and by diffusing light and liberality among their oppressors, or at length by his exterminating thunder, manifest his attention to the things of this world, and that they are not left to the guidance of a blind fatality."(**7**).

History actually proves Jefferson to be right in the choice of these two overpowering issues. His words quoted in the previous paragraph were quite ominous and prophetic. What horribly true words Jefferson spoke concerning the plight of the slaves. You could tell in reading the works of Jefferson that the overriding issue was winning the war against Britain. Unfortunately, their stand against slavery would have to take second place. You could also tell that Jefferson as well as other leaders wanted the slaves to be set free but they weren't willing to make that an issue above the survival of the Republic.

Had they concentrated on slavery and not the war with Britain, the war would have probably been lost or at least divided the nation in the 1780's. The Republic would have been divided with the northern colonies against slavery and the southern colonies seceding to form their own nation 80 years before that attempt was made during the Civil War with Britain still a part of the struggle. The northern colonies would have had no jurisdiction over the southern colonies, as was the case at the conclusion of the Civil War. The North may have never contended with the South for them to give up slavery and slavery would more than likely have continued even after the Civil War era. There never would have been an Emancipation Proclamation because the North would have had no jurisdiction over the South, as they would have been an independent nation. If there still had been a war in the 1780's it would have had to be with another nation, the South! Slavery would not have ended when it did and how it did at the end of the Civil War.

Abraham Lincoln said that "slavery was not distributed generally over the Union, but localized in the southern part of it."(**8**). Most of the north was opposed to slavery because they were more industrialized. Most of the south wanted slavery because they were mostly involved in agriculture and they needed the workers. However, America had a civil war and guess what? The North won! The curse of slavery was overcome and the slaves were emancipated!

Also, many of the northern churches were against slavery. "In the year 1827 a law was passed that made it illegal to own a slave in New York State. This law was supported by the churches. Due to the Underground Railroad, Western New York was very much against slavery. Hundreds of anti-slavery sermons were preached from the pulpits of the churches of all faiths."(**9**). Wow, talk about the lack of separation of Church and State! As those sermons were being preached, southern legal authorities were pursuing slaves that were from the south, but many people of the north helped in the freedom of the slaves. Through the Underground Railroad many slaves escaped to Canada.

My wife and I remember that African Americans went to high school in the north with Caucasians and also at our college in Rhode Island. My wife remembers them riding on her school bus and attending her school and graduating with her class in Connecticut. My family and my wife's family saw nothing wrong with personally visiting black Church congregations in the north. The north wasn't exempt from prejudice to be sure, because it was there as well, but there didn't seem to be as much of a problem with prejudice and racism as there was in the south. Having said that, no racial prejudice or bigotry is to be accepted anywhere at anytime.

When my family moved to Florida in 1955, I remember getting off the bus with my mother and siblings and seeing separate drinking fountains and restrooms for whites, and for those who were, as the word was used back then "colored." I remember not understanding that and never seeing that before. When I asked my mother about it I remember feeling uneasy that we would think that we were above the blacks because that was the first time I had seen segregation in the south. I felt so bad. My wife moved to Florida in that same year, before we knew each other. She saw the drinking fountains and restrooms and remembers feeling embarrassed as a white person that we would think we were better than the blacks. She felt terrible as she saw the blacks being treated in a degrading way.

I remember seeing blacks having to ride in the back of the buses after I had moved to the south. I asked questions about it. Around that same time, Rosa Parks was one who stood for the justice of the persecuted people in our country. She called attention to the discrimination in all of us, as she knew she could "overcome" by her faith and religion. She refused to give up her seat to a white man on a bus in Birmingham, Alabama and became the spark that helped move the civil rights movement. It was the highest form of nonviolent civil disobedience that could have been expressed. When she passed away she was the first woman and only the second black to lie in state in the rotunda of the Capital building in Washington, D.C. What an honor!

Segregation was indeed another blight against the southern states that affected the United States as a whole. Segregation was the south's answer to the Emancipation Proclamation. It was the law of the land in the south, but it was a BAD law. That bad law was even endorsed by Christians in the south, but it was still a bad law. The celebration of Juneteenth is a commemoration of the Emancipation Proclamation finally reaching the western area of the republic in Texas a couple of years after it was proclaimed. Segregation was effectively dealt with in a free society, a free society that helped the more sane individuals of Christianity realize and deal with its blight, even though shamefully it took another 100 years. That doesn't mean that there is no more prejudice in society, because there is, on all sides. Maybe we can't get rid of prejudice but hopefully we can confess it and forgive one another.

A great price was paid by the African/American community to help enact the Civil Rights Act of 1964. Dr. Martin Luther King Jr. tried not to instill a mob mentality but gave his life for non-violent protest. He encouraged the blacks to pray, march for freedom, and not retaliate or fight back as they fought for freedom from being treated worse than 2nd class citizens. His marches were birthed out of Christianity that was trying to correct a grave injustice. He was opposed to the black power movements following him that encouraged guns, violence, and moving civil rights ahead by force. It is unfortunate today that African/Americans are kept as "victims" by many leaders who continue to remind them of their plight, instead of instilling them with positive and affirming attitudes.

To be sure when Jackie Robinson joined the Brooklyn Dodgers Baseball team, he and eventually other black players had to contend with prejudice in the north. While there was no law against black players playing in Major League Baseball, he still had a tough time and he had to accept insults. He had to bite his lip. No finer man could have been chosen for that groundbreaking event. But he was slightly, just slightly more easily accepted in the north than what Martin Luther King Jr. was in the south, and what other southern blacks had to contend with. However, he still went through a harrowing time. In the north it took Jackie Robinson's strong gentlemanly courage and determination, and a stalwart Branch Rickey to help bring about the change that was necessary.

In the south it was a different story. It took riots to bring decency to the plight of southern blacks. It took an armed militia sent by President Dwight Eisenhower to confront the southern Democratic Governor George Wallace of Alabama to allow blacks into the school system, to stop a mob, and to ensure school integration. What a disturbing injustice to the community of African Americans! Segregation was in itself, very appalling and its change was long overdue. A strong message was conveyed that southern Mayors, Sheriffs, and Governors were no longer in charge.

The biggest unfortunate fact surrounding the civil rights movement is that it was birthed right at the beginning of an upheaval in America at a time that other "rights" movements began. A plague of "rights" have been spawned and will come back to not only haunt America but also the legitimate black "rights" movement that was originated under Dr. Martin Luther King, Jr. Far different than Dr. King, some of the "black rights" movements have been birthed without the foundation of Christianity. Some have nothing to do with Jesus Christ and have been birthed with the belief that Jesus Christ is either a myth, or He has not much to do with their organization. The message of Dr. King sometimes has to muddle through all the other right's messages in order to be clearly heard. These other right's movements divert attention away from the victory that belongs to Dr. King. What he did should have been the singular focus for the rights of racially depressed people everywhere.

As the 1ˢᵗ Amendment rights of an "anything goes" radical and various fringe movements gain a foothold in America, it will be coupled with an Antichrist spirit. The pendulum will have swung to bring in a moral decay and a corruption that would never have been a part of Dr. King's "I have a Dream." As much as we want to make everyone feel comfortable under the 1ˢᵗ Amendment umbrella, the series of "rights" that many are saying is freedom, have become a series of "wrongs." We are dealing with a "legion of rights" which makes it impossible to keep a moral balance in society and will help tear our nation apart. That's the sad part of our rights and freedoms.

Someone recently wrote that the Bible accepted slavery and that Jesus and the Apostle Paul never spoke about its abolition. In actuality, slavery was never a part of God's original design; it was the result of sin. In the book of Exodus, God was against the enslavement of Israel in Egypt and prompted them to be released from their bondage. Deuteronomy 23:15-16 says that if a runaway servant or slave came to you, you were not to return him but let him live with you and you were not to oppress him. Also, God lamented over those who were bought and sold into slavery as recorded in other Old Testament books of Joel, Amos, Obadiah, and Nahum. In the New Testament, Paul pleaded with Philemon for the emancipation of the slave Onesimus. The book of Revelation in chapter 18 speaks about the judgment and fall of the great city of Babylon and that no one buys her merchandise anymore, including its "slaves, and souls of men." Slavery has been a horrible blight on the American landscape and the world.

Another correction in America was the interment camps established during World War Two in 1941. Suspected Germans, Italians, and Japanese were ordered to move to a relocation camp and register with the government. There were approximately 40 interment camps in America for these nationalities. They were more like holding camps, not concentration camps. They had good food, were treated reasonably and respected. At the end of World War Two, they were eventually all released.

Past dreams of America have been fulfilled: the abolition of slavery, the destruction of fascism, and the ending of communism. All the peoples of the United States, Native Americans, African Americans and Whites, should forgive and celebrate how we've overcome past differences with each other or our country will be torn apart. President William Clinton apologized for slavery, and still we have a long way to go to reflect the changes that are needed as Americans. Christianity is God's answer to what has been wrong and what continues to be wrong with America and the world. It is the only faith that offers His own self to replace our death with His death. All of history that we are currently making must line up with God's Word or harsh days lay ahead for America.

MAINLINE CHURCH VERSUS EVANGELICAL CHURCH

There is such a disparity between the older mainline division of the Protestant Church and the newer Evangelicals in the Church. There always is a difference between any older traditional church or denomination and one that has less of a history. Even what we consider the mainline churches of today were at one time new and different from their predecessors. At one time they were more conservative in their teaching of Christ and morality but now they are more liberal. It is the same way in the Catholic Church as well, a division between those who are conservative and those who are liberal. There is a real division over what is sin and what is not sin. There is a real difference as to what are the most important subjects to emphasis in church doctrine and faith.

The problem is that man continually tries to lessen the impact of sin in our world. They try and make excuses for it. They will pick and choose the sin that deals only with the outer social ills of the day. For instance, many professional biblical scholars and teachers of the Bible, raise certain concerns and important issues of our day, such as "the care of individuals who are vulnerable and powerless, community integrity and justice, the economy, the establishment of peace, and the stewardship of the environment". They imply that these are the most important issues and that other issues such as homosexuality and abortion that are identified in political debates are not major concerns in the Bible, and in fact they say that they are not even directly addressed in the Bible.

My answer is that the social issues such as stewardship of the environment mentioned in the Garden of Eden as "replenish the earth", was not a major concern for the Old Testament prophets as was adultery, drunkenness, idolatry, pride, and disobedience to the commands of God. The message of repentance from immoral sin must always come before the concerns of the environment. As far as integrity of community is concerned, it should be encouraged in the context of a nation that is following God. The integrity of community would prevail if the nation was obedient to God's commands and was willing to continue to follow God. Such is not the case in America and that's why the integrity in communities is failing.

I will agree that the powerless, the vulnerable, and economic justice issues were major issues with God. God's Word tells us that.

Psalm 72:4 says, *"He will bring justice to the poor of the people; He will save the children of the needy, and will break in pieces the oppressor."*

God was upset with those in Amos 4:1 who, *"oppressed the poor and crushed the needy"*.

However, there was no attempt as in socialism to try and raise everyone to a certain level, making everyone financial equal. It was simply a means of helping the poor on their level. In Acts chapter two, it tells us that when Christianity began, many of the wealthy shared some of their goods with others. They did so, yet still retained many of their holdings, not giving everything away. Their ambition was simply to help the poor.

Acts 2:44-45 says, *"Now all who believed were together, and had all things in common, and sold their possessions and goods, and divided them among all, as anyone had need."*

THE POOR

As a little boy I remember when we lived in Sharpsburg, PA, my father and mother would feed the travelers that would ride the trains. Back then we called them "hobos" or "bums." They would come to my dad's storefront shoe repair business and my mother would give them a sandwich and a glass of milk. Also at my grandparent's home, a traveling man always came by for work that they knew drank too much alcohol. They would allow him to sharpen their kitchen knives and they would give him something to eat. Helping the poor was always a part of the conservative thought and practice.

In that great chapter in Isaiah that talks about fasting and praying for the poor and needy we read an interesting encouragement that will be a benefit to all those who are able to help the poor. Works that are humanitarian should be a top priority and we should not stop one who is stealing in order to eat.

Isaiah 58:10 says, *"If you spend yourselves in behalf of the hungry and satisfy the needs of the oppressed, then your light will rise in the darkness, and your night will become like the noonday."*

Proverbs 6:30 says, *"...do not despise a thief if he steals to satisfy himself when he is starving."*

The liberals are always saying that the conservatives are against helping the poor. They cite the various programs that the government wants to put in place to help them. The liberals haven't learned the lesson that most people are coming to the conclusion that the big government programs of the "New Deal" and the "Great Society" cannot be there to help everyone. The conservatives do not want the government to be the one to sponsor all these programs because they cannot afford them. They would rather have the private sector help take care of them, as financially difficult as that may be as well. In actuality, both the government and the private sector should do the best they can. For years private corporations and churches have been the ones to lead the way. And recently with "faith-based initiatives" the call to help in these areas has increased, putting great financial stress on those organizations. In the days of Jesus, they couldn't depend on the government for handouts. They had to be creative and help the poor from the Jewish private sector. Today, America and the other rich countries of the world must do their best to help the poorest people and those who are the most economically depressed.

Such was the case with the hurricane and floodwaters that hit New Orleans and the gulf coast in September of 2005. The local, state and federal government were slow at getting there, but the Salvation Army, Red Cross, Convoy of Hope, Samaritan's Purse, and many more private and Church organizations seemed to be much quicker in responding. How much longer the government and the private sector can continue to help during disasters is unknown. This burden will further add to the financial difficulties in the last days before Christ returns.

The liberals consistently cite the fact that Jesus talked hundreds or thousands of times about the poor. They're right. In fact, if Jesus hadn't said "you must be born again" in order to get to heaven, He might have said, "you must help the poor" in order to get to heaven. But the experience of Christ and the cross, and our faith in what He did for us on that cross must take precedence. In Matthew 26 when Mary anointed Jesus with very costly ointment, His disciples criticized the waste and said that they could have sold the ointment and helped the poor. It sounds like His disciples had some good liberal thoughts! Well, Jesus responded to them.

In Matthew 26:10-13 it says, *"When Jesus understood it, he said unto them, Why trouble the woman? For she hath wrought a good work upon me. For you have the poor always with you; but me you have not always. For in that she hath poured this ointment on my body, she did it for my burial. Verily I say unto you, wherever this gospel shall be preached in the whole world, there shall also be this, that this woman hath done, be told for a memorial of her."*

Notice that Jesus said that we would always have the poor with us. Of course the basic principle of Jesus was to help the poor but compared with the message of His death and burial, the message for their souls was more important than helping their physical need.

Jesus emphasized that our focus must be on Him. The message of salvation was so important and so powerful that it included everyone, even the dreaded tax collectors in the Bible who robbed from the poor. Salvation was for them as well.

He had the same basic message for Martha when in the Gospel of Luke it shows that her only concern was serving other people and not sitting down and listening to the words of Jesus as her sister Mary was doing. This is where we discover that doing good works is fine because "faith without works is dead." Therefore we must have faith that includes our works. If it comes however before being obedient to the words of Jesus, it is wrong.

> Luke 10:39, 41-42 says that Mary *"sat at Jesus' feet, and heard His word."* Jesus told Martha, *"Martha, Martha, thou art careful and troubled about many things: But one thing is needful: and Mary hath chosen that good part, which shall not be taken away from her."*

Feeding the poor and doing good deeds is awesome and absolutely necessary but there are various ways in doing so beside the government. Again, giving the gospel of Christ to others is as equally important as helping the poor if not more so. That is why we must place our first emphasis on preaching Christ as we help their physical and financial needs. The establishment of peace is something we should live for and strive for. It is not possible to guarantee it until Christ is absolutely and unequivocally accepted by at least the majority of the populace and leadership, if not by one and all.

I can share the concern for all the issues that my fellow clergymen raise. To do so and not consider the entire moral ills, and life and death social ills of our society is a shame. God is very interested in our spiritual welfare as well.

RICH HISTORY OF TRUTH

Some would say that the differences in our society prove the Bible is wrong because its stories and their tellers have it all wrong. The opposite is true. This proves the Bible is true. The differences only show the inaccuracies when you deviate from the accuracy of the historical Bible. When history is in conflict with the Bible, we must stay with the Bible. We must not prove the Bible is true by checking outside sources for comparison, but we must prove the outside sources are true by comparing them with the Bible, one of our oldest historical writings.

Once again, as far as differences in society as compared to the Bible are concerned, there are many stories of "Messiahs" in every culture. That doesn't mean that there is no Messiah. Just the opposite is true. The intrinsic nature of man demands he search for God and a Messiah that will lead him to God. Even Jesus predicted in the Gospel of Matthew that Messiah's would appear.

> Jesus said in Matthew 24:24, *"For false Christ's and false prophets will rise and show great signs and wonders to deceive, if possible, even the elect."*

Again, false Messiah's don't prove the inaccuracy of the Bible but rather its accuracy. That's because we know that these false leaders will increase in the last days. When any culture drifts from the original and one of the oldest sources of history and accuracy, generation after generation will hold to a certain element of truth. They will err however, when truth is treated as fable.

There has been a rich history of various revelations to the Church around the world and throughout the centuries. J. Dwight Pentecost said, "The history of dogma...is simply the system of theology spread out through the centuries." In other words, little by little, God has revealed Himself through the Church over the centuries.

The second century was "the age of Apologetics and of the vindication of the fundamental ideas of all religion." The early church leaders were explaining the early Gospel. The third and fourth centuries was the defense of "the Christian doctrine of God, and specially the doctrine of the Trinity." In the fifth, sixth, and seventh centuries we see a "long and distracting series of controversies." That surrounded the study of the doctrine of Christ, known as Christology. During the reformation period of the sixteenth century, the doctrine of Soteriology or salvation was brought forth, which was "the development of the doctrine of the Application of Redemption." It wasn't until the nineteenth century that the End-Time was revealed to the Church. Mr. Pentecost points out that Eschatology, or the end of all things "was not theologically conceived,"(**10**) but it was God letting His people know about the future. God said what I do "I reveal to the prophets."

God has allowed the history of truth to develop in phases for the benefit, growth, and maturity of the Church. Much of the Church has been lukewarm toward God but a remnant of the church has developed a better understanding of God through the centuries. Alongside the church is the world that has been writing a history that has been in opposition and disharmony with God. That puts history and the Bible in conflict. History and the church of the ages are crying for a convergence of thought and a correction of its past.

The book of Revelation will tell it's own story and is yet futuristic. It will unfold and bring upon America and the world some of the greatest devastation yet known to man. When history is so alienated from the Bible that is when you must ask the question, "Is God a God only of the past or is He also a God of the future?" Will we ever learn? In II Timothy it talks about those who are loaded down with sin, think that they know it all, but yet do not understand God.

II Timothy 3:7 says, *"Always learning and never able to come to the knowledge of the truth."*

Let us believe that we will come to the truth and that our culture will not clash with God's Word. We must have faith to believe that as Christianity has corrected itself for the good, that it will continue to impact America in a positive way. Let us pray as a church that America will be as the Prodigal Son who had determined that he had sinned against his father, went home, asked for forgiveness, and he was forgiven. Let us believe that America will weep for their wrong doing as Peter did after he realized his mistake after denying that he knew the Lord. God always had a message of acceptance for His people. As long ago as in the Old Testament, God was ready to receive His people back to Himself.

Joel 2:12-14 says, *""Even now," declares the LORD, "return to me with all your heart, with fasting and weeping and mourning." Rend your heart and not your garments. Return to the LORD your God, for he is gracious and compassionate, slow to anger and abounding in love, and he relents from sending calamity. Who knows? He may turn and have pity and leave behind a blessing."*

For those of us who are all part of the Church of Jesus Christ there are some important things to consider. God has a plan for the end of time. The world will seem to come to an end as God interrupts the Devil's maniacal plan to use man to destroy the world through war in an attempt to disrupt God's plan to set up His Kingdom here on earth. The restructuring of the world to fight against terrorism is what in part will lead to Armageddon. Warfare of unprecedented nature will be fought on the streets, in the air, on the waterways, and through the Internet. The worst is yet to come!

CHAPTER EIGHT:

21ˢᵗ Century Internet Global Warfare

—ⱮⱮ—

There is a warfare that is transpiring right in front of our eyes. It is all around us, on the Big Movie Screen, Satellite and Cable Television, and on the Internet. We are fighting in a demonized Western world. We are involved in a European and American cultural warfare that is reaching into our homes via the Internet. The electronic medium of cyberspace has now become our greatest source of communication. Its pace in reaching into every home is on the increase. Access into our homes is far different and greater over the Internet than what it was when television first came out. Many parents are alarmed at how easy it is for their children to be reached by some outside source without their knowledge, such as predators who are targeting the children.

The computer is the most amazing invention that the world has ever seen thus far. It is a machine and system that can store, process, and reference information like no other tool. Everyone seems to be enamored with their own personal computer. You can learn so many wonderful and helpful things on the Internet but it's almost as if we seek a relationship with a mechanized world rather than socialize with other physical beings.

We can view all kinds of scenarios on the Internet, both good and bad. We can play video games, view people in their homes, and find a date and a mate. We have pornography, scary violent games, where to buy a gun, and how to make a bomb. We have seen teenagers show and explain their entire actions on the Internet before they carry out a dastardly deed like a school shooting. There are violent video games that center on stealing cars and shooting cops. Hidden sex scenes can be found at the touch of the right button.

Of course the mad money makers are out to make a fast dollar. There is nothing wrong with making money but greed has led us to the piracy of property with monetary values via the Internet. It is very easy for copyrighted material to be stolen and distributed for illegal profit. Also, it is just as easy to invade someone's privacy by preying on the unsuspecting and viewing all kinds of personal information about them.

We have to ask ourselves, how much abuse are we willing to tolerate over the Internet in the name of freedom, and will major blackmail over the Internet be the juggernaut of the future? How many ticking time bombs are out there in America and elsewhere in the world that carries potential danger to us, and our family? How can we keep weapons out of the hands of dangerous people? The computer has become the biggest star in this struggle over the pureness of our families and the world. The computer, the Internet world and its virtual reality, has become the 'global village' of electronic communication. To top it all off, we are involved with a 21st Century Global Warfare over the life and death of our planet.

In the midst of man's work, inventions, riches, pleasures, and death, we must come to the astonishing conclusion that Solomon did.

He said in Ecclesiastes 1:8-9 says, *"...The eye is not satisfied with seeing, nor the ear filled with hearing. That which has been is what will be, that which is done is what will be done, and there is nothing new under the sun."*

Ecclesiastes 12:8 says, *"Vanity of vanities,"* says the Preacher *"All is vanity."*

THE IMPERFECTION OF AMERICAN FREEDOM

In the past, unsavory individuals and groups have used American freedom as their most powerfully potent weapon. Not too many people knew of the brazen and hideous underbelly of the evil regimes of criminals and racial groups. After the Civil War, racial hatred came out of the reconstruction of that period. The Ku Klux Klan was birthed during the 19th Century to resist the emancipation of the slaves, using terrorist tactics to suppress black people. Before World War Two, America was gripped by the Great Depression and some people were looking for radical solutions. Racial superiority was an easy message to deliver, as the Ku Klux Klan, which had quieted down, was re-established. Certain people believed that at the heart of every problem were the Jews that controlled everything or the blacks that needed to be suppressed. During the history of this time in America, explosive rhetoric was used to target Blacks, Jews, Catholics, and homosexuals. Some felt that the Jews were running the world through the images of mass media and entertainment. These accusers had a field day given some of the past racial and segregation feelings in America. Also during this time, American Nazi's wanted to take advantage of the social freedoms such as freedom of speech and assembly. Radical Americans used it to launch their style of hatred toward these classes of people.

Not only could the Ku Klux Klan and Nazism thrive, but today just about any other deviant thought, idea, or video can survive because of America's freedom. In its history, America has allowed or put up with such horrible and immoral behavior patterns as slavery, segregation, Nazism, and Communism. Today we endure abortions, homosexual unions and marriages, skinheads, gangster rap, and radio shock jocks. These are the extremists in our society that others have to deal with through strength of moral character. The imperfections that are developing in America are a brand of freedoms hiding itself behind the cloak of 1st Amendment rights.

Bernard Goldberg says, "Today, too many of those who should be protecting the culture are too busy applauding those tearing it down." In his book he cites a quote, "In the end there will be a price to be paid for this," says Herb London, the conservative professor and critic, "the price one always pays for ignoring evil. Some of the best potential minds will be decimated. Culture will be assaulted beyond repair and the nation will be undermined from within."(**1**). It's incredulous but we are on the precipice of a serious collapse in our society and America's great influence of freedoms will help spread this collapse worldwide.

Because of the tremendous power of its vast source of information, the Internet has become a massive intercontinental super-highway. Similar to Nazism in America that thrived under the cloak of freedom during its glory years, the dark side of the Internet today is running without restraint. The abuses that we are beginning to see on the Internet will only get worse worldwide as we are looking at just the tip of the iceberg of it's evil side. The Internet will be taking us to unparalleled heights when it comes to the abuses that will erode the moral foundation of America, all in the name of freedom without restraint. Liberal thinking wants to allow it to flourish as they will give license to any immoral behavior in the name of freedom.

The book of Ephesians talks about runaway sin because of the blindness of a person's heart.

Ephesians 4:17-19 says, *"This I say, therefore, and testify in the Lord, that you should no longer walk as the rest of the Gentiles walk, in the futility of their mind, having their understanding darkened, being alienated from the life of God. Because of the ignorance that is in them, because of the blindness of their heart; who, being past feeling, have given themselves over to lewdness, to work all uncleanness with greediness."*

INTERNET ISOLATION

Television has disconnected us as families but the Internet has done something further. It has brought isolationism to the family members and isolationism has brought loneliness and anger. The family has become a part of the Internet age as we have continued to isolate ourselves from family, friends, and personal relationships. Instead, we seek relationships through the mechanized means of the computer and the Internet as we lose our humanity. Consequently, we have lost the sense of family and we are fractured from the personal relationships we would have with parents, children, and siblings. We are infected with knowledge and communications skills of Internet language and yet we are languishing behind in skills of communicating with the everyday person we should remain in contact with. We are deprived of loving relationships with our peers, our families, and friends. The more we are skilled at talking to a screen, the more we have become ignorant and isolated.

All of this is leading to a depression and anger in our society of unprecedented proportions. We have deprived ourselves of the vehicle of love that can be returned by using our senses interpersonally. Instead, we give and receive love with instant messages and chat rooms, and we get enough e-mail that would tire any "pony express." We constantly occupy ourselves exclusively with noise instead of rest. There is no such thing as "quiet time" anymore. We have to have music or violent noise of some kind whether it's through television, cell phones, I Pods, CD and DVD players, or the Internet. All this has helped lead us to violence and anger in America.

AN ANGRY AMERICA (2)

Many have wondered where our anger has come from and why we possess such rage. Millions of people in America and around the world are beset by anger. It is problematic to families, businesses, and our culture, and it is symptomatic as we are ruled by an emphasis of personal rights and the protecting of our personal space. It had been suppressed but has now been building up for the past 40 years. This anger has grown because of the subjugation of spirituality in our society. There is no release in our culture as a whole to a higher power in order to decrease our anger and violence. Society has come under the control of the whims of the minority that see no harm in changing society from its religious roots. There is also a racial anger that has been rooted in America for hundreds of years that is systemic in a world of hatred and violence since time immemorial.

Our anger has made our behavior egregious and we have become aggressive in our mannerisms. Someone may do something that crosses some imaginary line of our own personal space. We are angry with our wives or children at home. We may take out our anger on our co-workers or bosses, store checkout clerks, and even people we don't know that may cut us off while driving. We will use any excuse for not being able to control our anger including road rage, that has now been medically diagnosed as "Intermittent Explosive Disorder." What each of us needs to do is take personal responsibility and maintain control over our behavior patterns. Regrettably, this out of control anger is seen in the sports arena and on the ball field, which is a big influence on society, particularly our children.

We are angry because of our insecurities, bankruptcies, fear, stress, the lack of self-image, and the lack of control over our surroundings and ourselves. Everyone is on edge. We become depressed and want to sue someone or some organization because we weren't treated fairly. We are supposed to control the decisions that we make and be responsible for the results of those decisions but our anger gets the best of us.

Our isolationism continues to lead us deeper and deeper into depression and anger in which there seems to be no return. We have moved away from family relationships and have jumped at the opportunity that television began to offer us since the 1950's. Now we don't know how to cope with self in the absence of relationships, so we seek it on the Internet. The growth of the Internet has continued this trend toward isolationism with programs that would never have been dreamed of by the average television viewer decades ago.

It's this isolation that has led us into loneliness, anger, and frustration. We don't know why we are angry but everyone is angry with others and it's reflected in the fact that we are losing our skills in dealing with other people. We are becoming used to the mechanized screen and being zoned out of simple and easy interpersonal relationships.

This depression and anger has spiraled completely out of control. When we become angry with our spouses, that anger many times leads us to divorce. Our children become angry with teachers and consequently they do poorly at school. There are killings of our children in school and of our judges in court. Suicide web sites are easy access to anyone that is beset by drugs or anger. They can find someone on the Internet who is pro-suicide who will guide them through the steps of taking their own life.

Anger and violence is depicted on television and on the movie screens. It is what seems to attract many viewers and influences them to do similar things they see. They learn anger from others such as their peers and parents and then encourage this anger as they turn on others because they are so much on edge themselves. That anger attracts them back to the Internet and into the computer screen of isolation, to the thrills of games of war and vengeance in order to launch their personal Internet wars. Anger fosters anger even after they leave the computer screen, only to return to it again to have what they think is solace, but find only bitter loneliness.

A chemical release in our brain may bring about this anger but there is an antidote for all of the rage and anger in this world and it comes from forgiveness through knowing Jesus Christ. There is a rage that is taking place in our culture that has separated us from the peace of Christ. Many are at war within themselves as they wage war with others. When Christ is given the open door to our heart, He changes our lives. Without Christ, this world will be deprived of an empathy that restrains them from anger and violence toward themselves and others.

PORN-NET

Pornography on the Internet has exploded. The problem is everywhere. It is a network of pornography that is far more sophisticated than pictures seen years ago. You may have seen them in the backyard, in the bedroom, or behind the scenes in some room to tickle your sexual appetite in an unwholesome way and prey on your innocence. Years ago you might stumble upon someone who would show you pictures that where unacceptable to the public in general. Those opportunities were few and far between and not as big of a problem as we are facing today. Those child predators of years ago were imprisoned in their own mind and destroyed lives of the ones they contacted. Today, the Internet has opened a highway of perversion, available at the click of the mouse. If one is not careful, the Internet can destroy all types of morally good boundaries and behaviors.

Today, you can see live scenes of sexual escapades of adults and children as anyone can develop any deviant Web site and display their sexual wares so that others can download the pictures. Just as the Internet is growing, so is this industry growing and it can become habitual because of its 24 hour a day enticement. Scenes of just about any imaginable taste have lured people into this practice from every imaginable profession. There is a vast addiction to pornography that is rapidly hitting the main stream of America. The Internet world of cyberspace needs to concern itself with moral cyber safety.

We won't have a moment's rest from the radical sexual and perverted agenda of pornographic predators that appeal to the pre-adolescent. These monsters are taking advantage of our children, children who are given too much privacy and who know too much about technology. These on-line predators enter chat rooms and know exactly how to contact the children. They come from all walks of life and can be any one of our neighbors. Many times, the chances of them being caught are very slim.

The Internet has been used for identification theft, the piracy of copyrighted movies and music, and also to lure vulnerable women and unsuspecting children. The latest technology has been used to attract lonely women for job offers, dating, seduction, or sometimes murder. Children have been tantalized away from their computer by a predator as an adventure, and either molested, raped, or murdered. Even video games aimed at our children and youth have been found with sex scenes and other provocative material in their graphics.

Now those who run the trafficking of pornography have made it available to subscribers of cell phones and small personal digital computers worn around the neck. This will impact our children because many of them now have these kinds of advanced wireless handheld devices. It will be very difficult to keep this kind of deviant behavior away from our youth and children. Playboy magazine and other sexually explicit organizations are behind this latest adventure. Thousands of pornographic images will be made available not only while in homes or offices, but anytime of the day or night on cell phones while traveling to and from those homes or offices.

After Playboy there has come a proliferation of multiple deviant magazines and behavior, and now the Internet can be easily fitted to a gutter lifestyle. This has helped lead us to the collapse of our marriages, abuse of our children, a rise in adultery, homosexuality, and sexually transmitted diseases. If in these sexually deviant magazines and on their Web sites they offer the prevention and solutions to the ills of sexually transmitted diseases that are so pervasive in our society, it would be like pouring their brand of gasoline on an already raging fire. They are offering more poison to our society than what we already have and are saying, "Here, I have the antidote for that poison I just gave you." Add to that, the growing crime of child sex trafficking that has become a worldwide problem most notably seen in the Far East, and you can see where our world is heading.

This has further isolated many individuals who are involved with this kind of practice and have clouded their rationale and severed their relationships that would be wholesome and acceptable by our culture. Our culture and our world is imploding from within and suffering because of the mayhem and confusion of the spiritual warfare with sin. With a lack of repentance and many people being easy prey, all of their evil behavior will contribute to the greater warfare to come.

You can judge today's society by how it entertains itself just as past civilizations have used entertainment during the days of their decline. The next big catastrophe beside the earthquakes and cultural dilemmas will soon take place in our world. It will be the warfare and terrorism strikes from radical terrorist groups through the Internet.

RUMORS OF WARS

The Bible says in Matthew 24:6, *"And you will hear of wars and rumors of wars. See that you are not troubled; for all these things must come to pass, but the end is not yet"*.

In the days of the Bible a rumor of an impending war would travel by a man on a horse or a runner who would deliver the news to the nation or to the King. It would take days for the rumor to arrive at its destination. For much of the 20th Century a rumor of a war would travel by armored vehicle, plane or by radio. Eventually videotape would announce the impending doom of war. That could still take many hours or even days.

Today, with television, satellites, and the computer, a rumor of an impending war could take just minutes or even seconds.

337

Never before in all of world history can so many people see the scripture "rumors of wars" fulfilled in their eyes all at the same time. Never before could so many people all hear of a rumor of war at the same time.

We see events that happen all around the world in an instant of time. We see dramatic pictures of war, funerals, and Royal weddings. In April of 2005, we were instantly plugged into the funeral of John Paul II. Television by satellite and the Internet made it a mass media event. Crowds were watching around the world for those who could not make it to Rome as part of the millions who came. For many, it felt like the funeral was the center of the universe as Kings, Presidents, Queens, and Prime Ministers came. It was termed the "largest Christian gathering in history". The television audience numbered in the billions. Such a happening wasn't even dreamed about for the average individual, but television, satellite, and the Internet have made that kind of a huge impact on society today.

Revelation 11 talks of another event that can be instantly seen when two witnesses for Christ will be killed by the Antichrist in Jerusalem.

> Revelation 11:7-10 says, *"When they finish their testimony, the beast that ascends out of the bottomless pit will make war against them, overcome them, and kill them. And their dead bodies will lie in the street of the great city which spiritually is called Sodom and Egypt, where also our Lord was crucified."* Then those from the peoples, tribes, tongues, and nations will see their dead bodies *three-and-a-half days, and not allow their dead bodies to be put into graves. And those who dwell on the earth will rejoice over them, make merry, and send gifts to one another, because these two prophets tormented those who dwell on the earth".*

Notice that people from all nations will be able to see their dead bodies. How is that possible? Of course, with news networks in the Middle East, everyone will be able to see them on television because of satellite, and they will see them over the Internet. The Internet will be a dramatic part of the end times, as the mastermind known as the Antichrist, will use instant communication to connect to the entire world in an instant of time.

THE BEGINNING OF THE END

As we approach the end we see God as the great motivator of life. He moves all the scenes in the end of time to His satisfaction. He is the Master Director placing the actors, the score, and the sets in a massive climax of power and grandeur as He brings about the completion of time according to His will. God is interested in people turning to Him and believing in Him. He does not want to turn His wrath on the world.

Psalm 103:8 says, *"The LORD is merciful and gracious, Slow to anger, and abounding in mercy."*

The disciples of Jesus were concerned about the end of the world so they came to Him and asked Him some pertinent questions. Jesus talked about a future apocalypse that would carry much sorrow as war, trouble, famine, and earthquakes would become frequent for the citizens of all nations. He was speaking of a future time of Tribulation that the world had never seen before. It will be a desperate time, as the most devastating horrors will befall the peoples of the world bringing great unrest and fear.

Matthew 24:7-8 and 21 say, *"For nation shall rise against nation and kingdom against kingdom: and there shall be famines, and pestilence, and earthquakes, in divers places. All these are the beginning of sorrows. For then there will be great tribulation, such as has not been since the beginning of the world until this time, no, nor ever shall be."*

First of all, as these things begin to happen on the earth, a picturesque scene is depicted in heaven. It is the redeemed of all the earth singing the praises of God and a song of salvation around the throne of the heavenly Father. Jesus was there because this group is none other than Christians of the earth who are now in heaven as the horrors of the Tribulation begin on the earth. They can be no one else. It is the Church of Jesus Christ whose individuals are Kings and Priests unto God according to Revelation chapter one. They are then seen around the throne in Revelation chapter five just before the Tribulation begins.

Revelation 1:5-6 says, *"From Jesus Christ, the faithful witness, the firstborn from the dead, and the ruler over the kings of the earth. To Him who loved us and washed us from our sins in His own blood, and has made us kings and priests to His God and Father, to Him be glory and dominion forever and ever. Amen."*

They are around the heavenly throne in Revelation 5:9-10, *"And they sang a new song, saying: "You are worthy to take the scroll, and to open its seals. For You were slain, and have redeemed us to God by Your blood Out of every tribe and tongue and people and nation, and have made us kings and priests to our God; and we shall reign on the earth."*

FOUR TERRIFYING HORSEMEN

While the saints of God are in heaven and around the throne, the book of Revelation openly exposes the four horsemen of the Apocalypse. One of the first things that will transpire on the earth is the horror of the Great Tribulation that begins in chapter six. We see these four horsemen as an entourage of devastation and a cornucopia of disaster as one by one their hidden agenda is revealed.

The first horseman is seen as one who would go forth and conquer. The context of evil that transpires in this chapter leads us to believe that this first horseman is none other than the personification of the Devil, the Antichrist. This is the first glimpse we have of him as he rises from obscurity. The picture of him is enhanced as his influence is seen as the Tribulation unfolds.

The second horseman that causes unrest to fall on everyone follows the Antichrist. Murder that is so much a part of our world today will be multiplied as he takes peace from the world. All around the globe and even in the civilized nations will be terrorism, mayhem, and confusion. We will have to fend of stalkers who will patrol not only the streets but also the Internet. Women and children will be unsafe, as the lack of peace will lurk at every corner. Police will be unable to keep up with the amount of sinful individuals who will be interested in helping to cause so much unrest in the world for the honor and prestige of evil.

The third horseman unleashes starvation and a dreadful famine encompassing the globe that will be as commonplace as plenty is in the Western world today. Similar to the flood of Noah's day it will affect every individual. Crop failures that will bring about a massive shortage of food will take place first in developing countries and then in economically strong countries as well. Money will be so difficult to come by and prices will be so outlandish that it will take practically the wages that are earned in one day just to buy daily food and necessities. This does not include all the extra things that are needed to exist. It is revealed in Revelation chapter thirteen that one must fit in with the economic structure of the Antichrist's system. One must participate in and receive the marking system placed on individual hands and foreheads, or you won't be able to buy or sell anything.

The fourth horseman carries the ominous task of distributing death and unleashing the horrors of hell. One quarter of the earth comes under their death grip. Multitudes of people are slaughtered in battles throughout the entire Tribulation. Death at the infliction of wild beasts signifies the spiritual horror and calamity that will fall on all the people of the world through brutish, cruel, savage individuals and circumstances. The collapse of cultures around the world begins to run rampant in a wild array of unparalleled chaos.

In the meantime, countless numbers of faithful followers of Jesus Christ will give their lives because they want no part in the death and destruction that the Antichrist is bringing. They are pictured as martyrs who were standing by the altar of God in heaven. They gave their lives during the Great Tribulation just as others in the past were killed who took a stand for God's Word and made it into the portals of heaven.

Revelation 6:11 says, *"Then a white robe was given to each of them; and it was said to them that they should rest a little while longer, until both the number of their fellow servants and their brethren, who would be killed as they were, was completed."*

Revelation 7:9, 14-15 says, *"After these things I looked, and behold, a great multitude which no one could number, of all nations, tribes, peoples, and tongues, standing before the throne and before the Lamb, clothed with white robes, with palm branches in their hands. These are the ones who come out of the great tribulation, and washed their robes and made them white in the blood of the Lamb. Therefore they are before the throne of God, and serve Him day and night in His temple. And He who sits on the throne will dwell among them."*

THE EARTH MOVES

The Bible describes events that will come to pass that seem to be powerful and frightening. All of heaven will some day be rolled up like a scroll and be dissolved and all the stars will seem to fall out of the sky as the collapse of the physical world will begin.

Massive earthquakes will be the order of the day as over and over again, earthquakes rattle the world. However, none of these earthquakes are as bad as the piercing wrath of God's presence that falls upon the world. Revelation chapter six describes an earth-shaking event that pictures an earthquake happening at the beginning of the Tribulation. It is probably indicative of what happens at other times during the Tribulation. It must involve something more than just a physical earthquake as it seems like the entire geological, political, cultural, social, and astronomical landscape changes right before everyone's eyes. What happens here in this chapter is the dynamic of a powerful God who is seeking vengeance on a disobedient earth and causes everything to be uprooted and shaken. Everyone tries to hide from the presence of God and from the wrath of the Lamb whom we know as the Savior of the world. They will seek shelter in caves and under landslides of rock thinking that physical death will shelter them from facing the spiritual death and wrath imposed on them by the Lamb of God.

> Revelation 6:12-17 says, *"I watched as the Lamb broke the sixth seal, and there was a great earthquake. The sun became as dark as black cloth, and the moon became as red as blood. Then the stars of the sky fell to the earth like green figs falling from trees shaken by mighty winds. And the sky was rolled up like a scroll and taken away. And all of the mountains and all of the islands disappeared. Then the kings of the earth, the rulers, the generals, the wealthy people, the people with great power, and every slave and every free person—all hid themselves in the caves and among the rocks of the mountains. And they cried to the mountains and the rocks, fall on us and hide us from the face of the one who sits on the throne and from the wrath of the Lamb. For the great day of their wrath has come, and who will be able to survive?"*

Later on we see more of the same. In Revelation chapter eight, powerful angels appear to gather the wrath of God in what seems like giant cauldrons, and cast that wrath to the earth with the end result being an earthquake. In chapter eleven toward the middle of the Great Tribulation, two great earthquakes are pictured. One earthquake strikes the city of Jerusalem as ten percent of the city is destroyed after the two witnesses of God that were killed by the Antichrist, ascend into heaven. These earthquakes seem to be coming from God as in that same chapter it says that God's temple was opened in heaven and another earthquake rattles the world. Toward the end of the Great Tribulation the last earthquake is felt as the Battle of Armageddon rages in full force.

INTERNET WARFARE

The warfare that will strike at the heart of the earth as the tribulation begins will evolve like a spider-like web that will descend upon earth and encage it as a steel trap. Powerful satellites, the encompassing Internet and all of its software programs will put the nations of war on a level playing field as global warfare rears its ugly head.

Before the end of the past century, with the advance of the computer, we began to conduct our wars with the touch of a button. Missiles and missile sites were manned with the computer age of technology that would allow missiles to reach their target within minutes or hours, depending on how far away the targets were. Today, nations with Intercontinental Ballistic Missiles will play a huge role in the fires and destruction that will plague the world at the time of Armageddon.

More nations are interested in possessing nuclear weapons and other weapons of mass destruction. In the near future, weapons of warfare will be made available or be under the control of not only nations but also groups of people or individuals on the Internet and via Satellite. Computer "hacks" from around the world will find it easy to be "worms" that will invade military installations. They will create havoc as in 2005 when someone broke the codes and passwords of the Pentagon and entered their military security systems. Many war-like video warriors, who will be inspired by Al Qaeda and other terrorist groups, will become a honeycomb of corruption. All of this will be a part of the landscape of destruction that leads up to and into the Great Tribulation.

Will players of seemingly innocent games of murder and destruction that are carried out in an imaginary war with a friend, now turn violent and dominate the air over our cities and its streets? Will a more heightened desire for destruction grip the minds of evil perpetrators? Will it be similar to what fell upon our innocent teens in our schools when some of them were wounded or mortally shot by mentally deranged individuals heavily equipped for chaos?

With incredulous incivility on the increase, individuals will resort to violence over trivial issues, as respect for others will diminish greatly. Bombs will be planted in subways, plane terminals, skyscrapers, super malls, and other public places. It will become unsafe to be in certain areas where people gather. Wars will be conducted, as armies of nations who are armed with sophisticated weapons and manned by computers will be facing off with other national armies sitting behind computer screens. Violence will be perpetrated over land disagreements, oil and gas reserves, and cultural issues just to name a few. The events of the 21st Century wars will all be interconnected because of the Internet.

Individuals who want to get into the act can man their own computer software programs of real live warfare as they download the commands for atomic, chemical, and biological weapons that have been marketed off to rogue countries. They can make weapons of mass destruction, have them planted somewhere in missile silos and then with the touch of a button activate them with their cell phone or computer. As they command them to explode they can watch it over the Internet. They can develop missile sites and launch those missiles to places that are miles away. Individuals, terrorists cell groups, and armies of the world who will be able to plot and recruit terrorists over the Internet will play into this final day dilemma. Terrorist bloggers who will carry a run-down of their dastardly deeds on the Internet, will post and trade information with other terrorist bloggers using vast international systems of technology and planning. The end times will see nuclear, biological, chemical, and even laser weapons of destruction carried out with pinpoint accuracy through satellite communications.

Wars that are carried out with the touch of a button are what can be seen in Revelation chapter eight as destruction rains from the sky. Hail and fire is poured down, as over 30 percent of vegetation are lost in the heat. A great mountain is also seen falling from the sky. In the Greek language of the Bible, this great mountain refers to something that rises in the air. It could be a volcano, or it may mean numerous or abundant things of intensity that would be violent, mighty, and strong. Could they be missiles that come plummeting from the sky? Over 30 percent of life and vessels in the oceans are destroyed. The same thing is seen as a great star falls upon the drinkable water. Again over 30 percent of waters are polluted and undrinkable. The devastation is so horrible that the sun, moon, and stars will not be able to be seen. Could this be a weapon, or weapons of mass destruction? What lies in store for the nations of the world during this intense time of The Great Tribulation as weapons can be dispensed as easy as pushing the "enter" key?

Wars that can be carried out with the touch of a button are seen in Revelation 8:7-12. *"The first angel sounded: And hail and fire followed, mingled with blood, and they were thrown to the earth. And a third of the trees were burned up, and all green grass was burned up. Then the second angel sounded: And something like a great mountain burning with fire was thrown into the sea, and a third of the sea became blood. And a third of the living creatures in the sea died, and a third of the ships were destroyed. Then the third angel sounded: And a great star fell from heaven, burning like a torch, and it fell on a third of the rivers and on the springs of water. The name of the star is Wormwood. A third of the waters became wormwood, and many men died from the water, because it was made bitter. Then the fourth angel sounded: And a third of the sun was struck, a third of the moon, and a third of the stars, so that a third of them were darkened. A third of the day did not shine, and likewise the night."*

THE THREE TERRORS

Then what the book of Revelation calls the three terrors is revealed in chapters nine and eleven. First there is unleashed the most horrific experience of demonic locusts and scorpions that rise to become legions of spiritual persecutors to shake the mental and soul-like nature of man. In what can only be described as demonic and evil supernatural hellish spirits, we see the unearthing from a bottomless pit, a hoard of burning tormentors that will wreak havoc upon an unsuspecting world. Smoke as a furnace rises and a great darkness covers the sun and chokes the air. It is like the smog of multiplied cities rising to engulf every region of the world. These evil tormentors were there to trouble men, women, and children with the sting of plagues that will bring about a delirium of confusion and horror. The pain of these hoards of demonic powers will be so internalized and so intense that people who are plagued by these forces wish to die but they can't. It will be a suicidal dilemma that defies description! This is the first terror!

Second is the massive movement of physical armies that number in the multiplied millions, 200 million to be exact. This organized army of regimented eastern fighters form a militia of killers that crosses the Euphrates River, swarms the desert and descends to the plains of Esdraelon near the ancient city of Megiddo in northern Israel. We believe that these vast armies will perhaps come from any or all of the nations representing China, Japan, Korea, and India, the most populated region of the world. They are there to fight in the Battle of Armageddon that is also described in Revelation chapter sixteen. This is the second terror!

Third comes the announcement in chapter eleven that seems to signal that all hope of evil triumphing either through the Devil, the Antichrist, or his False Prophet is lost. The voices of heaven speak prophetically as it announces in proleptic (described as already occurred) terms the anachronistic (something as happening in other than chronological, proper, or historical order) representation of the Kingdom of Christ. This scene doesn't actually take place until the end of the Great Tribulation but it is described as if it has already occurred. It is the anticipated day "when Christ shall assume the ascendancy and dominance of His long promised and eternal Kingdom."(3). All of a sudden, out of nowhere comes this dramatic and all-important announcement. This scene of pronounced blessing of the Kingdom of Christ is a deathblow to the fiends of evil and must rattle the nerves of all that are in the Devils kingdom. This is the third terror!

Revelation 11:15 says, *"There were loud voices shouting in heaven: The whole world has now become the Kingdom of our Lord and of his Christ, and he will reign forever and ever."*

ANTITHESIS OF CHRIST

While doing my preparatory work for ministry, I had a woman by the name of Charlotte Marie King as one of my Bible professors. She was a godly woman, stately in her appearance and regal in her presentation of the Word of God. She was someone that you could look up to and would want to emulate. She possessed all the qualities of Christianity that you would look for in anyone. I have fond memories of this master teacher who was charming and delightful to sit with in her classroom. She spoke of all the glories of a God that she not only presented, but also lived for.

In a book her husband authored that she gave as a gift to our mutual friend the Reverend Almon Bartholomew, she showed her constant dedicated devotion to teaching. She wrote the note "God bless you Almon, your friend and teacher, Charlotte M. King." Her husband, the Rev. H. Pierson King was the former Pastor of the First Baptist Church, in Hudson Falls, New York and he made an astonishing prediction and presentation of the Antichrist. "He is the embodiment of all that is lawless and evil; the personification of iniquity and the incarnation of blasphemy. His malicious activities will culminate in a reign of chaos and lawlessness. He will devastate the universe and corrupt humanity. He will cause righteousness to be a luxury. He will institute a reign of terror, unparalleled by past history, regarding neither man, nor tradition, nor precedent, nor law."(4)

The Antichrist is seen in Chapter thirteen of the book of Revelation as a reincarnation of every evil and diabolical idea of anti-truth and anti-god throughout history. Somehow the past systems of unrighteousness come alive in the form of this man of evil. He is depicted as someone who comes back to life after a pronouncement of death. All of the past evil of the system of Babylon filled with religious confusion will be resurrected to appear in the form of this man of sin as the Antichrist. He will receive the endorsement of the religious leaders and will head the final day empires of evil. He is metamorphosed to appear as the last day answer to solve all the world's ills. He will unleash unparalleled persecution against Christians and Jews who name the name of Jesus Christ. He makes war with the saints who are described in the Bible as believers in Jesus Christ.

Revelation 13:3, 7 says, *"I saw that one of the heads of the beast seemed wounded beyond recovery—but the fatal wound was healed! All the world marveled at this miracle and followed the beast in awe. And the beast was allowed to wage war against God's holy people and to overcome*

*them. And he was given authority to rule over every tribe
and people and language and nation."*

He will institute a system of economic record keeping around
the world for the disbursement of food and goods. A computerized
mark will be required instead of a credit card or cash. This mark can
be tied in directly to bank accounts. He will have access to personal
accounts using a scan of mechanized means to detect a computer
chip placed under the skin either on the right hand or on the forehead. With technology what it is today, it will be so minute, it won't
even be noticeable.

Revelation 13:16-17 says, *"He required everyone—great
and small, rich and poor, slave and free—to be given a mark
on the right hand or on the forehead. And no one could buy
or sell anything without that mark, which was either the
name of the beast or the number representing his name."*

The computerized age will have reached its diabolical maturity
during this time. A replica of evil will not only be characterized in
every imaginable act of the Antichrist, but his False Prophet will
duplicate the Antichrist's exact person as an idol is made of him
to be worshipped. Just as many people idolized and practically
worshipped Adolf Hitler during World War II, so the Antichrist
will exude the same characteristics. He will welcome the idoliza-
tion and worship of the masses. There is a spirit of Antichrist in the
world today but the Antichrist of the book of Revelation will be the
pantheon of all Antichrist luminaries that have appeared since the
beginning of time. An image of the Antichrist will be erected that
will seem to possess animated life. His computerized voice will be
enhanced so that the Antichrist can be worshipped whether he is in
the presence of his adoring subjects or not. Masses of people will
plan to make annual pilgrimages to worship his image in the centralized place where it is erected. This will be of particular horror to the
Jews because this image will be placed in the Temple at Jerusalem
that is newly built during the time of the Tribulation. That image is
referred to in the Bible as an Abomination, something that is detest-

able. This of course is after the Jewish Temple is built during the Great Tribulation as mentioned in the book of Revelation.

Revelation 11:1 says, *"Go and measure the temple of God and the altar, and count the worshipers there."*

The Antichrist will have a False Prophet that will speak for him. He will have the authority to exercise mesmerizing hypnotic powers so that all will come under his spell and worship the Antichrist. How will the world know that he is a false prophet? False religions and cults are known for their jaded view of Christ, lowering Him to less than Divine and relegating Him to a man who just did good deeds. In a similar way, the world will eventually know that the Antichrist is not the Christ. His initial clandestine actions will be recognized, and those actions will eventually expose his false nature. Once the Antichrist is idolized, the reaction of the people and the reversal of his hero worship will be as swift as the rejection of the true Messiah Jesus Christ 2000 years ago. When the Antichrist elevates himself as God, the world's reaction will be similar. The difference is the Antichrist "will be the direct antithesis of Jesus Christ. As Jesus was the representative, in person, of the cumulative forces of heaven and deity, so will the Antichrist be the representative, in person, of the cumulative forces of Satan and hell. The Christ was the Masterpiece of God. The Antichrist will be the masterpiece of Satan. One was profoundly divine. The other will be confessedly and shamelessly diabolical."(**5**).

The Antichrist image will be computerized and idolized as seen in Revelation 13:11-15. *"Then I saw another beast coming up out of the earth, and he had two horns like a lamb and spoke like a dragon. And he exercises all the authority of the first beast in his presence, and causes the earth and those who dwell in it to worship the first beast, whose deadly wound was healed. He performs great signs, so that he even makes fire come down from heaven on the earth in the sight of men. And he deceives those who dwell on the earth by those signs which he was granted to do in the sight of the beast, telling*

*those who dwell on the earth to make an image to the beast
who was wounded by the sword and lived. He was granted
power to give breath to the image of the beast, that the image
of the beast should both speak and cause as many as would
not worship the image of the beast to be killed."*

How and when all of this evolves in the last days is still a mystery.
Beside the physical war that will transpire, our cultural warfare
will become worse as predators of innocent people will dominate
the Internet landscape. Pornography and indecency will become
common place. We do know that we are heading for troubling times
and the mysteries of God spoken of in the Bible will be revealed.

ARRIVAL AT ARMAGEDDON

General Douglas MacArthur made some powerful remarks at the
signing of the Instrument of Surrender of the Japanese at the end of
World War Two. He said in part, "Men since the beginning of time
have sought peace. Various methods through the ages have attempted
to devise an international process to prevent or settle disputes between
nations. From the very start workable methods were found insofar as
individual citizens were concerned, but the mechanics of an instru-
mentality of larger international scope have never been successful.
Military alliances, balances of power, leagues of nations, all in turn
failed, leaving the only path to be by way of the crucible of war.
We have had our last chance. If we do not now devise some greater
and more equitable system, Armageddon will be at our door. The
problem basically is theological and involves a spiritual recrudes-
cence and improvement of human character that will synchronize
with our almost matchless advances in science, art, literature and all
material and cultural developments of the past two thousand years. It
must be of the spirit if we are to save the flesh." (**6**)

Our world is reeling and shuddering in preparation for the intensity of the final war of the world. It will be plagued by an enormity
of force and power in the last days. The book of Revelation reveals
a quadrilateral announcement of the Battle of Armageddon after the
Great Tribulation unfolds of which the Antichrist plays a major part.

Exactly how far away this battle is we're not sure but the book of Revelation clearly annunciates the final battle as being brutal and awesome. Four times the battle is described as seven last plagues are unleashed upon the world. Horrifying sores upon man, polluted ocean and drinking water, scorching sun and darkness will find their culmination in the Battle of Armageddon. The following four chapters in Revelation reveal the terrible scene.

Revelation 14:19-20 says, *"So the angel swung his sickle on the earth and loaded the grapes into the great winepress of God's wrath. And the grapes were trodden in the winepress outside the city, and blood flowed from the winepress in a stream about 180 miles long and as high as a horse's bridle.*

Revelation 16:15-16 says, *"Take note: I will come as unexpectedly as a thief! Blessed are all who are watching for me, who keep their robes ready so they will not need to walk naked and ashamed. And they gathered all the rulers and their armies to a place called Armageddon in Hebrew."*

Revelation 17:14 says, *"Together they will wage war against the Lamb, but the Lamb will defeat them because he is Lord over all lords and King over all kings, and his people are the called and chosen and faithful ones."*

Revelation 19:17-19 says, *"Then I saw an angel standing in the sun, shouting to the vultures flying high in the sky: Come! Gather together for the great banquet God has prepared. Come and eat the flesh of kings, captains, and strong warriors; of horses and their riders; and of all humanity, both free and slave, small and great. Then I saw the beast gathering the kings of the earth and their armies in order to fight against the one sitting on the horse and his army."*

It is God that directs the battle armaments of His enemies and confuses them as they come against Him and the saints of God in battle. It is God that is the victor in the War of the World. The world will see God's Son Jesus Christ and the scars that were inflicted on Him at the cross of Calvary. The memory of these scars will return to everyone's mind, as the agony that was inflicted on Him was as if it had happened just days before. Everyone will weep in bitterness as they realize that it is Jesus Christ who is the Lord of the earth that is returning.

> Zechariah 12:10-11 says, *"And I will pour out on the house of David and the inhabitants of Jerusalem a spirit of grace and supplication. They will look on me, the one they have pierced, and they will mourn for him as one mourns for an only child, and grieve bitterly for him as one grieves for a firstborn son. On that day the weeping in Jerusalem will be great..."*

God's rage will catapult our planet into the age of Armageddon. It is His enemies that will feed on His mighty wrath as they become drunk on a potion made up of His justice and authority. It will be God's balances of Justice at work.

> Psalm 75:8 says, *"For in the hand of the LORD there is a cup, And the wine is red; It is fully mixed, and He pours it out; Surely its dregs shall all the wicked of the earth Drain and drink down."*

All the armies of the world will be gathered to this great battle through the influence of the evil, miracle working spirits that are sent by the Devil, the Antichrist, and the False Prophet. Out of their mouth will spew vindictive and enticing words of war, as armies will be swayed to join the fray to battle one another.

> Revelation 16:13-14 says, *"Then I saw three evil spirits that looked like frogs; they came out of the mouth of the dragon, out of the mouth of the beast and out of the mouth of the false prophet. They are spirits of demons performing miraculous signs, and they go out to the kings of the whole world, to gather them for the battle on the great day of God Almighty."*

All of this is a fulfillment of what the Prophet Joel said. It is just the opposite of what we envision when Christ comes to set up His Millennial Kingdom of rest. Instead of a world that is ready to beat their swords into plowshares, God announces just the opposite and rises up to impose His justice in an already declared war!

Joel 3:9-10, 16-17 says, *"Proclaim this among the nations: Prepare for war! Wake up the mighty men, let all the men of war draw near, let them come up. Beat your plowshares into swords and your pruning hooks into spears; Let the weak say, 'I am strong.' The LORD also will roar from Zion, and utter His voice from Jerusalem; The heavens and earth will shake; but the LORD will be a shelter for His people, and the strength of the children of Israel. " So you shall know that I am the LORD your God, Dwelling in Zion My holy mountain. Then Jerusalem shall be holy, and no aliens shall ever pass through her again."*

"The Antichrist will mobilize his armies. Each nation will contribute its quota of soldiers. The great coalition will create the most wonderful fighting machine ever organized. The genius of a super-man will back the enterprise. It will be the most audacious act man has ever attempted. It will be a worldwide militaristic organization mobilized for the express purpose of refuting the imperial claims of Jesus Christ. It will be a gigantic uprising against Almighty God. It will be a colossal array of millions upon millions of armed warriors, perfectly drilled; fired with diabolical hatred, and sensitive to the faintest order of their commander, the Antichrist. Hatred, anger, jealousy, and crime will break out in all quarters. The armies of the Antichrist will be successful against their opponents. Hope will perish."(7).

The Battle of Armageddon will be a juggernaut that will engulf the entire region of Palestine beginning with the plain of Megiddo in the north and sweeping to the streets of Jerusalem in the south. All of the villages and the hamlets between those areas will come under the cruel destruction of the Antichrist and his armies. The cruelty of the Battle of Armageddon will be so fearsome that the book of Revelation describes the aftermath of that battle as a trail of blood that is nearly 180 miles in length and deep enough to nearly swamp a horse. That stretch of territory will be so bloody, it will make William Sherman's march from Atlanta to the sea during the Civil War look like a Sunday afternoon walk in the park.

The battle will reach its fiercest peak as armies from the north in Russia and Europe will arrive at their destination in the Middle East through the Mediterranean Sea and over the Caucasus Mountains. The armies of the east will then march in with great crescendo. The armies from Arabia and Africa will also play their part. Jesus will return to earth, fight in the Battle of Armageddon and defeat the nations of the world.

All of the religions of the world from Hinduism, Buddhism, Sikhism, Confucianism, Islam, Christianity, to Judaism will be riding in the name of their religion and their god to fight a war that will climax at Armageddon. The Hindu religion that relies on the law of Karma to reach higher levels of existence through reincarnation and believes in many gods as manifestations of their one creator god Brahma, will have to acknowledge the one true God who created all things. The Buddhist religion that also believes in reincarnation, the understanding of the Four Noble Truths, and that one must go through the eightfold path to end suffering will realize that there was only one God and Savior worthy enough who suffered and died for the sins of the world. The followers of Sikhism that believe in one God and rely on the practice of devotional singing and prayer will see Jesus the intercessor revealed before their eyes and will be thrilled to sing, "Jesus, name above all names." The religion of Confucianism with its great emphasis on knowledge and right relationships will then realize that there is only one with the true knowledge and love for the world. Islam that gives only cursory respect to Jesus as one of their major prophet's will have to conclude that He is the one that their religious faith had misguided concepts about. Much of Christianity whose faith many times over the years had been tepid at best, will suddenly awaken to what they had as part of their core belief, and how much they let slip through their fingers as a Church that was plagued by a "lukewarm spirit." The Jews will

be startled to see that the one whom they have ignored for centuries is the one that will become the heart and soul of the world.

Christ will be victorious over all the religions of the world and over every evil of paganism. The world will then pray "O for a thousand tongues to sing, my Redeemer's praise, the glories of my God and King, the triumphs of His grace. My gracious Master and my God, assist me to proclaim, to spread through all the earth abroad, the honors of thy name."

None of the writings of the Buddhist, Hindu, Islamic, and Confucius religions have shown the history of the world as the Bible does. All of the writings and teachings of these religions will have to bow to the teaching of Jesus Christ. All religions including atheism will understand that their beliefs, cultures, lifestyles, and indeed their world will collapse, unless they reach the overwhelming conclusion that Jesus Christ is the God that they must bow and give allegiance to.

Philippians 2:10-11 says about Jesus, *"God also has highly exalted Him and given Him the name which is above every name, that at the name of Jesus every knee should bow, of those in heaven, and of those on earth, and of those under the earth, and that every tongue should confess that Jesus Christ is Lord, to the glory of God the Father."*

Christianity, Judaism, Islam, and the other religions of the world will have their spiritual differences and disagreements settled at the Battle of Armageddon. And what is the purpose of the battle of Armageddon? Does God take pleasure in seeing people suffer through war and calamity? Is it an angry God who delights in destroying a creation that He thinks has turned evil? Does He have a penchant for destruction that won't be satisfied until His inclination toward disaster finally comes to an end? No, none of the above! He doesn't declare the war of Armageddon, He interrupts and finishes it. His purpose of including Himself and the saints of God in that war is to stop all war. His desire is for a creation that will acknowledge and know Him as God and honor Him above all else in the earth. His heart and desire will be for the land that we call Palestine, for the Jews and the Arabs, for the Middle East, for the Christians, and the entire world to know Him.

Psalm 46:9-10 says, *"He makes wars cease to the end of the earth; He breaks the bow and cuts the spear in two; He burns the chariot in the fire. Be still, and know that I am God; I will be exalted among the nations, I will be exalted in the earth!"*

Ezekiel 39:21-22 says, *"I will set my glory among the nations; all the nations shall see my judgment which I have executed, and my hand which I have laid on them. So the house of Israel shall know that I am the LORD their God from that day forward."*

MYSTERIES

In Revelation 17 the Antichrist is seen as part of a great mystery to be revealed in the last days Great Tribulation. In that chapter, the Antichrist as a beast is supporting the weight of a woman of prostitution that is called "Mystery Babylon." Before we speak of this great event it would be important that we try and understand what the word "mystery" means in God's Word and how it has been used in the Bible.

The word "mystery" in the Bible is a derivative from "to shut the mouth, a secret, or a religious truth that man can know by revelation alone, and yet cannot fully understand". It means that there is always a hidden, secondary, or secret meaning behind what can be clearly seen. It could contain a dual meaning or an undisclosed truth such as an association of some kind.

There are a number of scriptures that talk about mysteries in the Bible, and the New Testament explains many of those mysteries that only the searching heart would find and understand. Jesus told His disciples that not all of His listeners would understand His teachings because their spiritual ears were closed and their spiritual eyes could not see. He told them that He would speak to them in Parables or mysteries and that He had given to them the hidden message that was the key to understanding the kingdom of God. It would be revealed to those disciples who ardently searched for it.

It says in Matthew 13:10-11, *"And the disciples came, and said unto him, Why do you speak unto them in parables? He answered and said unto them, Because it is given unto you to know the mysteries of the kingdom of heaven, but to them it is not given"*.

In the book of Romans the Apostle Paul reveals the mystery behind the Gentiles being saved and that the Jews are temporarily overlooked in God's salvation plan. The dual hidden mysterious meaning is that both the Gentiles and then eventually all of Israel as a nation will be saved. The Jews cannot see it right now because their eyes are closed to it, but that is the mystery or the hidden message in understanding how both Jews and Gentiles can be saved and prepared for the kingdom of God. It was a part of God's eternal purpose and had been kept well hidden as a secret but would be revealed at the proper time that the Jew, Gentile, as well as everyone can be saved. It was dropped on the earth as a bombshell after it had been in the heart of God since time immemorial.

In Romans 11:25-26 it says, *"For I would not, brethren, that you should be ignorant of this mystery, lest you should be wise in your own conceits; that blindness in part is happened to Israel, until the fullness of the Gentiles be come in. And so all Israel shall be saved: as it is written, There shall come out of Zion the Deliverer, and shall turn away ungodliness from Jacob"*.

Ephesians 3:8-9 says, *"Unto me, who am less than the least of all saints, is this grace given, that I should preach among the Gentiles the unsearchable riches of Christ. And to make all [men] see what [is] the fellowship of the mystery, which from the beginning of the world hath been hid in God, who created all things by Jesus Christ"*.

In another great mystery for those who would believe it, Jesus Christ was both God and man. The hidden truth is that He was divine and yet human. Hence, another mystery! Even the wisdom of God and His will is spoken of as a mystery and you have to search for it.

Romans 16:25-26 says, *"Now to Him who is able to establish you according to my gospel and the preaching of Jesus Christ, according to the revelation of the mystery kept secret since the world began but now made manifest, and by the prophetic Scriptures made known to all nations, according to the commandment of the everlasting God, for obedience to the faith."*

We read in I Corinthians 2:7, *"No, the wisdom we speak of is the secret wisdom of God, which was hidden in former times, though he made it for our benefit before the world began".*

Ephesians 1:9 says, *"For he has made known to us in all wisdom and insight the mystery of his will, according to his purpose which he set forth in Christ".*

Colossians 1:26-27 says, *"The mystery that has been kept hidden for ages and generations, but is now disclosed to the saints. To them God has chosen to make known among the Gentiles the glorious riches of this mystery, which is Christ in you, the hope of glory."*

Understanding the Godhead requires a person to especially acknowledge both God and Christ. Believing that God could become a man and save the world is a mystery that can only be revealed if you will search for it in order to try and understand it. Even the Godhead is a mystery but it is supported in the book of Colossians as knowledge that can be understood.

Colossians 2:2-3 that says, *"that their hearts may be encouraged, being knit together in love, and attaining to all riches of the full assurance of understanding, to the knowledge of the mystery of God, both of the Father and of Christ".*

The Bible goes on to further explain the incarnation of Christ as a multiple mystery as it is revealed from His birth until His ascension. It is a mystery by which Christ came to this earth to be presented as the Savior and received back to His glory He originally had in heaven. It must be believed on and accepted by faith as a step by step unfolding mystery that reveals the eternity of God as seen in Christ.

That wonderful passage is found in I Timothy 3:16, *"Without question, this is the great mystery of our faith: Christ appeared in the flesh and was shown to be righteous by the Spirit. He was seen by angels and was announced to the nations. He was believed on in the world and was taken up into heaven".*

Also, there is a beautiful teaching about marriage that compares a husband and wife's relationship as indicative of the relationship that Christ has with His Church. The hidden meaning behind the love in a marriage is the mystery of the great love that Christ has for the Church.

In Ephesians 5:31-32 we read, *"For this cause shall a man leave his father and mother, and shall be joined unto his wife, and they two shall be one flesh. This is a great mystery: but I speak concerning Christ and the church".*

Then there is the mystery of the resurrection of all of the believers in Christ that is mentioned in I Corinthians. The Gospel of John and the book of I Thessalonians support the resurrection as well.

I Corinthians 15:51-52 says, *"Behold, I tell you a mystery: We shall not all sleep, but we shall all be changed, in a moment, in the twinkling of an eye, at the last trumpet. For*

*the trumpet will sound, and the dead will be raised incor-
ruptible, and we shall be changed."*

John 5:28-29 says, *"Do not marvel at this; for the hour is
coming in which all who are in the graves will hear His voice
and come forth—those who have done good, to the resurrection of life, and those who have done evil, to the resurrection
of condemnation."*

I Thessalonians 4:16-17 says, *"For the Lord Himself will
descend from heaven with a shout, with the voice of an arch-
angel, and with the trumpet of God. And the dead in Christ
will rise first. Then we who are alive and remain shall be
caught up together with them in the clouds to meet the Lord
in the air. And thus we shall always be with the Lord."*

This mystery that is mentioned in these scriptures endorse the
fact that the dead will be resurrected and be with the Lord as well as
those who are alive. It involves a bodily change from the corruptible
life to the incorruptible, meaning the process of death is reversed.
It also involves a bodily change from the mortal to a life of immortality, meaning death is not the "final answer." All of these mysteries
have plenty to do with 21st Century Internet Global Warfare in the
end of time as the Saints of God serve Him and prepare for the
Battle of Armageddon.

MYSTERY BABYLON

The biggest and most important mystery for the end time is the
reference to "Mystery Babylon" in chapters seventeen and eighteen
of the Book of Revelation. This mystery reveals to us the final gasp of
breath in the mighty Babylon of old, as its destruction becomes one
of the greatest victories of God. As mentioned in a previous chapter,
Mystery Babylon contains a variety of interdependent elements of
false religions and faith as Babylon had in the Book of Genesis.
She appears riding on the political back of a beast-like creature, as
a woman who has prostituted herself with the leaders of the very

nations that the Antichrist represents. This woman is called Mystery Babylon with good reason. Instead of a faith that is the true religious representation of God on the earth, this woman has committed spiritual adultery with the political systems of the world. She has endorsed all of the world's evil. Instead of spiritually influencing politics, politics was influencing her spirituality and she had become a monstrosity. That's what gives her this mysterious quality.

This woman and the Antichrist together become the resurrection of an unholy union. The Beast that is the Antichrist stems from and is part of the Babylon system that is empowered again for the time of the Great Tribulation. He represents the empires of the old worldly authority, power, ruin, loss, and war. The woman, who is the embodiment of religious authority, represents the drunkenness, offense, and blasphemy of everything that is impure in her relationship to the world. The two of them together become the great "Mystery Babylon" and unleash a plethora of evil upon the earth that has never been seen before. This woman wouldn't be mysterious if she wasn't riding on the back of the beast and drunk with the fornication with the world through the leaders of the nations. Without that relationship, she would be pure and holy. Revelation 17 shows their union and also how this union is met with disaster.

Revelation 17:3 and 5 say, *"So the angel took me in spirit into the wilderness. There I saw a woman sitting on a scarlet beast that had seven heads and ten horns, written all over with blasphemies against God. A mysterious name was written on her forehead: Babylon the Great, Mother of All Prostitutes and Obscenities in the World."*

Revelation 17:16-17 concludes, *"The scarlet beast and his ten horns—which represent ten kings who will reign with him—all hate the prostitute. They will strip her naked, eat her flesh, and burn her remains with fire. For God has put a plan into their minds, a plan that will carry out his purposes. They will mutually agree to give their authority to the scarlet beast, and so the words of God will be fulfilled."*

The above scriptures are a picture of the result of a religious and political mix that is difficult to accomplish and maintain. Their preposterous joining together is unholy and mysterious. When the Church and the State unionize and become inseparable that's when the danger occurs.

In the first 175 years of the United States we have seen a premium relationship between religion and politics. It was a gentleman's agreement between a young nation and their leaders being guided by a rational and relational understanding of a higher power's influence. It was a burgeoning American Church offering its blessing and care. It was not a union but a mutual, caring, respectful, and gentlemanly understanding.

In the Old Testament there was a delicate balance between the religious and political elements of Jewish society. They mutually respected each other and were allowed to flourish and yet they did not interfere with the other's office. What we see in the last days as revealed in the book of Revelation is a world that accepts a counterfeit religion that will merge itself with the political systems of the world.

What happens in Revelation is the casting off of this immoral union. The fact that these two entities are tied together in close union but yet are separate makes it easy for one to cast off the influence of the other. We see a picture of politics casting the Church off its back, similar to what we are seeing here in the United States today. Instead of the Church being allowed to flourish as we have enjoyed for the first 175 years of America, that trend has reversed. It has brought a downswing of religious liberties as the state is attempting to cast the Church off its back.

In an indictment that God had against the nation of Israel in the book of Amos and before He allowed serious punishment to be inflicted upon them, He said some rather remarkable and astounding words. These words say that when God and His people were walking together in agreement, they had a special relationship. God goes on to say that is what makes it imperative that they are punished, because they should have known better but yet they sinned! Israel was known and chosen by God but still they disobeyed. That type of relationship can be spoken of about any nation that has a special kind of closeness with God and yet falls into the trap of committing cultural sins in the world. The indictment was clear to the nation of Israel as revealed in the following scripture.

> Amos 3:2-3 says, *"You only have I known of all the families of the earth; Therefore I will punish you for all your iniquities." Can two walk together, unless they are agreed?"*

From the very beginning, Babylon in the Old Testament book of Genesis had become a center of idol worship that was designed by Satan as a distraction from the worship of God after the fall of Adam and Eve. This idolatrous worship soon engulfed all the nations of the world. It was a form of spiritual fornication that set the nations aflame with a passion for false faith and worship. What happens to Mystery Babylon in the Book of Revelation is seen as the climax of what religious and political Babylon has done over the centuries. From a religious standpoint, it would be called ecclesiastical harlotry.

This woman is described as being drunk with the blood of the saints. Some expositors say that she was drunk because she was the perpetrator of many of the evils throughout the centuries that was inflicted on Christians around the world. If that is the case, I believe that John was also startled because she was so victimized in her past as her enemies had inflicted so many of her Prophets and Apostles with martyrdom. She was drunk not only in the sense that she was the perpetrator of various forms of evil, but that she was also the persecutor's victim.

John was truly amazed as to why she was riding on the beast with seven heads and ten horns, and why she was so intoxicated with the political representatives of the entire world's kingdoms and powers. He wondered why she was so affiliated with their politics. He saw in her the beauty of her martyrs as well as the devastation of her debaucheries. It was a mismatch made in hell. She was an enigma. She was filled with fornication because of her compromise with the nations, its politics, its kings, and drunk because of her martyrs. She was drunk with both those whom she martyred as enemies, and those who were martyred by her enemies. John wondered at what he saw, he was awed! There was a hidden, secondary, or secret meaning behind what could be clearly seen! In the eyes of God, it is a mystery of purity and impurity, of commitment and compromise, of zeal and disfavor.

Just as there were the seven heads, or seven kingdoms of the beast, the book of Revelation describes this woman as sitting on seven mountains. Both of these representations correspond with the imperial kingdoms throughout the ages of time and the religious ages of the church that correspond with those kingdoms.

They are both going to come to an end in the book of Revelation. Mystery Babylon is the climax of both the systems of false faith and the system of politics since the beginning of time. The Antichrist finds his end in the book of Revelation as the climax of the political scene that began in the book of Genesis. The religious woman is destroyed as the politics and sin that she has corrupted herself with, eats her alive!

As Babylon comes to an end, all across the regions of the world leaders will cry out in desperation to maintain control of what little time and power they have left. The fall of Babylon will be the total collapse of political and religious ideology. There will be insurrections, as nations begin to implode. Confusion instead of sanity will reign as head of state. Horror will grip families in neighborhoods of cities, as crime and financial ruin will take its toll and help bring the collapse of the system of Babylon. Personal bank accounts will be wiped out. Fear will rise to torment the living as the living will envy the dead. Babylon's collapse will begin even before Christ returns. It will be complete as He masterminds His actions of war from the Mount of Olives as He returns to fight in the Battle of Armageddon. He defeats His eternal foe called "Lucifer," "Satan," the "Devil," that "Old Dragon."

Mystery Babylon had become the amalgamation of the political and religious systems of the world. The cry is made throughout the universe that the mighty Babylon has been deposed and destroyed. This is a picture of the end of all the evil powers of the nations and all of the counterfeit religious influences.

The description of "Mystery Babylon" shifts from a woman prostitute that represents religious systems to the appearance of a city that is in great peril. Both are a symbolism of a religious and political system in trouble. Notice in Revelation chapter eighteen when John talks about the fall of this city, what her characteristics are. When Babylon falls she becomes a home for demons and a haunt for every evil spirit. All the nations have drunk the maddening wine of her adulteries. The kings of the earth committed adultery with her, and the merchants of the earth grew rich from her excessive luxuries. Her sins are piled up to heaven, and God has remembered her crimes. In her heart she boasts, 'I sit as queen; I am not a widow, and I will never mourn.' By her magic spell all the nations were led astray. In her was found the blood of prophets and of the saints, and of all that have been killed on the earth. Christ returns to "wipe clean" the world's plate of religious and political gluttony just as a city would be swept clean after the filth and debris of a flood or a tsunami.

SECOND COMING OF JESUS CHRIST

Terrorism through terror cells or warfare seems to be the "thorn in the flesh" of the world as it is racing toward a continued rise of fear and anxiety. The 2nd Coming of Jesus Christ will stop the spiral toward destruction and annihilation. The coming of Jesus Christ is biblically predicted, and it is essential in order for God to conclude the events of time. Just as there was a beginning to man, it is logical to conclude that there will be an end to man and all his labors here on earth. The Lord intervening in the process of the end of time is within the scope of understanding for the Christian. The Bible says that the Lord is coming back to earth to bring judgment on its inhabitants as all war and terrorism will find their judgment in the Battle of Armageddon. It's that unknown quantity of war against a faceless nation of terrorism that will expand and engulf all nations and lead the world to war.

There are some that say Christ is not coming and the end of the world is nowhere in sight. That kind of thinking could be delusional because the Bible makes the point very clear that the Lord is coming to disrupt the plans of man. He will bring the beginning of the end of this world even as terrorism and war are at its highest level and it will come when everyone least expects it.

I Thessalonians 5:2-3 tells us *"For you yourselves know perfectly that the day of the Lord so comes as a thief in the night. For when they say, 'Peace and safety!' then sudden destruction comes upon them, as labor pains upon a pregnant woman. And they shall not escape."*

There certainly have been false prophets announcing the end of the world that has made people laugh at the possibility of the 2nd coming of Christ. We shouldn't worry about the end time if our heart is right with God but the cavalier attitude that is so prevalent today is explained in the book of Peter. What they laugh about becomes their theory for the rejection of His Coming.

II Peter 3:3-4 says, *"First of all, you must understand that in the last days scoffers will come, scoffing and following their own evil desires. They will say, Where is this 'coming' he promised? Ever since our fathers died, everything goes on as it has since the beginning of creation."*

The Revelation of Jesus Christ will occur in the form of His Second Coming to the earth, as He and all the saints of heaven will break into the plans and ambitions of a world that is intoxicated with death and destruction. As the warriors of the various nations gather together for the Battle of Armageddon, suddenly the alarm of a trumpet will sound. A new and different battle cry will be heard within the battlefield. Christ will return to the earth with a dazzling array of power and brilliance. All that He will have to do is speak the word and the Battle of Armageddon will be over in a millisecond of time. All of the world's war machine and the Church's counterfeit religion will have to surrender to the will of the one who sits on the horse in triumphant victory.

Revelation 19:11-15 says, *"I saw heaven standing open and there before me was a white horse, whose rider is called Faithful and True. With justice he judges and makes war. His eyes are like blazing fire, and on his head are many crowns. He has a name written on him that no one knows but he himself. He is dressed in a robe dipped in blood, and his name is the Word of God. The armies of heaven were following him, riding on white horses and dressed in fine linen, white and clean. Out of his mouth comes a sharp sword with which to strike down the nations. He will rule them with an iron scepter. He treads the winepress of the fury of the wrath of God Almighty."*

The saints of God would have already been resurrected according to scripture previously mentioned in this chapter. They will be with Christ as He returns. They will still be reveling in the glow of the Marriage of the Lamb as they return with the Lord after they have attended that marvelous ceremony. That ceremony is when the Church will be eternally wed to Christ similar to a wedding ceremony we may have on earth. These are Christian believers that have been in heaven in preparation for this moment. While the Great Tribulation is taking place on the earth they are in heaven with Christ and return with Him at His 2nd Coming. The book of Revelation indicates that they are wearing the garments that speak of the holiness that comes from the Lord. Notice that it is the same saints who are the Church, and who have attended the Marriage of the Lamb in their wedding garments. They will be returning with Him from glory wearing those same wedding garments. The Church had been taken up into heaven in order to return in victory with Christ.

Revelation 19:7-8 says, *"Let us rejoice and be glad and give him glory! For the wedding of the Lamb has come and his bride has made herself ready. Fine linen, bright and clean, was given her to wear. (Fine linen stands for the righteous acts of the saints.)"*

Revelation 19:14 says, *"The armies of heaven were following him, riding on white horses and dressed in fine linen, white and clean."*

In the great timetable of God's relevant calendar, all other important events of history are past. The creation of the angelic beings to do God's bidding was glorious but did not complete the voluntary intuitive and responsive worship worthy of a Creator God. The fall of Lucifer, the creation of the universe and its inhabitants, and the formation of a called out family and nation brought about a fulfillment of worship that was worthy of His Sovereignty but did not complete the process of reconciliation of a lost and dying world. The incarnation of the Son of God, His life, death, burial, and resurrection and the establishment of the Church of Jesus Christ fulfilled the redemption process but did not restore the Kingdom back to God. These events are all marked as momentous occasions that are mighty and powerful happenings, but one more event is necessary for the fulfillment of the righteousness of God.

It is the Second Coming of Jesus Christ that is the most important date that far surpasses all of the other events brought about by a Sovereign God. It is the most anticipated event of the entire history of the universe. It completes all that God has worked toward, and it restores all of creation back to God. No other event is as important as the Second Coming of Jesus Christ and the establishment of His Kingdom. What a glorious and momentous occasion!

Every eye will see Christ as He returns to the earth. Those in the central part of the globe in and around the equator will see Him, as well as those in the regions of the north, south, east, and west. Both the Eastern and Western Hemispheres will behold this marvelous entrance of the Christ, the Savior of the world. Of all the characteristics of a wonderful exhibition of His glory that He will display, it is His omnipresence that will be greatly enhanced for this dramatic 2nd Advent of Jesus Christ. Everyone's eyes will be on Him everywhere around the world.

Revelation 1:7 says, *"Behold, He is coming with clouds, and every eye will see Him, even they who pierced Him. And all the tribes of the earth will mourn because of Him."*

We can only imagine with wonder as the sky will seem to open as the Red Sea did for the Children of Israel when they were fleeing Egypt and heading for the Promised Land. Except for the clouds He is coming with, all the clouds of the earth will roll back forming a clear day for the appearance of Jesus Christ. The entire atmospheric heavens as far as the eye can see, and the entire cosmos, will be literally filled with the saints of God. They will be coming from the Marriage of the Lamb in heaven, as the adoring Bride of Christ who accompany their Creator.

The return of Jesus Christ will be as swift as lightning. The glare of His glory will penetrate every eye, as the entire heavens will be filled with His presence. The thunder of his movement from east to west will pierce every human ear as the noise of His power destroys every foe.

Matthew 24:27 says, *"For as the lightning comes from the east and flashes to the west, so also will the coming of the Son of Man be."*

Satan will be helpless and will not be able to engage the saints of God in a battle in the air as he has been confined to the gravity of the earth after he was cast out of the heavens. His dastardly deeds will conclude because of the death of Christ on the cross, just as Jesus predicted in the Gospel of John that they would. His participation in the crucifixion of the Christ will seem like a vision that will come back to haunt him as his once powerful persuasive temptations will become an empty shell. Christ is here!

John 12:31-32 says, *"Now is the judgment of this world; now the ruler of this world will be cast out. And I, if I am lifted up from the earth, will draw all peoples to myself."*

JUDGMENT OF THE NATIONS

There is coming a future time when God's glory will cover all of the heavens and His influence will be so immense that He will stand and measure the earth as He drives the nations out from His presence. God will judge the nations of the world according to Matthew chapter twenty-five. At the conclusion of the Great Tribulation and after Christ's return to the earth, all the nations will stand before

Christ. Beginning with the Battle of Armageddon they will surrender to Him as the world enters the millennium.

The nations will stand in rigorous judgment as Christ will test their sincerity and willingness to serve God during the Millennium. The nations who fail His test will be placed on the left of Christ and declared to be the unacceptable "goat" nations. Their name and authority will cease to exist as nations and their remembrance will be cast into hell and not be allowed to continue through the millennium. Their authorities will be forever lost in eternity. They will fail because they have not ministered to others as if they were doing it to Christ.

The nations who pass His test will be placed on the right of Christ and declared to be the acceptable "sheep" nations. These are the nations who have ministered to others as if they were doing it to Christ. These nations will be given a place in the Kingdom of God and their names will be forever remembered and allowed to continue through the millennium to rule with Christ as He rules. The following verses explain what He says to those "sheep" nations.

Matthew 25:34-36, 40 says, *"Then the King will say to those on His right hand, 'Come, you blessed of my Father, inherit the kingdom prepared for you from the foundation of the world. For I was hungry and you gave me food; I was thirsty and you gave me drink; I was a stranger and you took me in; I was naked and you clothed me; I was sick and you visited me; I was in prison and you came to me.' And the King will answer and say to them, 'Assuredly, I say to you, inasmuch as you did it to one of the least of these my brethren, you did it to me.'"*

After the final acts of God in which He makes the devastation of the Tribulation a thing of the past, He establishes His throne during the Millennium as a time of 1,000 years of rest. Then will be brought to pass the many scriptures that cite the fact that the earth will enter into that millennial time of rest when Christ shall rule and the saints of God will rule with Him. Two such scriptures are found in Isaiah that speaks about the overwhelming peace that will be in the world at that time.

Isaiah 2:2, 4 say, *"Now it shall come to pass in the latter days that the mountain of the LORD'S house shall be established on the top of the mountains, and shall be exalted above the hills; And all nations shall flow to it. He shall judge between the nations, and rebuke many people; they shall <u>beat their swords into plowshares, and their spears into pruning hooks</u>; Nation shall not lift up sword against nation, neither shall they learn war anymore."*

Isaiah 11:6 says, *"In that day the wolf and the lamb will live together; the leopard and the goat will be at peace. Calves and yearlings will be safe among lions, and a little child will lead them all."*

NEW HEAVEN AND EARTH

Then their will come the most anticipated event after the return of Jesus Christ to the earth, the moment God re-creates heaven and earth. All of God's children will see the form of God sweeping His hand across the vast expanse of a wasted universe to enact a new beginning. Today's concept of global warming in the world that we have ruined will have met its match as the environment comes under the control of God. The old heaven and earth will be swept away in a crucible of fire.

II Peter 3:10 says, *"But the day of the Lord will come as a thief in the night; in the which the heavens shall pass away with a great noise, and the elements shall melt with fervent heat, the earth also and the works that are therein shall be burned up."*

The difference between the first creation in the book of Genesis and the re-creation of heaven and earth in the book of Revelation is that this time the redeemed of the Lord will be there. They will be able to see these mighty feats preformed! God will not be re-creating heaven and earth in the vast void of timelessness and space where life is empty and still. He won't have to speak worlds into reality without the watchful eye of a Creation that willingly adores Him, because we will be a part of that eternity. All of His adoring subjects will behold Him speak a new heaven and earth into existence and sense the shuddering power of His voice. He will bring us into the eternal dimension of a world that is vastly different than the one we know as time and universal measured coordinates of space will be non-existent. Our spirit, which at that point is eternal, is united with God's eternal Spirit as an outgrowth of His eternity that He meant for us from the beginning of time. We will live forever as our knowledge of good and evil will have been redeemed as evil will become something of the past.

Isaiah 65:17 says, *"For behold, I create new heavens and a new earth; and the former shall not be remembered or come to mind."*

Revelation 21:1 says, *"Now I saw a new heaven and a new earth, for the first heaven and the first earth had passed away. Also there was no more sea."*

New galaxies will then be created that will be just as innumerable in the heavens as in the first act of creation. His words will fill the universe of universes as His voice dwarfs the constellations. Just as God's energy has had the power to create, it has had the power to destroy. Part of this destruction has been the ultra violent collisions that created black holes in space and absorbed much of the energy of the universe where even light could not escape. At the future re-make of the universe, His authority and power will reverse the energy and expansiveness of those black holes, as they spew the death of stars back to life.

As He creates a new heaven and a new earth He will speak three words to signal their completion, "It is done!" This will be the 3rd time that He would have used those dramatic and dynamic words of completion. The 1st time was at Calvary when He said in John 19:30,

"It is finished." The 2nd time will be at Armageddon when an angel proclaims with a loud voice to sin and evil in Revelation 16:17 "It is done," "enough is enough." The 3rd time will be in Revelation 21:6 when He re-creates heaven and earth.

The first time those three words were uttered was on the cross when Jesus cried, "It is finished." Those three words marked the culmination of all the sacrifices of generations of worshippers seeking redemption through the blood of animal sacrifices. The toil, labor and works as seen in those sacrifices were simply a representation that could not make anyone perfect in the eyes of God. Since then, millions of people have found the completion of their lives in those three words on the cross, "It is finished." All of those sacrifices are never to be needed again as they point to the cross of Christ, the perfect sacrifice that is complete in Him. It was an end to all acts of self-righteousness, as the redeemed could now trust in the righteousness of God. His words made us perfect in His righteousness because He spoke those three words. The death of Christ on the cross was a one-time event that is never to be repeated again. God dealt with the sin question and provided a remedy by substituting Himself vicariously for a Creation that could not be free from the dilemma of sin that they found themselves in. All of redemption is complete in Christ. All roads to salvation and all windows on the path to enlightened righteousness lead to Christ. "It is finished!"

The second time those three words will be spoken will be on another level when the total embodiment of sin and evil finds their conclusion as they are destroyed at the Battle of Armageddon. A voice out of the throne room in heaven cries, "It is done!" Every evil thought, sinful act, each murder and hateful intent, all disobedience, every willful prideful action, all war, and cultural evil will find its end after those three words are spoken, "It is done!" That's the demise of sin! The penetration of evil into the thought process of man will never plague him again. From God's throne room will come those awesome words in victory over sin, "It is done." The destruction of the Antichrist and the False Prophet will then take place as they are cast into the Lake of Fire. Even after the Millennium and after a final assault on God's people, the Devil will finally join the Antichrist and the False Prophet in that Lake of Fire. Sin will be over! The end of all evil is assured.

> Revelation 20:14-15 says, *"And death and hell were cast into the lake of fire. This is the second death. And whosoever was not found written in the book of life was cast into the lake of fire."*

The third time we hear those words is when heaven and earth are re-created. When the earth was formed the first time, God did not say, "It is done," He said, "It is good." He was pleased with creation but in the back of His mind must have been the possibility of a runaway world that would soon fall into sin. His plans to remake the heaven and earth were still on the drawing board. Satan, who had fallen because of his sin of pride was soon to be released on a yet to be made world that would eventually have to be recreated in the end of time. That gracious act of remaking the world would come about after the death of the Son of God who was "slain before the foundation of the world," and God's creation would have an opportunity of redemption. I don't believe that God had to remake the world in the book of Genesis after the fall of the Devil and before Adam and Eve was created. I believe that God has reserved the making of a new heaven and earth for yet a future time. We can still anticipate the event that we will behold!

The collapse of the known world in and of itself will never happen apart from a loving God who allows it to happen. Its virtual collapse will only become a reality as it falls into the hands of a loving God as He articulates His mercy and His justice. It is the act of God that brings the return of Christ and a new heaven and earth, as the former earth does not collapse but passes away by the hand of God.

Any making of a new heaven and earth was in God's long range plans and is what we are still looking for. God remakes the world, we see him perform this action with an unbelievable torrent of power, and we will be there to hear Him proclaim those awe inspiring words, "It is done." It is then that we will enter into an eternal rest and be a part of the overwhelming worship of the mighty Creator God.

God will answer the profound question as to why He made the entire universe and it all sat so empty. We will ask, "was there ever life on other planets?" A still more provocative question He must answer is "what did he do for the billions of years of eternity past, indeed from infinity before the worlds, and man and angels? What took up His time?"

In the heaven of heavens we come to realize a world where God will wipe away all tears from everyone's eyes. There will be no more death, no more sorrow or crying, or pain. We will be in the eternal city of God where we will not need the sun or the moon, for the light of the Glory of God will be the light everywhere and will be the light for everything.

Revelation 22:20-21 says, *"He who testifies to these things says, "Surely I am coming quickly." Amen. Even so, come, Lord Jesus! The grace of our Lord Jesus Christ be with you all. Amen."*

Part of the words of George Frederic Handel's "Messiah" describe the climatic conclusion of the world under the power of God through Jesus Christ:

> The kingdom of this world
> Is become the kingdom of our Lord,
> And of His Christ, and of His Christ;
> And He shall reign for ever and ever,
> For ever and ever, forever and ever,
> King of kings, and Lord of lords,
> King of kings, and Lord of lords,
> And Lord of lords,
> And He shall reign,
> And He shall reign forever and ever,
> King of kings, forever and ever,
> And Lord of lords,
> Hallelujah! Hallelujah!
> And He shall reign forever and ever,
> King of kings! and Lord of lords!

And He shall reign forever and ever,
King of kings! and Lord of lords!
Hallelujah! Hallelujah! Hallelujah! Hallelujah!
Hallelujah!

BIBLIOGRAPHY

—⟋⟍—

Chapter One

1. Reverend Paul Beck, Pastor of Christ Chapel, Centerville, Massachusetts
2. American Institute of Physics, "Einstein: Image and Impact" http://www.aip.org/history/einstein/voice1.htm
3. NOVA, Science Programming on air and online, Frank Wilczek, Theoretical Physicist, http://www.pbs.org/wgbh/nova/einstein/expe-text.html
4. NASA, Exploration, "The Big Bang Theory," http:/liftoff.msfc.nasa.gov/academy/universe/b_bang.html
5. Institute for Creation Research, "The Big Bang Theory Collapses," Duane T. Gish, Ph.D, http://www.icr.org/index.php?module=articles&action=view&ID=343
6. Time Almanac 2006, With Information Please, Time Inc. page 663
7. "The Christian View of Science," Dr. D. James Kennedy, Coral Ridge Ministries, Ft. Lauderdale, FL.
8. God and Science, Rich Deem, "One Flew Over the Cuckoo's Nest," http://www.godandscience.org/apologetics/flew.html
9. "The Biblical Flood and the Ice Epoch," Pacific Meridian Publishing Company, Donald Wesley Patten, pages 20 and 105

Chapter Two

1. Illustrated World History, Hammerton and Barnes, "Emerging of the Nations," page 399
2. Copyright, George F. Will. Originally appeared in Newsweek, May 9, 2005, p. 72, "Aspects of Europe's Mind."
3. Copyright, George F. Will. Originally appeared in Newsweek, May 9, 2005, p. 72, "Aspects of Europe's Mind."
4. Morton Kondracke, July 14, 2005 column in Roll Call newspaper, quote from Robert Leiken, of the Nixon Center

Chapter Three

1. Time Almanac 2002, With Information Please, Time Inc. page 796
2. EveryStudent.com, April 20, 2006, "Jesus, Religions, and Just War," Paul Copan, http://www.everystudent.com/wires/justwar.html
3. Compiled from wire reports, Niagara Gazette Newspaper, 2005, Niagara Falls, NY
4. Institute in Basic Youth Conflicts, "How to make an Appeal," Bill Gothard

Chapter Four

1. Timeline of Terrorism, http://www.simplytaty.com/broaden-pages/terrorism.htm
   History of Terrorism, http://www.crimsonbird.com/terrorism/timeline.htm
   The History Place, Genocide in the 20th Century, http://www.historyplace.com/worldhistory/genocide/bosnia.htm
2. Interesting Facts about Iraq, http://users.ameritech.net/used-2bbear/interesting_facts_about_iraq.htm
3. Unveiling Islam, Kregel Publications, Ergun and Emir Caner, page 221

4. Reprinted from "War on Terror." Copyright © 2002 by Dr. Grant R. Jeffrey. WaterBrook Press, Colorado Springs, CO. All rights reserved. Page 82

5. Reprinted from "War onTerror." Copyright © 2002 by Dr. Grant R. Jeffrey. WaterBrook Press, Colorado Springs, CO. All rights reserved. Page 81

Chapter Five

1. Department of Health and Human Services, Centers for Disease Control and Prevention, http://www.bt.cdc.gov/disasters/earth-quakes/prepared.asp

2. Time Almanac 2006, With Information Please, Time Inc. Continental Drift and Plate-Tectonics Theory, page 487

3. "The Biblical Flood and the Ice Epoch," Pacific Meridian Publishing Company, Donald Wesley Patten, pages 65-66

4. "The Biblical Flood and the Ice Epoch," Pacific Meridian Publishing Company, Donald Wesley Patten, page 68

5. Time Almanac, 2002, With Information Please, Time Inc. page 491

6. Department of Health and Human Services, Centers for Disease Control and Prevention, http://www.bt.cdc.gov/disasters/volca-noes/facts.asp

Chapter Six

1. Sermon in Syracuse NY, Dr. Charles Crabtree, Assistant General Superintendent, Assemblies of God, Springfield, MO

2. Thomas Jefferson Writings, Merrill D. Peterson, editor, Letter to Danbury Baptist Association from Thomas Jefferson, January 1, 1802, page 510

3. Thomas Jefferson Writings, Merrill D. Peterson, editor, Letter to Danbury Baptist Association from Thomas Jefferson, January 1, 1802, page 510

4. Thomas Jefferson Writings, Merrill D. Peterson, editor, Second Inaugural Address, Thomas Jefferson, March 4, 1805, page 518

5. Thomas Jefferson Writings, Merrill D. Peterson, editor, Revisal of the Laws: Drafts of Legislation, "A Bill for Establishing Religious Freedom," Thomas Jefferson, page 346

6. Thomas Jefferson Writings, Merrill D. Peterson, editor, "The Autobiography, Revisals of the Law," Thomas Jefferson, page 40

7. Original Intent, Wall Builder Press, David Barton, pages 13 and 19

8. "The Rebirth of America," Arthur S. DeMoss Foundation, "The Bible and the Dawn of the American Dream," John Whitehead, pages 35-37

9. Thomas Jefferson Writings, Merrill D. Peterson, editor, "The Autobiography, The Congress in Philadelphia," Thomas Jefferson, page 8

10. Reprinted with permission, Faith and Finances, issue three, volume two, Summer 2005

11. Thomas Jefferson Writings, Merrill D. Peterson, editor, Second Inaugural Address, Thomas Jefferson, March 4, 1805, page 518

12. Reprinted with permission by Charisma Magazine, Copyright February 2000. Strang Communications. All rights reserved. Jim and Lori Bakker.

Chapter Seven

1. Reprinted with permission, Faith and Finances, issue two, volume two, Spring 2005

2. Second Inaugural Address, Abraham Lincoln, March 4, 1865

3. Reprinted with permission by Charisma Magazine, Copyright November 2000. Strang Communications. All rights reserved. Jack Gaines and John Hatch

4. Reprinted with permission by Charisma Magazine, Copyright November 2000. Strang Communications. All rights reserved. Jack Gaines and John Hatch

5. Thomas Jefferson Writings, Merrill D. Peterson, editor, "The Autobiography, Republican Legislature," Thomas Jefferson, pages 33-34

6. Thomas Jefferson Writings, Merrill D. Peterson, editor, The Autobiography, Revisals of the Law," Thomas Jefferson, page 44
7. Thomas Jefferson Writings, Merrill D. Peterson, editor, Answers to Jean Nicolas Demeunier, Thomas Jefferson, pages 590-592
8. Second Inaugural Address, Abraham Lincoln, March 4, 1865
9. Under Three Flags, Raymond F. Yates, used with permission, Brock Yates, pages 215 and 126
10. Things to Come, Zondervan Publishing, J. Dwight Pentecost, pages 166-167

Chapter Eight

1. 100 people who are screwing up America, Harper Collins Publishers, Bernard Goldberg, page 28
2. Lewiston Assembly of God Sunday School class, David Livingston, teacher
3. The Imperial Hope, H. Pierson King, page 125
4. The Imperial Hope, H. Pierson King, pages 123
5. The Imperial Hope, H. Pierson King, page 123-124
6. http://www.freedomdocuments.com/macarthur.html
7. The Imperial Hope, H. Pierson King, Pages 159-160

LaVergne, TN USA
06 March 2011
219002LV00001B/9/A